THE LAST SHAMAN

THE ARAKMBUT OF AMAZONIAN PERU
Andrew Gray

The Arakmbut are an indigenous people who live in the Madre de Dios region of the southeastern Peruvian rainforest. Since their first encounters with missionaries in the 1950s, they have shown resilience and a determination to affirm their identity in the face of difficulty. During the last fifteen years, the Arakmbut have been under threat from a gold rush that has attracted hundreds of colonists onto their territories. This trilogy traces the ways in which the Arakmbut overcome the dangers that surround them: their mythology and cultural strength, their social flexibility, and their capacity to incorporate non-indigenous concepts and activities into their defence strategies. Each area is punctuated by the constant presence of the invisible spirit world, which provides a seamless theme connecting the books to each other.

Volume 1
The Arakmbut: Mythology, Spirituality, and History

Volume 2
The Last Shaman: Change in an Amazonian Community

Volume 3
Determining Identity and Developing Rights:
Development and Self-Determination among the Arakmbut of Amazonian Peru

Drawing by Tomás Arique

THE LAST SHAMAN

Change in an Amazonian Community

Andrew Gray

Berghahn Books
Providence • Oxford

First published in 1997 by

Berghahn Books

Editorial offices:
165 Taber Avenue, Providence, RI 02906, USA
Bush House, Merewood Avenue, Oxford, OX3 8EF, UK

© Andrew Gray 1997

Library of Congress Cataloging-in-Publication Data

```
Gray, Andrew, 1955-
    The last Shaman--change in an Amazonian community / Andrew Gray.
        p.   cm. -- (The Arakmbut of Amazonian Peru ; v. 2)
    Includes bibliographical references and index.
    ISBN 1-57181-874-X (alk. paper)
    1. Mashco Indians--Social conditions.  2. Mashco Indians-
  -Religion.  3. Mashco mythology.  4. Shamanism--Peru--San José del
  Karene.  5. Social change--Peru--San José del Karene.  6. Gold mines
  and mining--Peru--San José del Karene.  7. San José del Karene
  (Peru)--Social conditions.  8. San José del Karene (Peru)--Economic
  conditions.   I. Title.  II. Series.
  F3430.1.M38G77  1996
  306'.089'983--dc20                                        96-13120
                                                                CIP
```

British Library Cataloguing in Publication Data

A catalogue record for this book is available from the
British Library.

Printed in the United States on acid-free paper.

CONTENTS

TABLES

FIGURES

MAPS

SERIES PREFACE

The Arakmbut are an indigenous people who live in the Madre de Dios region of the southeastern Peruvian rainforest. They are one of seven Harakmbut peoples all of which belong to the same linguistic family and which number in total about two thousand people. Despite having been known as Mashco and Amarakaeri during their forty years of contact with Peruvian national society, the people of the community of San José del Karene, with whom I have lived periodically since 1980, request that they be known as 'Arakmbut'.

Since their first encounters with missionaries in the 1950s, the Arakmbut have shown resilience and determination to affirm their identity in the face of difficulty. For the last fifteen years, the Arakmbut have been under threat from a gold rush that has attracted hundreds of colonists onto their territories.

This trilogy traces the ways in which the Arakmbut strive to overcome the dangers that surround them: They use their mythology to reinforce cultural strength; they demonstrate social flexibility in the face of alien peoples; and they show a discriminating capacity to incorporate positive non-indigenous concepts and activities into their defence strategies. Each of these factors reflects the constant presence of the invisible spirit world, which provides a theme connecting these books to each other.

The mythology of the Arakmbut is extremely important to them and to the way in which they perceive the world. On my departure from the community of San José del Karene after two years in 1981, I was told by several elders that I should write up my material around the three central myths. The first volume of this trilogy looks at each of these myths in order to introduce different facets of Arakmbut life.

The first myth, 'Wanamey', tells of the origins of the Arakmbut, the visible world and their social and cultural existence. It provides the impetus for a discussion of Arakmbut social organisation, which is based on various overlapping principles such as gender, age, residence, patrilineal descent and marriage exchange.

The second myth, 'Marinke', tells of the relationship between human beings, animal species, and the invisible spirit world. The visible and invisible worlds interconnect in ways that parallel social relations within the community, and this accounts for the constant presence of spirits and soul-matter in Arakmbut daily life.

The third myth, 'Aiwe', describes the abduction of an Arakmbut child by white people (Papa) who threaten his people with destruction, yet provide the means for their survival. It looks at the history of Arakmbut contact with outsiders, and charts the effects of the rubber boom and the period that the Arakmbut spent in the mission of Shintuya. After their dramatic escape in 1969, the Arakmbut founded their present communities.

The book ends with a discussion about the relationship between myth and history, showing how the Arakmbut recreate their myths at dramatic moments in their history. The conclusion reflects on power relations, the significance of the spirit world, and the relevance of the political concept of self-determination. Furthermore, embedded within Arakmbut myths are strategies for defence against colonisation. By looking at Arakmbut social organisation, cultural diversity, and historical experience, the first volume shows how myth provides a bridge linking the visible and the invisible worlds.

The second volume looks at the changes that have taken place in the community of San José del Karene between 1980 and 1992 in order to establish the two main dynamic factors involved in social, political, and cultural change – shamanism and politics. The book begins at the outset of the gold rush, with the death of the last great shamanic dreamer in the community. It continues by investigating the invisible world and the different techniques used by the Arakmbut to make contact with the spirits in order to promote the well-being of the people. Food production and curing are used to illustrate the complicated web of communication linking animals, spirit, and human beings to ensure Arakmbut growth and health. In both cases, a profound knowledge of Arakmbut biodiversity is necessary to enable a shaman to influence spirits.

Arakmbut politics is based on an understanding of the relativity of the social world, linking together the contrasting dynamics of desire and generosity. Through numerous daily encounters, the Arakmbut build up opinions, make decisions, solve disputes and acknowledge skilled persons through titles reflecting their prestige.

Arakmbut politics is in constant flux, shifting its emphasis from one social principle to another.

The period from 1980 to 1992 witnessed a marked change of social organisation within the Arakmbut community of San José del Karene, from a comparatively hierarchical to a more egalitarian pattern of life. The book offers multiple explanations for the changes, including the influence of the gold rush, the cumulative effect of the domestic cycle within the community, and the presence of the spirit world.

The book demonstrates that Amazonian communities are not fossilised settlements but that they are, and have always been, highly dynamic. The patterns of change over the last fifteen years in San José reflect shifts that have taken place throughout its history. The generating factor for this change comes from the invisible world, which enters both political and shamanic fields of activity. The conclusion explains why the death of the shaman provides a key to understanding the changes that have taken place and continue to take place in the community.

The third volume looks at the Arakmbut's growing awareness of their rights as indigenous peoples to their territories and resources. This awareness has risen concurrently with the growing development of indigenous rights internationally. The book takes the concepts of territory, people, cultural identity, government, development, and self-determination and looks at their emergence in a non-indigenous framework, juxtaposing them with their relevance in an Arakmbut context. The result is a mapping between indigenous and non-indigenous perspectives. Fundamental concepts such as 'territory' and 'peoples' broadly cohere, whereas concepts such as 'development' or 'self-determination' are present in practice but not expressed verbally.

While there is no necessary matching between human-rights concepts and indigenous perspectives, the Arakmbut quickly grasp the meanings of the terms as they become relevant to their practical conditions. With the violation of their rights, the Arakmbut are beginning to use the concepts of human rights as a means for defending their lives. The conclusion is that whereas non-indigenous human rights legislation receives its legitimacy by judicial means, the Arakmbut find their legal system legitimised through the spirit world. Whether through access to resources, expression of cultural identity, potential for development and the assertion of self-determination, the spiritual features of Arakmbut life are a constant presence. For non-indigenous observers, the invisibility of the spirit world makes it appear non-existent; however, overlooking its importance prevents outsiders from understanding and appreciating its significance in the Arakmbut struggle for survival.

The perspective adopted here is one of an outsider who has been invited into the periphery of Arakmbut social and cultural life in order to explain the complexities and depths of their views of the world to others. The discrimination that the Arakmbut suffer is based on ignorance and lack of respect on the part of non-indigenous people, who consider their territories and existence as a people to be fair game for predatory colonial expansion. These books are not meant to explain away the Arakmbut into tidy packages, but to use the non-indigenous imagery of structures and processes to understand the importance of their survival in the future as a people and to express solidarity with their struggle against adversity. The conclusions here are not timeless truths, but the particular views of a person on the margins of their world.

Each of the three main Arakmbut myths is divided into three parts corresponding to the head word, the centre word, and the whole word. Although each section is independent, it also fits into a series. As with the internal structure of the myths, so with the relationship between the myths themselves: each one looks at a different aspect of Arakmbut life from within a similar framework. The theme which links them together is the blending or separation of the human, animal, and spirit worlds in the face of the constant threat of outside forces – harmful spirits and non-indigenous peoples.

A trilogy is thus an appropriate structure for writing about the Arakmbut, and these three volumes fit together within the framework of their mythology. Each book takes a theme that relates to the three Arakmbut myths analysed in the first volume: creation and organisation of social and cultural life; growth and change in the relationship with the animal and spirit world; and the relationship with non-indigenous peoples, the threats they introduce, and the ways in which the Arakmbut can combat or avoid the dangerous consequences of invasion. However the relationship between the volumes like so much of Arakmbut life, involves the superimposition of layers of meaning covering different aspects of the triadic relationship.

The first aspect is the narrative form which starts from one situation and draws the listener through a variety of experiences to a new set of conditions at the end. Both artistically and ceremonially, a triadic narrative structure is common to many cultures. The famous anthropological example consists of rites of transition marked by three phases: separation, liminality, and reincorporation. The directional nature of these triadic rituals makes them as linear as the triadic narrative convention found so frequently in Victorian novels. The meaning comes from the sequence.

A different view of triadic structures comes from a more spatial perspective, which places less importance on the sequence. Arakmbut myths are 'cubist', in that any section or theme can be taken out of the main structure and transformed into a new story, showing the original narrative from another angle, or complementing the theme. This cubist or sculpturesque point of view is illustrated in Lambert's observation about Eric Satie:

> Satie's habit of writing his pieces in groups of three was not just a mannerism. It took the place in his art of dramatic development, and was part of his peculiarly sculpturesque views on music ... . It does not matter which way you walk round a statue and it does not matter in which order you play the three Gymnopedies' (Constant Lambert, *Music Ho!* 1948:92).

Another aspect of the triadic structure of Arakmbut myth is the way in which each part 'eavesdrops' on the others, picking up themes and characters who reappear in different guises, drawing our attention to various facets of the stories. In this way the myth becomes a triptych in which each 'panel' makes sense in term of its similarities to and differences from the other two parts. John Russell points out that the painter Francis Bacon has frequently painted in groups of three (1985:127): 'Bacon in his triptychs plays over and over again with the idea of the eavesdropper – the figure who looks across to the central panel and directs our attention to it.' Arakmbut myths demonstrate this element through thematic cross-currents, which appear as the shifting of meaning within a framework of imagery such as birth/death, growth or cooking.

Each Arakmbut myth combines narrative, multiple perspectives, and thematic cross-currents, all of which take the listener into different domains, looking at the world from a variety of angles. The three volumes here also share the three aspects of Arakmbut triadic relationships within their mythology. From one perspective, the three volumes constitute a narrative moving from the first volume's description of the difference between mythical structure and historical process, to the second volume's account of the process itself and the third volume's demonstration of the struggle as to who controls history.

The three books can be seen as cubist in that there is a common element in each volume that is investigated from three different angles. This is the position of the spirit world, which is a constant articulating presence for the Arakmbut in their everyday life, as guarantor of mythical knowledge, as cause of the generative process of change and as the legitimiser, arbitrator and guardian of acceptable behaviour.

The final triadic aspect of Arakmbut mythology that connects these three volumes is the constant movement from one aspect of the triptych to another. In each of these three volumes there is information that adds, reflects and comments on the material contained in the others. The creation myth of Wanamey reappears regularly through the pages, pointing to the main crises of Arakmbut existence; the constant relativity operating between human beings, animal species, and spirits appears in different guises throughout the visible and invisible worlds according to the contexts such as the myth of Marinke, in curing rituals or when hunting; and the invasions arising from the gold rush have mythological connotations in the story of Aiwe and appear as a trigger for change with the emerging consciousness of indigenous identity.

In this way, these three volumes fit together as a trilogy, providing an interpretation of Arakmbut experience from a peripheral perspective and trying as far as possible to reflect the aims of Arakmbut mythology – to draw attention to the importance of the invisible spirit world in the present struggle for survival.

PREFACE

Returning to Arakmbut territory in 1991 was unnerving. I had known about the gold rush in the southeastern Peruvian rainforest since 1979, but assumed that, after the mining fever had died down, the indigenous peoples of the area would once again be in control of their lands and resources. Instead, as the canoe nosed its way up the Karene river on the trip to the Arakmbut community of San José, the situation was clearly worse than ever; it was like slipping through a time warp into the rubber boom of the last century.

On both sides of the river, coloured blood-red by the sandstone silt, were the dazzling white beaches, pockmarked with rows of mining placers, each manned by gangs of highland workers brought into the area to work for their colonial patrons. The sounds of picks, shovels, and the wheelbarrows depositing cascades of pebbles onto the mining sieves echoed across the river in an arhythmic cacophony, accompanied by the constant murmuring of the small motors which pump up water to wash away the stones, leaving minuscule particles of gold dust in the black sand.

As the canoe passed closer to the shore, the grim faces of the workers looked up – most were young adults, but a wizened face or the diminutive shape of a child of maybe no more than ten years were also clearly visible in most work gangs. A hundred yards upstream the patron and his managers crouched by the river, panning the results of the previous days washing, their broad-brimmed hats keeping off the sun and marking their status as masters of the domain.

After two hours, passing the mouth of the river Pukiri, the colonists became less frequent and for the last half-hour, the river seemed as peaceful as it used to be. The deep green of the rain forest framed the riverbanks, bird song took over from the gold pumps; and then the Arakmbut community of San José appeared, perched at the top of the blazing red cliff, the same as ever. Well, almost: there were a few more canoes with outboard motors and some new houses sported corrugated iron roofs. Several highlanders were walking through the village; some Arakmbut households employed their own gold workers – most of them escaped from the patrons downriver. The villagers were older, except for those who are so old that they have always looked the same.

This book is about change; however, in an Arakmbut context this means not simply a comparison of socio-cultural differences over time, but a reflection on the reaffirmation of continuity with the past. The Arakmbut of San José have changed markedly over twelve years, but the dynamic processes of change have not made them unrecognisable. Their sense of being Arakmbut is as strong as ever. When discussing this one day, an elderly member of the community said to me, 'We have to change to stay the same.' This paradox provides a challenge to understanding Arakmbut life which has reappeared throughout anthropological history.

San José del Karene is the Arakmbut community in the lowland Peruvian rainforest where I have spent most of my fieldwork periods. The Arakmbut are one of seven peoples who speak the Harakmbut languages of the Madre de Dios region of Peru. My first visit to the area, between 1979 and 1981, provided material for my doctoral thesis (Gray 1983); during a brief period in 1985, I looked at the relationship between the Arakmbut local economy and the world economy in the light of the gold rush in the Madre de Dios (Gray 1986); a further year between 1991 and 1992 consisted of an investigation into indigenous rights in an Arakmbut context.

The 1991-92 visit was very different from the visit twelve years previously, not only because conditions among the Arakmbut had changed, but also because my circumstances had changed. On this occasion, I lived with Sheila Aikman and our son Robbie as a household. Rather than sharing a house with the Arakmbut, we were provided with a dwelling of our own, although we continued to eat and cook with them. This provided us with more independence and with more resources at our disposal; it was not necessary for me to work gold and I devoted more time than previously to analysing my material with people in the community.

The Arakmbut were surprised that we wanted to return for such a lengthy period. They are aware that San José appears isolated to outsiders and assume that, on the whole, all visitors can be classified as the young (anthropologists), those forced to live there (functionaries), or seekers of self-sacrifice (priests). The fact that we had chosen to settle with them again provoked considerable discussion and speculation.

During the year I worked extensively to gather new material and to double-check my findings of ten years earlier. For the period of a month I translated a large draft of my previous material to an Arakmbut university student who was on leave, and cross-checked his reactions with those of other members of the community. As we discussed the material, it became apparent that there were discrepancies between what I had seen in 1979 and the situation twelve years later. Part of the explanation for this was misunderstanding, but there were other areas, particularly politics and shamanic insights, which had clearly changed during the intervening period.

By comparing the similarities and differences between my earlier data and the extensive additional information from 1991 and 1992, certain patterns began to appear. This book is the result of the comparative work and traces the processes and dynamic aspects of Arakmbut community life. By outlining the internal features of Arakmbut socio-cultural change and continuity with the physical and spiritual threats which face the Arakmbut from the outside, I have sought to throw light on the tenacity of resistance among indigenous peoples and on their ability to defend their territories and cultures from destruction.

This defence is vital nowadays, when physical, social, and cultural genocide faces so many indigenous peoples throughout the world. The invasions of indigenous peoples' territories are the principal threat to their survival. Accompanying this is the emerging market economy, which is a two-edged sword for indigenous peoples. As long as it operates in harmony with their lives and aspirations there need be no ill-effects; however, once indigenous peoples lose collective control over their relationship with the market, a form of self-focused individualism takes over which undermines community relations and quickly erodes the apparently resilient socio-cultural organisation.

Indigenous peoples' lives are dynamic and subject to change from many directions, but this does not mean that their lives are exclusively determined by external forces. On the contrary, people make decisions in a context of discussion and practical activity within their communities. The threats from external colonisation may exaggerate fluctuations which already exist, but unless the limits which identify the people as a socio-cultural community collapse completely, extinction need not take place. Through the flexibility of their social and cultural organisation, they can be remarkably resilient in the face of tremendous external threats. The Arakmbut do not live according to static fragile structures which snap when threatened, nor do they live in fluctuating contingencies which allow for no order. These theoretical exaggerations obscure our capacity to see indigenous peoples as threatened but at the same time capable of determining their own future.

Throughout my work with the Arakmbut, I have encountered epistemological questions when collecting, interpreting, and organising the multivocal information they have given me. The material is not necessarily consistent, but changes according to a perspectival relativity whereby the Arakmbut share or differ in their views of the world according to particular socio-cultural criteria. These perspectives can be connected to social positions but they are also frequently matters of opinion or interpretation. Once I had grasped that there is not one version of Arakmbut life, my own methodological position became even more difficult.

Whereas I strive to understand what the Arakmbut have taught me, I can see that the results which I publish here are no ultimate view of their world any more than there is one correct indigenous perspective. This book rests on a personal and a necessarily marginal perspective which arose from my encounters with the Arakmbut. All aspects of Arakmbut social and cultural life are subject to interpretation, but I have tried as far as possible to avoid placing myself in a partisan position. Nevertheless, not every Arakmbut will agree with all that is written here, but everyone will agree with certain aspects.

This work is not completely relativistic because there are certain phenomena about which all Arakmbut are in agreement – such as the existence of spirits or the main categorical divisions of the world into forest and river. However, its findings cannot be absolute either, because any attempt to explain the information invariably encounters personal objections of interpretation from different Arakmbut. Even beginning to document what the Arakmbut think is fraught with problems and one can easily find that the effect becomes a fragmentary series of loosely connected pieces of information, ideas, and perspectives. Shamanic activity among the Arakmbut consists of seeking inspired frameworks which make sense of the irreducible complexity of change. The Arakmbut emerge from the text as a people struggling to control their destiny as far as they can in the face of countless threats from both the visible and invisible worlds.

Much of the data has come in the form of myths, stories, and songs that have been recorded and translated by Arakmbut speakers, while more material has been provided in Arakmbut and Spanish through conversations with different people, usually on an informal basis. The Arakmbut are not partial to interviews and preferred a non-interventionist style of fieldwork where they offered information when they thought that I was ready to receive it or needed to be corrected. My language skills in Arakmbut are sufficient for daily life but certainly not proficient enough to understand the subtleties of shamanic interpretation, and so for some of the material I received assistance in translation and understanding from several people. Throughout these volumes I have decided not to transcribe the Arakmbut texts of the myths and the songs. Whereas I apologise to the linguists familiar with Harakmbut, I think that vernacular texts should be the object of more specific studies such as Helberg (forthcoming). Furthermore, Arakmbut students are still working on an orthography which is generally acceptable and would like to work on the texts in detail themselves. Copies of all the tapes from which the myths and songs have been taken are deposited in San José and at the offices of FENAMAD (the Federación Nativa de Madre de Dios y sus Afluentes) in Puerto Maldonado.

Whereas the case studies come from my first period in the field, all the information on curing chants, songs, and many of the shorter myths come from 1991-92. Where the difference in time is significant, I have indicated the source and date in the text. I have also tried to avoid undue repetition of the material in my previous volume on the Arakmbut, although it has sometimes been necessary to summarise earlier findings in order to place the current information in context and to ensure that this volume can stand independently.

The spirit world of the Arakmbut lies at the very centre of this study because change is not just physical but is itself bound up with a causality which embraces invisible phenomena. Soul-matter is invisible and constitutes a fundamental part of the Arakmbut experience of reality. The difficulty in looking at the spirit world is either to avoid it because of its metaphysical complications, or to overemphasise its importance so that it becomes a reductionist tool, replacing ecological, economic, cultural, or linguistic determinism as yet another ultimate explanatory device.

For the Arakmbut, the invisible spirit world is a reality which provides the means of understanding their lives. Through dreams and visions, spirits provide those possessing shamanic skills with the analytical tools which they need for explanation. In contrast, non-Arakmbut see the spirit world as an element to be explained because it is an ideological and fictional construct of Arakmbut imagination, separate from the real world. This book attempts to resolve this problem by approaching the spirit world from the perspective of shamanic practitioners. Their relationship with the spirit world and the political implications of their thoughts and activities provide a context in which both Arakmbut and non-Arakmbut can appreciate the complexities and intricacies of existence.

For this reason, certain parts of the text describe strange occurrences and coincidences which some may prefer to dismiss or disregard. However, if readers can suspend their disbelief for a while, they will broaden their perception by means of a sympathetic reading of Arakmbut insights into their own universe.

Acknowledgements and Intellectual Property Questions

To thank the Arakmbut seems somewhat lame, as without them this book could not have been written. Their patience, encouragement, influence, and friendship not only affected me while I was there but has taught me the importance of the indigenous struggle throughout the world. I feel immense gratitude to them which will always draw us together.

Similarly, to thank Sheila Aikman and our son Robbie for their support does not express how much of them is in these pages, and how much they have done for me. Whether in the field or in Europe they have provided the inspiration for this work; in particular, I would like to draw attention to Sheila Aikman's perceptive comments on my discussion of gender. I should also thank my father who provided us with refuge on our return from Peru in 1981 which enabled much of this material to be written and analysed.

Dr. Peter Rivière helped transform what was a 'large shapeless object' when I first came back from the field into a thesis. His guidance, technical advice, and anthropological insights were not only important when writing my thesis but have remained a major inspiration. Several chapters from my thesis appear in this text (the death of the shaman and the discussion on curing, in particular) and so I would also like to thank my examiners, Dr. Stephen Hugh-Jones and Dr. Robert H. Barnes, for their crucial suggestions on the text which I followed when writing this book, and also Dr. Joanna Overing for her helpful comments and her enthusiasm for my work. Dr. Dan Rosengren and Professor Kaj Århem from Gothenburg University have kindly read and commented in detail on the manuscript, providing me with many critical insights.

In Peru there are countless people who have helped me in my work: Thomas Moore, Lizzie Wahl, Klaus Rummenhöller, Heinrich Helberg, and Didier Lacaze all have extensive knowledge about the

Harakmbut and have provided me with essential insights and the benefits of their work which are particularly clear in the third part of this book. The Universidad Pontificia Católica del Perú provided me with an affiliation in both 1979-1981 and again in 1985. I should thank both Juan Ossio and Teófilo Altamirano for their encouragement.

Indigenous organisations such as the Asociación Interetnica de Desarrollo de la Selva Peruana (AIDESEP), the Federación Nativa del Madre de Dios y sus Afluentes (FENAMAD), and the Asociación de Estudiantes Indígenas del Madre de Dios (ADEIMAD) have all had members and officers over the last ten years who have been of great assistance. In 1991 and 1992 I was affiliated with FENAMAD, to which I am very grateful for providing me with credentials enabling me to visit indigenous communities in the area. Furthermore, members of ADEIMAD have taken a great interest in my work and have helped me very much with comments on the text, specifically Elias Kentehuari, Hector Sueyo, and Tomás Arique, who also provided the diagrams for the text.

Other people whose help has been of great value are the staff at the Centro Eori, Puerto Maldonado, who have discussed many of the themes in this book with me; Jaime Regan and the Centro de Amazónico de Antropología y Aplicación Práctica (CAAAP), who were a great support when I arrived in Peru in 1979; Padre Adolfo Torralba and Mixtel Fernández, who are Dominican priests, and Robert Tripp from the Summer Institute of Linguistics, all of whom have provided me with much stimulating conversation and inspiring comments from their experiences with the Arakmbut.

In Europe I should mention the International Work Group for Indigenous Affairs (IWGIA) in Copenhagen which provided me with many of the opinions I developed between writing my thesis and this final version of the book. I would like to thank Jorge Monrás from IWGIA who provided all the maps and diagrams. IWGIA is currently working on a programme of support for the Arakmbut and regularly publishes material on their current situation. IWGIA can be contacted at: Fiolstraede 10, 1171 Copenhagen K, Denmark.

I would also like to mention members of the Department of Social Anthropology at the University of Gothenburg, who gave me many opportunities to try out my ideas. My work in Peru was financed in 1979-1981 by the then Social Science Research Council and in 1985 by a grant from the Danish government development agency DANIDA. In 1989, thanks to Georg Henriksen, the Bergen research programme, 'Social Organisation Systems of Knowledge and Resource Management, supported my research from Norwegian Research Council grant 550.88/013. The final sections were written in 1990-91 while I was on an IWGIA research programme supported by DANIDA. To these bodies I am extremely grateful.

However this acknowledgement does not answer the question of intellectual property or the protection of Arakmbut cultural heritage. The Arakmbut of San José have provided most of the information contained in this book and its perspective predominantly shares their orientation. Nevertheless, members from other Arakmbut communities have checked some of the information, and although there are discrepancies in detail, the main results are broadly similar. For this reason the information here, outside of its interpretation, is part of the Arakmbut cultural heritage.

Because Arakmbut is a collective tradition, it would be inappropriate to attribute each piece of evidence personally. The only exception has been the acknowledgement of Ireyo, who is known and respected for his knowledge as myth teller and chanter. On the basis of my discussions with the community, I am aware of no information in this text which has been told to me in confidence. After extensive talks with members of San José, other Arakmbut communities, and FENAMAD I have received broad support for publishing this book. This in no way obliges them to agree with my particular interpretation.

*   *   *

This book is dedicated to the memory of Professor James Littlejohn from Edinburgh University, who was a constant inspiration to me during my formative years in anthropology.

Scenes from Arakmbut life

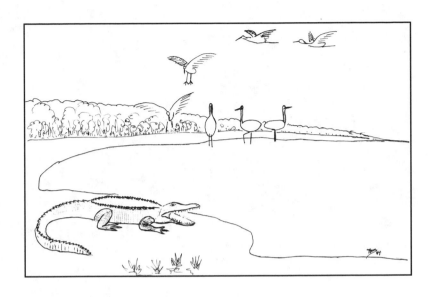

Drawings by Tomás Arique

INTRODUCTION

In lowland South America, the apocryphal anthropological traveller seeking enlightenment visits an indigenous community. Asking the people if there is a great thinker or wise person who knows the customs and traditions or who is in contact with the spirit world, the response is, 'Oh yes, we had one, but unfortunately, the last shaman died several years ago.'[1] The implication of this frequently-heard tale of the 'last shaman' is that when shamans die, communities transform their cultural identity. Gradually, their distinctiveness as a particular people takes on less significance and the death of the shaman becomes a cultural death-knell.

The story comes to mind when I recall a San José Arakmbut community representative telling a curious visitor in 1992 that their last great shaman had died over ten years ago. The irony is that, in this case, the story was correct because I had been living in San José when it occured. The shaman died on 23 December 1980. He was not only greatly respected within the community but was treated by all Arakmbut with admiration and reverence. His death was traumatic for the community and provided the catalyst for changes which, twelve years later, continue to affect the people of San José. During times of political difficulty, the Arakmbut resignedly interpret the death of the shaman as heralding the end of their community life which will be replaced by external influences from the national society. However, at times of resistance they consider that his life and ideas have been dispersed throughout the activities of the

1. Although the term 'shaman' originates in an Asian context, it is now used throughout the world (Eliade 1951) to refer to techniques by which practitioners make contact between the visible and invisible worlds. In a South American context, a useful approach is that elaborated by Campbell (1989:110) which sees 'shamanism' as a series of qualities or techniques which enable a person to carry out visionary and healing activities.

members of the community, reinforcing their confidence in their heritage and their spirituality. This book takes the death of the shaman as the starting point for an analysis of change within a Peruvian Amazonian community.

The most apparent changes among the indigenous peoples of lowland Peru over the last twenty years or more consist of the incorporation of certain initiatives from the national society into community life: the construction and registration of a school or health post; an increasing awareness of a common identity with other indigenous peoples and connections to local and national federations; the increasing use of Spanish as opposed to indigenous languages; the development of community identity and territorial demarcation; and an expansion of production activities into the cash economy.[2]

The Arakmbut include all of these features in their community life; however, change in San José is more complicated than simply a process of adding external influences. For example, since only 1980, the community of San José has become spatially more dispersed, clan factions have broken up, and households are more independent. The comparatively hierarchical political organisation among the adult men has become more egalitarian, while the overt influence of women has gained prominence. Whereas the community as a whole is less united in defence of its territory than it was in the early 1980s, tensions and violence within the community have noticeably decreased.

It would be simple to explain these changes as the effect of external factors. Outsiders are now regularly staying in the community: lay missionaries run the school; highland gold miners work with Arakmbut households; some young Arakmbut have married outsiders; anthropologists come and go; and representatives of the local native federation pay periodic visits. However, these influences cannot be seen as causing the changes which take place in Arakmbut daily life.

2. It is important to establish that this process of incorporation should not necessarily be seen as assimilation into national society but rather concerns features which indigenous peoples choose to draw into their community lives. This is not to say that assimilation does not occur; rather that it should not automatically be taken for granted. Features of daily life in the Amazon such as schools, the cash economy, or health posts can be found throughout the Peruvian rainforest but each people or peoples relate to them according to their own priorities. Sometimes this involves utilising an already existing indigenous socio-cultural framework and sometimes it involves developing more innovative ways of incorporating external features into their lives. A particularly innovative example appears in Gow's 1991 study of the lower Urubamba in the central Peruvian rainforest.

The Arakmbut live in active communities which are constantly changing for a multiplicity of reasons. Social life is not stable; the Arakmbut experience a multitude of constantly shifting internal community relationships by which everyone interprets and reinterprets daily events. Even when influences come from outside, change is not necessarily imposed; in many cases the Arakmbut actively choose to reformulate their lives. They incorporate external influences into their own experience, on Arakmbut socio-cultural terms, making them resonate with their history, mythology, and the invisible powers of the spirit world. This book tries to unravel some of these complexities in order to show the Arakmbut as a people striving to control the dynamic processes through which they live.

Approaches to Change in Anthropology

How and why social and cultural life changes have been preoccupations of anthropological study since its inception. During the second half of the nineteenth century, the proponents of historical evolutionary thought considered that culture developed through the internal dynamics of human creativity (Kuklick 1993:75). Tylor, for example, saw change arising from peoples' increased knowledge and use of innovation (1871:I); Morgan took a similar line, entitling the first part of *Ancient Society* (1877) 'The Growth of Intelligence through Inventions and Discoveries' (Kuper 1988:66).

Although the evolutionary thinkers conceived of culture as a universal concept embracing all humanity (Holdsworth 1994:68), the generating factor for change was primarily individual and operated on the basis of a gradual progression in the capacity and rationality of human thought. This was fundamentally internal to a society, because even influences from the outside had to be received and reproduced from within.

Marx's contribution to the discussion of change shifted the emphasis onto the internal dynamics of the political economy, seeing historical processes as generated by contradictions within the community (Marx 1977:167). Although his approach focused primarily on capitalist economies, the use of internal socio-political dynamics in analysing potential for change has been influential in the structural Marxist anthropology of the 1970s (Friedman 1975; Kahn & Llobera 1981).

In contrast to the evolutionary thinkers of the last century, diffusionists in the 1900s argued that change arising from external sources is far more significant in understanding the dynamics of social and cultural formations. By adopting a more historical and culture-specific orientation, diffusionists such as Rivers in Melanesia (1914) made geographical comparisons showing that cultures consisted of mixtures of peoples and posited the influence of immigration as an explanatory factor of change. Diffusionists argued that the external inter-relationships of any people provide the generating factors for change (Kuklick 1993:125).

In practice, most evolutionary thinkers accept some diffusionist elements in their arguments while diffusionists were also prepared to accept some evolutionary features of change. This has been particularly noticeable in the development of approaches to social change in lowland South America, where both tendencies coexist. In the 1950s there was a discrepancy between the use of the 'evolutionary' style of classification in Steward and Faron's survey of the native peoples of South America (1959), and those which saw the colonising frontier as generating change in indigenous communities (Murphy 1978). Since then, the distinction between those who see colonisation as a significant factor in explaining change and those who see change as arising from the potential within each social formation has taken various forms.

Colonisation and Change

The 1970s witnessed a period in which these two tendencies became inter-twined in South America. Studies by Ribeiro (1970) and the collection by Dostal (1972) looked at the importance of differential power structures whereby the state imposes itself on indigenous peoples who slowly lose their cultural identity by means of a process which Ribeiro calls 'ethnic transfiguration'. Indigenous peoples are effectively incorporated by the colonising frontier into a system which embraces both the dominating state and the oppressed indigenous peoples (Varese 1972:11). In this way internal and external factors become part of a new system.

In spite of the blending of internal and external factors, the ethnic transfiguration approach still emphasises indigenous communities as entities which become changed through contact with the state, rather than taking internal dynamics into consideration. Since the 1980s, however, studies in lowland South America have broken away from viewing internal community relations as passive victims of external change, whether economic, political, or religious. Indigenous communities have been seen as comprising new configurations blending internal socio-cultural factors with outside influences (Stocks 1981; Taylor 1981; Henley 1982; Rosengren 1987; Gow 1991). Through interaction with the colonising frontier, new aspects of ethnic identity and political ideology have emerged in the changing historical conditions of Amazonia. This has had the effect of breaking away from the notion that Amerindian people live in communities completely separate from the outside world (Urban & Sherzer 1991:1).

The majority of indigenous peoples in the Amazon have regular contact with outsiders, whether missionaries, colonists, or researchers, while indigenous organisations and federations represent communities both nationally and internationally. Furthermore, hundreds of small-scale development projects regularly pass through indigenous non-governmental organisations. Whereas only a few thousand people appear to remain comparatively isolated in the Amazon, over one million indigenous Amerindians are connected to the wider national states of the area.

Taking this argument further, the global neo-Marxist approaches of writers such as Wallenstein (1979) look at international processes of the world economy and how they relate from national to global levels. This initiative is particularly useful in looking at the effects of boom and bust economies in the Amazon and the connections between local demands in an international context. However, a global view does not explain or account for local initiatives, which can too quickly be seen as passive responses to external conditions rather than active initiatives arising from local communities.

The implications of the global approach is to question the very distinction between 'internal' and 'external' change. To some extent, all indigenous peoples are connected with local, national and international economic systems and to presume that there are internal and external systems of change can overemphasise a separation into two spheres. Nevertheless, indigenous peoples are not completely integrated into the local, national, and international economy; they are part of a struggle to define and recreate their relationship with the state. This process of definition and asserting identity necessitates some distinction between 'internal' and 'external'. Thus, while accepting that there is an integral connection between indigenous peoples and external interest groups, this cannot override their distinct identities, socio-cultural formations, and approaches to political mobilisation.

The dynamics of the international economy provides some useful insights, but change as a dynamic generating process and the configuration where the global meets the local is elusive. Current writings which broaden out from the purely economical approach, however, are providing interesting connections on political and ideological grounds. For example, the weakening of the nation state in conjunction with the rise of 'Fourth World' movements has been usefully analysed by Friedman in his work on the native Hawai'ian people (Friedman 1994).

In spite of the recognition that local communities mutually interrelate with the national society and global economy, little discussion of indigenously produced change has arisen from lowland South America. The majority of ethnographies in the area have concentrated on describing social and cultural life as it is, rather than as a dynamic process. This has, to some extent, reinforced the idea that the lowland South American native communities are 'cold societies' or 'peoples without history'. One reason for this is that works of Amazonian ethnography frequently cover small spans of time and historical studies of the Amazon are often considered as having limited use.

Nevertheless, historical studies in the Amazon have been increasingly gaining ground as ways of demonstrating the development of contact between indigenous peoples and the growth of the state. Although this history is largely based on outside sources, which are often a part of the colonisation process itself, accounts of past events in lowland areas have been detailed and provide useful insights into the context of state contact with indigenous peoples (Hemming 1978, 1987; Rivière 1995). Another development in historical studies of lowland South America has worked towards placing indigenous peoples firmly within the broader context of historical and geographical conditions (Gray 1987; Whitehead 1993).

In addition to writing history as the activities of people, there is also another approach to change; namely, history as interpretation (Lévi-Strauss 1969). This semantic approach to history looks at how people conceptualise change and compare different versions of their past, linking these interpretations to their identities (Hastrup 1992; Davis 1992). The interpretation of events is here emphasised over the activities of people over time (Gow 1991).[3]

Indigenous Change

In contrast to historical studies and the significance of colonisation, some authors have looked at change from the context of indigenous

---

3. These approaches to history in Amazonia were juxtaposed in the previous volume on Arakmbut myth and history.

communities themselves. This has taken several forms. Århem (1989), for example, compares the social organisations of peoples in the Guyanas and the Tukanoans of Colombia and Brazil. The contrast between the Guianan cognatic, comparatively egalitarian, system (c.f. Rivière 1984) with the more hierarchical patrilineal clans of the Tukanoans provides several potential areas for comparison with the Arakmbut material. Århem describes two 'intermediary' cases – the Macuna, who are closer to the Tukanoans, and the Maku, who are closer to the Guianas – both of which could potentially take on features of the other over time.[4]

Several studies have looked at the relationships between indigenous peoples either prior to colonisation or in spite of colonisation. The diffusion of ideas from one indigenous people to another can be demonstrated in Amazonian Peru and throughout Western Amazonia. The accounts of the Asháninka, for example (Weiss 1975) show the presence of Quechua imagery, particularly in spirit classification. The Arakmbut talk of the Inca Manco, and demonstrate clear cases of mythology and songs passing from one people to another throughout the Madre de Dios (Gray 1987). Nevertheless, these observations do not seek to explain the socio-cultural changes taking place in any one people in terms of another, but rather to assert that indigenous peoples relate not only with the nation state and the colonising frontier, but also with each other.

The internal socio-cultural dynamics of indigenous peoples' lives is more difficult to ascertain. Some writers have analyzed the domestic cycle of a household or family over a period (Maybury-Lewis 1979; C. Hugh-Jones 1978). Here each person, or production and reproduction groups within the community, undergo the process of changing position from youth to marriage, procreation, old age, and death. This could involve changes in residence, participation in initiation rituals, reclassification by name or relationship term, and constant redefinition of the constituent elements of the community. This form of change is perceived as a part of the social formation and does not constitute a challenge to the system as a whole.

The possibility of major structural changes in Amazonian societies where large-scale shifts take place between one aspect of social organisation and another have been touched upon by some authors. Murphy (1978), for example, looks at structural changes among the

---

4. Arakmbut social organisation contains both hierarchical and egalitarian aspects, although these terms must be understood relatively. This a feature has been noted in other parts of Western Amazonia (Chaumeil 1993).

Mundurucú, but he analyses dynamics in terms of reactions to external phenomena rather than looking at internal processes of change.

Internal processes which lead to social change, such as access to resources, decision-making, informal communication, and subtle or gradual shifts of emphasis in social organisation, have been discussed in terms of certain specific social areas, particularly marriage. For example, the work of Kenneth Kensinger (1984) has drawn attention to the variety of possibilities available for interpreting and choosing marriage alliances. Furthermore, a recent article by Dean (1995) tackles the question of brideservice in Western Amazonia and looks at the processes by which marriage decisions are negotiated, not only prior to but also after the union. This insight can be broadened to many other areas of social life – indeed to all collective decision-making.[5]

Some authors have looked at indigenous peoples' own conceptualisations of change. A recent example is discussed by Rival (1993), who compares Huaorani perceptions of fast and slow growing trees with cycles of peace and war among the Huaorani. By embracing indigenous notions of change with the internal dynamics of social life, this book attempts to place the processes of Arakmbut change into the historical context of the gold rush which has taken place in the Peruvian Amazon during the last twenty years.

Methodological Considerations

The approach adopted here tries to juxtapose the internal process of change within the general framework of an Arakmbut social and cultural formation with the dramatic changes arising from the gold rush over a period of twelve years. However, a methodological difficulty can arise from the incompatibility between a structural configuration and the processes of change operating at the same moment. The description of a configuration at one historical moment does not necessarily reflect change; yet in the attempt to capture process, order is reduced to flux. This sociological version of the Heisenberg principle is difficult to avoid.

5. The distinction between changes which take place through interaction and the broader structural change, referred to here, is similar to Firth's discussion of organisational and structural change (Firth 1951). The distinction is useful providing that daily activities or organisational change, the longer-term cycles of social life (domestic or life), and the broader shifts of structural emphasis are not necessarily treated as different types of change but rather as different processes within one broad continuum.

One possible way to approach this problem is to look at the situation in a community such as San José del Karene in 1980 and in 1992 and then 'subtract' the difference, resulting in a structural approach comparing moments as frames in a film, or cards in a pack (Firth 1959, Lévi-Strauss 1974). The structural shifts appear as 'transformations'. However, structural analysts have also tried to look at process within transformation. This was a feature of studies influenced by Marx in the 1970s (Friedman 1975; Godelier 1977; Seddon 1978). The combination of structural transformations and internal processes provided a useful way of trying to resolving the problem. In retrospect, the mechanistic models gave the impression that structure gained over process.

Whereas the structuralism of Lévi-Strauss urged us to look at models rather than the 'empirical reality' (Lévi-Strauss 1963), the 'postmodern' approach urges us to understand that those very models are as complex and 'contingent' as the so-called empirical reality (Best and Kellner 1991). Postmodern approaches to social life may have rediscovered the importance of contingency, but too much reliance on event can lead to an 'anti-structure' which converts order into incoherent moments of creativity. Thus, too much emphasis on structural formations and concepts leads to mechanistic models which blur experience into patterns of structure, whereas too much emphasis on process and event dissolves form into an aleatoric and unpredictable basis of experience.

The eclectic approach used here, however, uses the above theories and methodological constraints not so much as factors which should be avoided in order to create something new, but as tools for illuminating change in an Arakmbut community.

Socio-cultural Change and the Arakmbut

Certain aspects of the dynamics of Arakmbut social and cultural life have already been studied in the volume on myth and history. The main myths in the Arakmbut canon provide a lens for illuminating principles of social organisation, the cultural conceptualisations of existence and death, and historical relationships with other indigenous and non-indigenous peoples. The previous volume juxtaposes the synchronic and diachronic features of Amazonian ethnography illustrated above: the dynamic configuration of an Arakmbut community in the twentieth century Peru and its creative and interpretative relationship to history.

The approach adopted here goes further because it traces dynamic processes within and without Arakmbut community life, and uses them to see how the social formation changes in practice. The Arakmbut live in a dynamic, changing world which is constantly redefined in relation to other members of the community, their neighbours, non-indigenous outsiders, and the spirit world. The Arakmbut universe is in constant flux and provides regular challenges to the communities in interpreting, reinterpreting, and anticipating events. By controlling this potential chaos, the Arakmbut establish order in their lives and try to ensure that they can determine their future and fulfil their desires.

There are two sets of qualities which are particularly significant in establishing this form of control: political and shamanic. Political qualities are about decision-making, responsibility and mobilising people to think beyond their specific needs and interests; shamanic qualities are about communicating with the spirit world, which oversees all Arakmbut productive and reproductive activities. This book looks first at shamanic activities and then at the political sphere of Arakmbut life in order to demonstrate the ways in which people strive to make sense of the world and utilise it for their own welfare and that of others. In order to achieve this they utilise an already existing socio-cultural framework which is sufficiently opaque to allow flexibility and creativity of interpretation. As these interpretations are accepted or rejected by others in the community, changes occur. Occasionally, certain events are so significant for the Arakmbut that they act as a catalyst for generating change because, at periods of crisis, new activities and interpretations are at their height.

The account of the death of San José's shaman precedes a discussion of shamanism, the dynamic relationship between the visible and invisible worlds, and the means of communication between the two realms. The close relationship between species, spirits, and humans on an everyday basis establishes the means for looking at dreaming and curing practices which strive to retain health and order in a community constantly facing sickness and death.

A case study on curing introduces the complicated political dimension of shamanic activities. Subsequent chapters analyse these in terms of Arakmbut notions of desire and generosity which are the main qualities that give rise to prestige. They are placed within a framework of Arakmbut social perspectival relativity and the connection between the political and shamanic domains at a personal level through the soul *(nokiren)*. This information is then used to show how social life is articulated through informal encounters at different times during the day. After reviewing the shamanic and political aspects of Arakmbut community life, the focus shifts to the changes which have taken place over the last ten years.

The period of change reviewed in this book covers the twelve years from 1980 to 1992. Twelve years is a short moment in history but, by comparing changes with documentation from earlier periods, it has been possible to put together a hypothesis about the directions in which Arakmbut socio-cultural life has moved in the last fifty years or more. This study takes two aspects of Arakmbut life as a basis for looking at change: relations between the visible and invisible worlds and the daily interactive encounters which take place between people. These two sets of relationships are the bases of the dynamic processes which define the boundaries of social and cultural categories and which also undergo shifts according to events which take place in the community.

The final chapters examine three areas which illustrate aspects of change in an Arakmbut community. The first looks at the effect of external colonisation. In 1980 there were a hundred illegal gold colonists on San José's territory. In spite of receiving legal recognition of 23,000 hectares in 1986, there are currently 443 colonists on the community's lands. One third of the beaches on San José's titled territory are in the hands of colonists who refuse to allow the Arakmbut to work gold. The increase in colonists has lead to a marked dwindling of gold and game resources which has had severe repercussions for Arakmbut households. Their response to this problem has triggered internal changes within the community.

More specific influences of colonisation arise in the question of technological innovation. The Arakmbut themselves have been mining gold for over fifteen years, which has provided them with sporadic returns and an increasing reliance on the market economy. Now each Arakmbut household has a source of cash income which has enabled the workforce to buy equipment and labour. The extension of gold technology, such as motor pumps, has had the effect of making each household group more independent. Furthermore, some Arakmbut have found it possible to hire workers from the Andean highlands to mine for them.

The activities of missionaries have also induced change among the Arakmbut. The permanent presence of missionary teachers in San José since 1983 has provided an alternative view of socio-cultural organisation based on principles derived from the national society. This has undoubtedly opened up possibilities within the community for changes in cultural orientation which are conducive towards integration into the Peruvian state.

- 11 -

Colonisation, new technology, and missionisation through education have had an enormous influence on changes within San José. However, to attribute all change to outside influences ignores the internal dynamics of community life as well as the fluctuating relationships which the Arakmbut have with the spirit world. This myopia does not help an understanding of change from an Arakmbut perspective and consequently reinforces the view that indigenous peoples do not change themselves but are changed by circumstances.

The second aspect of change looks at internal contradictions (or tensions) within Arakmbut social life. Conflicts and alliances between households are based on clan and kindred relations, affines, gender, post-marital residence and age, all of which operate simultaneously in a community and are emphasised by people with different interests. Everyday encounters emphasise these aspects of social organisation to a different degree and during periods of crisis such as a difficult marriage negotiation, illness, or death, countless discussions about behaviour, relationships, and community solidarity take place. These interpretations of events can change the organisation of a community for many years. The effect should not be to detract from the significance of influences from the national society, but rather to draw attention to the internal dynamics which exist in Arakmbut social life. These dynamics constitute the Arakmbut people's own capacity to make decisions and to try, as far as possible, to control their future.

Sometimes this form of control is clearly impossible in situations such as a catastrophic decimation of population. The Arakmbut faced this forty years ago, immediately prior to, and after, their first contact with non-indigenous people. Disease caused an enormous loss of life and, during the period, 40 percent of the elderly generation died. The repercussions of this population decline can still be felt today in terms of fear of illness, suspicion of outsiders, and concern about the loss of indigenous knowledge. The cause of the depopulation was the disease brought by non-indigenous people, but it was intimately connected with hostility from the spirit world.

It is impossible to grasp the multi-dimensional features of socio-cultural change among the Arakmbut without looking in more detail at the spirit world. This third area of change dynamics focuses on how the invisible domain acts on the visible world through spirit activities, patrolling the boundaries of the acceptable in ways tightly connected to personal behaviour. Without communicating with and understanding the spirit world, the Arakmbut socio-cultural formation could rapidly collapse and they would be unable to defend their lives from the constantly encroaching outside world.

The Arakmbut knowledge about the existence of spirits is something which missionaries have been unable to eradicate in forty years of proselytisation. Sorcery, the presence of hostile spirits, and the power of dreams are so strong that everyone, from Harakmbut university students in Lima to the most pro-missionary member of the community, is certain of their existence. The effect of the invisible spirit world on the visible has a profound influence on change because the two worlds are intimately connected. The state of a person's soul reflects his or her behaviour and relationships with other people. The result is a transcendental relationship with the invisible world which cross-cuts the influence of the nation state or the colonising frontier, all of which add to the internal dynamics of daily community life.

The Arakmbut do not reduce explanations of change to any one factor. On the contrary, they blend personal, social, and spiritual elements into the ways they initiate or respond to events. The emphasis of any one explanation of change over another varies according to the context. This book looks at several of these contexts to catch a glimpse of the extraordinary panorama of reasons, which range from the human to the non-human and from the visible to the invisible.

Ethnographic Background

The Madre de Dios of southeastern Peru consists of 73,402 km^2 containing three provinces: Tambopata, Manu, and Tahuamanu (see map 1). The region is currently the focus of intense gold mining activity which has attracted over forty thousand colonists and workers from the highlands, thereby doubling the permanent population (CAAAP, 1992:8) and causing considerable problems for the indigenous peoples of the region. Map 2 shows indigenous communities in the Madre de Dios from nineteen different peoples making up a total indigenous population of 10,000 (Rummenhöller & Lazarte 1991; FENAMAD pers. comm.).

The Madre de Dios contains four linguistic families: the Arawak-speaking Matsigenka; the Panoan Amahuaca and Yaminahua; the Tacanan Iñapari and Ese'eja; and the seven Harakmbut peoples. Furthermore, there are indigenous peoples who were brought into the area during the rubber boom at the turn of the century: Ashāninka (Campa), Shipibo-Conibo, Kichwa Runa del Napo (Santarosinos), and Cocama. In recent years, two other groups have appeared sporadically – the Yora (a Panoan group also called the Nahua) and the Mashco Piro.

Map 1: General map of Peru indicating other indigenous peoples neighbouring the Harakmbut.

• Towns
∼ Rivers

The Harakmbut, who number between 1,500 and 2,000 people, are the largest indigenous language family in the Madre de Dios (d'Ans 1973; Ribeiro & Wise 1978; Lyon 1976; Helberg 1989). They consist of seven peoples (Wachipaeri, Sapiteri, Pukirieri, Arasaeri, Arakmbut [Amarakaeri][6], Amaiweri [Kisambaeri], and Toyeri) whose homeland originally consisted of six hundred thousand hectares, stretching between the rivers Inambari and Upper Madre de Dios (see map 3).

The Arakmbut, consisting of approximately 850 people, are the largest Harakmbut people and live in the central area of Harakmbut territory in the five communities of Boca del Inambari, San José del Karene, Barranco Chico, Puerto Luz, and Shintuya (see map 3). This work is based primarily on research in San José del Karene, although comparisons have been included with other communities when relevant.

The Arakmbut are divided into seven exogamous clans (Yaromba, Idnsikambo, Wandigpana, Masenawa, Singperi, Embieri, and Saweron) whose names pass from father to children. They have a symmetric prescriptive relationship terminology while marriage alliances are arranged by an ego-centred category called the *wambet,* consisting of a father's and mother's immediate kin. Each person contains invisible soul-matter (nokiren) which provides the means for contacting the world of the spirits through dreams and visions.

Indigenous peoples of the Madre de Dios have had regular contact with the highlands since pre-Colombian times. The Incas still feature within the Arakmbut mythological repertoire. The first reference specifically to the Arakmbut appeared in a document from 1907 in which Olivera talks of the 'Marakaeri' who live in the headwaters of the Colorado (Karene) river. Although the Arakmbut had no direct contact with the devastating destruction wrought by the 'caucheros' of the rubber boom, the indigenous peoples escaping genocide from slave raids on the main Madre de Dios river moved

6. The Harakmbut peoples were originally erroneously labelled 'Mashco' by those who first encountered them. The term Mashco eventually became narrowed down to refer to one people living between the rivers Karene and Upper Madre de Dios. However, they considered the term Mashco an insult and the name Amarakaeri was accepted until recently. The name Amarakaeri is used by outsiders and, according to some, refers to the headwaters of the Karene, where they are thought to have originated. Others say that Amarakaeri is a term of abuse used by the Wachipaeri and the Matsigenka. During my stay in San José in 1991-92, the elders asked me if I would refer to them by their indigenous name 'Arakmbut' from now on, a request which I have respected (for more on this see Volume 3, chapter four).

Map 2: Indigenous communities of the Madre de Dios.

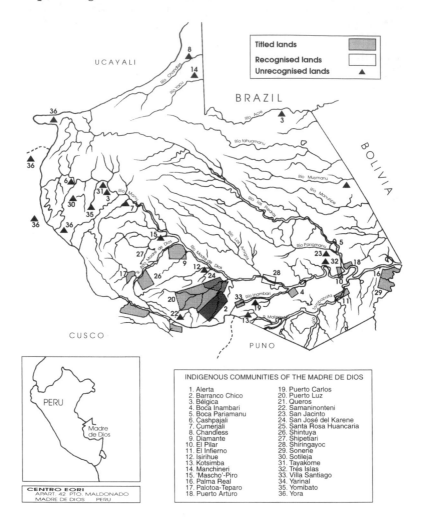

INDIGENOUS COMMUNITIES OF THE MADRE DE DIOS

1. Alerta
2. Barranco Chico
3. Bélgica
4. Boca Inambari
5. Boca Pariamanu
6. Cashpajali
7. Cumerjali
8. Chandless
9. Diamante
10. El Pilar
11. El Infierno
12. Isirihue
13. Kotsimba
14. Manchineri
15. 'Mascho'-Piro
16. Palma Real
17. Palotoa-Teparo
18. Puerto Arturo
19. Puerto Carlos
20. Puerto Luz
21. Queros
22. Samaninonteni
23. San Jacinto
24. San José del Karene
25. Santa Rosa Huancaria
26. Shintuya
27. Shipetiari
28. Shiringayoc
29. Sonene
30. Sotileja
31. Tayakome
32. Tres Islas
33. Villa Santiago
34. Yarinal
35. Yomibato
36. Yora

CENTRO EORI
APART. 42 PTO. MALDONADO
MADRE DE DIOS   PERU

Map 3: Harakmbut communities in the Madre de Dios.

i. PRECONTACT

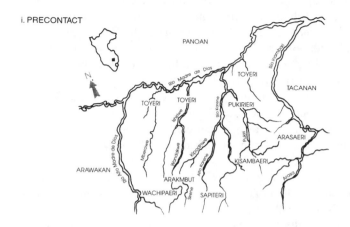

ii. CURRENT COMMUNITIES

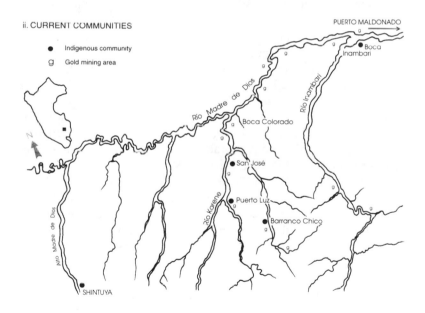

upriver to seek safety. The subsequent conflicts between the different Harakmbut peoples are still referred to as 'the Great War'.

Shortly before their first encounter with non-indigenous peoples, the Arakmbut were divided into two groups. The Wandakweri lived in the headwaters of the Ishiriwe river in seven communal houses or malocas *(hak)*. Each maloca held about fifty or more individuals who slept around a central area used for rituals and dancing, particularly the fiestas for the two male initiation ceremonies (*e'ohotokoy* and *e'mbaipak*). The people also shared garden work, cultivating a diverse variety of crops in a pattern of concentric circles. The men spent most of their time hunting or fishing while the women worked together in the gardens.

The other Arakmbut group – the Kipodneris – lived in five malocas on a parallel affluent of the Karene river, sharing a similar life style of hunting, fishing, gathering, and horticulture. Both the Wandakweri and Kipodneri Arakmbut differ in dialect, and there are distinctions in details of myth and ritual. Nevertheless, the two groups have always been in contact with each other and consider themselves closer than the other Harakmbut groups, whom they refer to as 'Taka'.

The Dominicans began proselytising in the Madre de Dios in 1902 and, over the next thirty years, made inroads with the Matsigenka in the upper Madre de Dios and the Ese'eja in the lower reaches of the same river. The Arasaeri, Toyeri, and Wachipaeri were brought or attracted to the missions during the 1920s and 1930s (Fernández Moro 1952) while a large-scale Wenner Gren Foundation expedition to the Karene (Colorado) in 1940 encountered the Sapiteri, Kisambaeri, and Pukirieri (Fejos 1941).

In 1950 the Arakmbut, who lived in the headwaters of the Ishiriwe on the Wandakwe river, moved towards the upper Madre de Dios and began to receive metal goods from the missionaries from plane drops or deposited on a trail leading towards the mission of Palotoa. During 1953 and 1954, the Dominicans crossed from the Alto Madre de Dios to the upper Ishiriwe and, with a Wachipaeri translator, made the first direct mission contact with the Arakmbut. Within three years the Arakmbut were suffering considerably from yellow fever, eye disease, and influenza. Gradually they made their way to Palotoa mission for help. They were eventually settled in the reduction-style mission of Shintuya which was established in 1957. After twelve years in the mission, the Arakmbut found themselves enmeshed in a complicated series of conflicts with other indigenous people and the priests. In October, 1969, a group escaped overnight and went downriver to found the community of San José del Karene.

They were followed in 1971 and 1973 by Barranco Chico and Boca del Inambari (Torralba 1979).

Meanwhile, the Kipodneri Arakmbut had been contacted by the Protestant organisation the Summer Institute of Linguistics. Although they briefly went to Shintuya for six months in 1958, the community eventually settled in the headwaters of the Karene on the Wasoroko, initially at Puerto Alegre and, later, further downstream at Puerto Luz (Moore nd). Since the late 1970s, all the Arakmbut communities have been washing gold on the beaches of the Karene or Inambari. There is no gold at Shintuya and so the community there has, with support from the mission, begun to carry out lumber work and cattle raising (Fuentes 1983).

In 1982 the Native Federation of the Madre de Dios (FENAMAD) was established, comprised of representatives from all the communities in the region (Wahl 1985; Moore 1985). FENAMAD carries out a wide variety of activities. It provides communities with political support, particularly concerning territorial rights; seeks funding for economic projects to reduce dependency on the national society; and provides programmes in cultural strengthening. Since 1993, the Harakmbut Council (COHAR) was established as an ethnic sub-organisation of FENAMAD, linking the seven Harakmbut peoples. COHAR channels the work of FENAMAD more directly to the Harakmbut communities.

This gradual political organisation of the indigenous peoples of the Madre de Dios is constrained through a constant lack of resources and difficulties of communication. The challenges of co-ordinating the indigenous struggle of nineteen different peoples over such a vast area are enormous. Nevertheless, the process of political mobilisation, although gradual, illustrates the dynamism which exists in the indigenous communities of the Madre de Dios and which this book aims to demonstrate in detail.

* * *

In December, 1980, during my first period in San José, I was living in the house of a widower who had temporarily left the community to work gold downriver. The shaman (*wayorokeri* – dreamer) had been unwell for several days and I had visited him regularly; for a while he seemed to be improving. Then, on the morning of 23 December, just before midday, I heard grief-stricken cries coming from his house, and a train of events began which coloured the history of the whole community for the next twelve years and beyond.

Chapter 120

THE DEATH OF THE SHAMAN

Death is distressing and dangerous, particularly the death of someone venerated. When the most powerful shamanic practitioner in San José del Karene died, the community was thrown into political and spiritual turmoil. The history of the shaman has been entwined with the fate of the Arakmbut of San José since their first contact with missionaries in the 1950s; his thoughts and ideas were refracted through the people and his knowledge of curing defended their health. In periods of crisis, his ability to interpret dreams gave him unrivalled authority as an advisor. His death left a vacuum which the Arakmbut still sense in times of adversity.

Psyche – 'a Man with Shamanic Qualities'[1]

Psyche was indistinguishable from any other member of the community; he worked gold, drank fully during the fiestas, enjoyed jokes and stories, cared about his relatives, and tried not to arouse anger in others. He was unobtrusive in daily community life, although his slender frame, prominent cheekbones and receding hairline indicated that he was an elder who should be respected. During political meetings he would sit or stand at the back of the company and say little. However, occasionally, after an evening meal, Psyche could be seen walking through the village to the hut of a sick person and, a

---

1. The Arakmbut do not like to utter the names of the dead and so I have called the shaman Psyche, which is similar to but distinct from his actual name. 'Psyche' also conveys the sense of gravity which his name inspired, as well as its mythological connotations.

moment later, the soft murmur of a curing chant *(chindign)* would float through the night.

At other times, Arakmbut visited him in his house at the far end of the village near the path to the cemetery, where they would consult him about personal problems or their general welfare. He would lie down on the bench outside his house for a short period, dream, and on awaking give his opinion, formed after consultation with his spirit contacts. At informal encounters with other members of the community, Psyche would advise, warn and interpret the cosmological implications of events and behaviour.

Psyche was a *wayorokeri* – an interpreter of dreams.[2] In troubled times, he knew the necessary precautions the community should take from the messages he received in his dreams. The information came from the *ndakmbayorokeri* or *ndakyorokeri* spirits ('good dream beings'). These spirits are associated with certain species with which a wayorokeri builds up a special relationship during his life. The ndakmbayorokeri take the form of attractive young women who tell the dreamer of the most appropriate time to hunt or fish, warn him of future events, and in particular help him to cure.

Psyche was also a *wamanoka'eri* – a curer and diagnostician of illness. His methods were based on insights revealed in dreams or arrived at by observing similarities between symptoms of a sickness and animal behaviour. If his diagnoses were correct, when he sang the curing chants (chindign) related to the species, the sick person would recover. Psyche was astute at interpreting the social or cultural transgressions which caused illness and was therefore considered to have both knowledge and vision.

A sign of shamanic efficacy is a successful curing and Psyche was sufficiently skilful that he was renowned far beyond the community

2. Barriales and Torralba (1970:45) follow Alvarez (1946:11) in describing a Uay-orokeri as a shaman who cures by taking invisible darts from a patient's body. The definition of wayorokeri in San José corresponds with that of Califano (1978a:421) who calls him a 'dreamer' or 'one who knows how to dream'. He is also a prophet. The term *watopakeri* (cf. Califano ibid.) or *topakari* is not known among the Arakmbut and is a rarely used Wachipaeri word.

    In this book I take a broader definition of 'shaman' than Califano (1982), who argues that, unlike other Harakmbut peoples, the Arakmbut have no shamans because the practitioners do not travel to different worlds. This is correct in the sense that shamans do not fly to different spheres in the universe. Nevertheless, I think that their capacity to travel in dreams and visions within the invisible world is sufficient grounds to use the term. Furthermore, as the present approach sees 'shamanism' as a set of qualities, techniques, and facilities concerned with communicating with the invisible world, I think that 'shaman' is appropriate in this context.

of San José del Karene. Other Arakmbut communities were more cautious in their eulogies of the benefits of his skills, because they knew that his techniques could be used to harm the enemies of San José. The beneficial shaman of one community can be feared in other communities as a sorcerer.

Psyche's Life

Psyche was born in about 1920 on the Wandakwe, a tributary of the Ishiriwe, in one of the seven Arakmbut communal houses which straddled the course of the river. He was a Wandakweri Arakmbut who belonged to the communal house of the Kukambatoeri ('those who live where coca grows'). His patrilineal clan name was Yaromba.

During his youth, Psyche discovered that he had the capacity to communicate with the spirit world. One day he was waiting by the river to catch boquichicos (carp-like fish) when, to his amazement, he was surrounded by different species of fish who suddenly spoke. They told him that they were spirits from the river and they wanted to communicate with him in dreams so that he could become knowledgeable. In his dreams and visions he frequently repeated this experience and gradually became proficient at understanding their messages. The spirits began to advise him where to hunt and fish, which enabled him to establish a reputation as a great hunter. Whenever he went to the forest or river, he always returned laden with game. As the spirit relationship developed, Psyche began to show expertise in curing and providing advice for the community.

After missionary contact, a yellow fever outbreak in 1957 forced the Arakmbut of the Wandakwe to seek medicines from the priests at Shintuya where they remained for twelve years. However, during this period, conflicts between the different Arakmbut maloca groups, the Wachipaeri, and the priests intensified to such an extent that Psyche's group separated from the majority of the mission and moved to a site a few hundred yards downstream. Psyche was deeply concerned about threats of sorcery and realised from his dream messages that they must escape from the mission in order to survive. The account of the escape (presented in its original form in Volume 1) was an exodus from the mission to another part of Harakmbut territory. Psyche's dreams directed them to the river Karene, and in 1969, they reached the river Pukiri.

Life was not very satisfactory there because the Arakmbut had no crops and had to start horticultural cultivation with no seeds. They made contact with the Kipodneri Arakmbut, who lived upriver at Puerto Alegre, and received some support, but after a conflict over an elopement, relations deteriorated into violent confrontations. Psyche played a vital part in defending his people by using his power over the weather to harass the raiding parties of Puerto Alegre. In 1974/5, after several floods, Psyche relayed a message from the river spirits to the Arakmbut telling them to move to the present site of San José, high on a cliff above the Karene.

During the 1970s, San José was divided into two parts. Two residential groups comprising survivors from several pre-1957 maloca groups had joined together in the community. The Wakutangeri ('those who live upstream') and the Kotsimberi ('those who live near the aguaje palm') had built their houses in two clearings divided by a short path through scrubland. The Idnsikambo clan were preeminent among the Wakutangeri group, and Psyche's clan, the Yaromba, was more influential among the Kotsimberi, along with the Masenawa. The residential groups and clans provided the main political rivalries within the community. In spite of his allegiance to the Kotsimberi/Yaromba part of San José, Psyche was always concerned for the welfare of all its inhabitants. He managed to override rivalries within the community, thereby ensuring his respect and popularity.

Table 1.1: Clan and residence formation of San José in 1980[3]

Residence Groups	Kotsimberi	Wakutangeri
Clan dominance	Yaromba	Idnsikambo

Psyche's life spanned the traumatic period from first contact with the Dominican priests in the Wandakwe through the time spent in the mission of Shintuya to the founding of the native community of San José del Karene. His capacity to communicate with the spirit world enabled him to provide advice and direction to the Arakmbut in the difficult decisions they had to make. During Psyche's final illness the Arakmbut frequently discussed his past life and came to realise how dependent they were on him. His part in the history of the community was crucial to them and his death threw the whole village into disarray. Some people even doubted whether San José would survive as a community.

---

3. This distinction disappeared around 1986 when a family from the Kotsimberi half moved to the community of Barranco Chico to live with other close kin. The result is that Barranco Chico is now the Kotsimberi Arakmbut community and San José is completely Wakutangeri.

Psyche's Illness

In October 1980 Psyche's health began to deteriorate. He complained of pains in his heart, so he stopped smoking and working gold and remained mostly in his house in the community. This appeared to help and his condition improved until December, when he was unable to keep his food down, lost weight, felt swelling in his intestines, and experienced piercing pains like sharp sticks penetrating his stomach.

No one knew how to explain this. The symptoms were those of an illness caused by the river spirits, but previously the river spirits had told him that they had no wish take away his life until his hair had receded to the top of his head; this had not yet happened. Psyche had neither hunted too much nor transgressed the social morality of the community. For this reason, the initial response was to treat his illness as the work of a sorcerer *(chindignwakeri),* which is usually the first reason given by the Arakmbut to explain misfortune.

Several severe storms took place over San José in mid-December and the people became afraid at night. Thunder and lightning are considered dangerous when the community is undergoing some crisis because they mark the presence of harmful spirits. The weather led to another hypothesis concerning Psyche's illness: river spirits, who unite when they are harmful, were gathering together to visit the community at night in order to take Psyche to their riverine underworld (Seronwe). The spirits liked him and wanted his presence in their abode.

In subsequent weeks these explanations were debated and discussed by the people and the sick man himself. According to the context and the social relations involved, the explanations altered. To this day no one is really sure whether his illness arose from sorcery or other causes.

The Prophecy

Two days before his death the shaman made a prophecy to the men who were most respected in the community. He explained that he would die earlier than he had expected because the river spirits wanted to take him to Seronwe. He was going to live there with his spirit wife, in a house with his own chacras (gardens) and domesticated animals. Whereas a death is normally very dangerous because the spirits of the dead can harm the living, the community were not to be afraid as he had no intention of causing any harm. Psyche said that he would remain in Seronwe for the duration of the wet season *(wawiyok)* and that the rain would be unlike any previously experienced. Thunder and lightning would be followed by a flood greater than any witnessed in the forest before; the river Karene would run straight and all the Amikos (non-indigenous people) in the Madre de Dios would be drowned. Only the Harakmbut would survive.

While he was in Seronwe, no one from San José should fish because he would be living with spirits of the river, some of whom were fish themselves. After the cataclysm, the dry season would arrive *(wambayok)* and Psyche would reappear in San José in the form of a bird. He would alight in the central patio of the village, and although no one then knew what species he would take on, everyone would recognise him. He would remain in contact with the community forever, returning to advise and warn people when they had problems. In the future they should call him either with the aid of ayahuasca or in their usual dreams and visions.

Attempts to Save his Life

After this prophecy Psyche appeared more relaxed. However the community did not want him to die and, after persuading him that he might live a little longer, used several methods to try to save his life. A Sapiteri shaman, famous for his curing abilities, was called from the river Pukiri. He was considered an outsider by the Arakmbut and so there was some uncertainty about him, but he knew songs and orations for curing and also how to prevent harmful spirits approaching the sick man. The Sapiteri shaman remained in San José for a few days but said that he could do nothing because his skill lay in curing illnesses caused by forest rather than river spirits. The Arakmbut in San José, however, were suspicious that perhaps this powerful shaman wished the sick man harm.

Meanwhile, Psyche's family tried to cure him by giving him a mixture of resins to drink, blowing tobacco over him, and hitting him with isanga nettles, but without success. They also gave him non-indigenous medicines such as tablets, vitamins, and salts. Several people suggested taking him to the hospital in Puerto Maldonado, three days downstream, but he said he was sure he would not survive the journey and preferred to die in his community.

Psyche's Death

A little before midday on 23 December cries were heard from Psyche's house. His wife was shouting a death chant in a long drawn out rhythm: '*Ndoedn opewadn! Ndoedn opewadn!*' *Opewadn* is the formal relationship term for 'my spouse' and is heard on occasions such as initiation ceremonies or marriages.[4] In his hut, stretched out on the floor, Psyche lay dead. His wife covered him with a blanket, constantly singing the death chant. Then she took all of their belongings out of the house and placed them in two piles; one consisted of her own things and the other of those of her husband, including his clothes, bows, arrows, blankets, and tools. The widow's brother, who was her only relation in the village, then began to set fire to the pile of Psyche's possessions. Meanwhile she went to the kitchen at the side of the house and brought out all the pots, pans, and cutlery, which she broke with an axe. In this manner the dead man's personal property was destroyed.

During the destruction of Psyche's possessions, two men who had not gone to work gold that day decided to inform the rest of the community about the death. At that time the two residence groups in San José, the Wakutangeri and the Kotsimberi, worked gold in separate placers. The Wakutangeri had left the village a few months before and were living at a temporary gold encampment one hour downstream from San José, while the Kotsimberi (Psyche's group) were working gold at a placer sufficiently close to the community to return every night from work. The two men canoed downriver to tell the news to the Kotsimberi but did not continue further on to inform the Wakutangeri who were further downstream, as there would not have been time for the messengers to return for the burial.

The Kotsimberi returned to San José immediately. Psyche's Yaromba kin entered the house first, followed by men from the other clans, while the women remained outside of the house watching. A low discussion then ensued to clarify the arrangements for the burial.

The Burial

Outside Psyche's house was a narrow path leading to the cemetery *(ku'mbarak),* which was rarely used because of the danger from spirits who lurk there. When alive, Psyche could warn the community should the dead threaten to attack from their graves. The men and the widow set out along the path to the cemetery, looking at the condition of the

---

4. *Opewadn* literally means 'she/he who sits next to me' as opposed to the usual word for spouse, *watoe,* which means 'she/he next to me'. *Opewadn* can be contracted to *opedn.*

track to see if there were prints of animals or signs of any wandering spirits. As they analysed the ground, they cleared the undergrowth.

Eventually they reached area of the dead, which contained various signs of previous Arakmbut burials such as rough mounds, wooden crosses, and personal mementos. The grave of a girl who had died recently had part of her clothing still hanging from a wooden covering, while at the head of another grave lay the remains of balsa ashes, burnt and left for a day to see whether the spirits responsible for the death had walked over the spot, leaving tracks such as animal prints. The men then began to look for a site where they could dig the new grave, and there was some discussion as to where the best place was, but the widow made the final decision. All were concerned lest while they dug they should encounter the bones of a dead body, which could wreak harm upon the community.

The younger men dug a grave about one metre in depth while the others sat on the ground, the widow apart, and, more relaxed, the elders began to talk of the new shamanic and political situation in the community. The Kotsimberi half of the village, with their predominance of Yaromba clan, considered that Psyche had been the traditional leader *(wairi)* of the whole of San José and that someone from their group should take over his position. The Wakutangeri half, dominated by the Idnsikambo, already held the state-recognised offices of President, Secretary, and Treasurer of the community and were referred to within the community as *wantupa.* The Kotsimberi wanted to ensure the continuation of a balance of power between the two sides. They feared that with their spiritual leader now dead, the Wakutangeri might extend their shamanic influence through their recognised skills in the use of the hallucinogenic plant, ayahuasca, which they had introduced into the community some years previously. Although old Harakmbut shamans were not opposed to ayahuasca, they considered it an easy way to contact the spirit world that avoided the patience and discipline of a long-term spiritual visionary experience.

When the grave was dug, they returned to Psyche's house. The Yaromba men entered the house and picked up the body, which was wrapped in his best blanket. The body was placed in a 'coffin' of pona wood which had been made out of his bed and tied with creeper. The dead man's classificatory brothers then raised the coffin to their shoulders and carried it slowly to the cemetery path. But on the path, they suddenly began to run, the men first and then the women. The last hundred metres were covered so quickly that the coffin was already in the grave by the time the women arrived. Everyone present began to throw soil onto the coffin. Emotions began to spill over; the men cried quietly, while the women, standing to the side, wailed and shouted *'Nowenda chimbui! Nowenda chimbui!'* which means 'grief for my brother-in-law!'

When the grave was almost filled, the widow suddenly became wild with anger and grief. She hit the men, screaming insults at those who had made the grave and then, grabbing a long stick, she began to beat Psyche's dog, which had followed the cortege to the cemetery. The creature lay almost dead, and her brother-in-law quickly killed it and threw its body in the bushes. The grave was now filled and a mound of earth rose above it, onto which the spades and machetes which had been used in the burial were placed. Everyone returned to the village and entered their houses in silence.

The Wake

After eating, the women and children went to bed because they were afraid that the spirits who visit a community to celebrate a death could harm them. Any unfamiliar noise outside was considered to be the presence of a dangerous spirit. Meanwhile the men went downriver to the small shop of a highland colonist, where they bought rum and cherry brandy. Whereas the women had displayed their feelings more demonstratively than the men at the burial, the men showed their emotions at the wake when they returned from the store. Throughout the night they became increasingly drunk, sang, cried and shouted *'Nowenda wamambuey!'* or *'nowenda enchipo!'*, depending on whether they were brother or brother-in-law of the dead man. Anyone who wanted to fight was immediately stopped by the others. They mourned Psyche's passing in song, in stories, and particularly through reminiscences, speaking of his life and deeds; then they began to discuss the reasons for his death and the consequences of the catastrophe. The men were still drinking as dawn broke and the women joined in as they emerged from the houses.

Psyche's closest relatives then prepared to destroy his house. Enormous flames shot into the air as his home caught fire and eventually burned to the ground along with his kitchen. A group of women related to his widow killed all his chickens and cooked them in enormous pots. When they were ready they brought them to the wake and everyone ate the chickens in communion outside the charred remains of Psyche's house.

As they were eating, a great flock of birds passed overhead and a cry of *'Kapiro! Kapiro!'* (heron) went up. A shudder of excitement passed through the assembled Arakmbut because herons are river birds considered to be the domesticated animals of river spirits. As all dead people have their 'chickens', everyone knew that the chickens which they were eating had been transformed into river birds to precede Psyche's nokiren (soul) to Seronwe. They discussed how his dog and chickens had been killed for his use in the other world under the river. Finally his chicken hut was burnt and the lemon tree outside his house cut down. All his property was destroyed except the chacras which were also the property of his widow – she would need food when she moved temporarily to live with her deceased husband's brother.

Dispersion of the Community

As the ashes of the chicken hut settled, the canoes of the Wakutangeri half of the village could be heard arriving. They had taken a day off from working gold and had come to San José to collect their weekly supply of yuca and plantains and to visit Psyche. The Kotsimberi told them the news and asked why they had not come earlier. They should have sensed or dreamed of the danger to his life if they had been proficient in shamanic skills. The widow showed great emotion verging on anger.

The two halves of the community then sat down and drank together, whereupon the Wakutangeri went to the cemetery to visit the grave. As on the previous day, the women cried and shouted while the men wept quietly. The Wakutangeri introduced the first signs of Catholicism when one young man, recently returned to the community after a period conscripted into the army, placed two candles on the earth mound and a wooden cross at the head of the grave, referring to Psyche as a 'saint'. Others prayed, and they began to return to the village.

On the path from the cemetery some of the Kotsimberi kinsmen of the dead man began an anxious discussion with the influential Wakutangeri men regarding future leadership of San José, but nothing was resolved. After drinking for an hour or so, the Wakutangeri returned to their camp downriver.

The Kotsimberi remained in San José and sobered up over the rest of the day. After sunset, noises were heard in an unoccupied hut and, later, mysterious footsteps passed by, pots and pans fell over of their own accord, and whispering voices filtered through the air. Over the following days, as these noises continued, the people became too uneasy to remain in San José and decided to move downriver to make a semi-permanent gold camp in the style of the Wakutangeri. They found a site and by the New Year of 1981 had moved to the camp of Santa Rosa.

After a death, the river and forest spirits come to the village for a fiesta where they spend day and night celebrating the death. During these feasts the vomit of the spirits causes the river to rise and foam appears on the surface. People should avoid the community at all costs during this period because the spirits can easily enter a person's house as a breeze and cause severe illness. Anyone who happens to see one of the spirits will die soon afterwards.

San José was therefore abandoned for two and a half months after the death of Psyche, to leave the houses free for the spirits to enter. One night after the evacuation a man stopped off in San José while returning from a trip to the neighbouring Arakmbut community of Puerto Luz. He arrived in the gold camp the following day, shaken, and told of hearing conversations of spirits and their footsteps in the night. Arakmbut from both gold encampments occasionally had to return to the village to collect yuca and plantains from the chacras. Whenever they returned, they always saw a single heron circling over San José, which signified that the spirits had not yet stopped their celebrations and the nokiren of the dead man was still there.

Political Consequences of the Death

When the two halves of the village met after the burial, relations began to deteriorate and the political consequences of the death began to have their effect as the implications of the prophecy were interpreted and reinterpreted. The principal manifestation of the conflicts was accusations of sorcery. No one claims to know how sorcery is done, because to a large extent, the knowledge is the act. Accusations are always directed at people whom the accusers dislike or fear and consequently indicate current political relationships. Initially Taka (non-Arakmbut) sorcerers were blamed for the death of Psyche, but in the months after, accusations were directed against persons with prestige, influence, and position in the opposite halves of the village. The motive for the murder was considered to be hatred *(ochinosik)* of the dead man. Several people with close relatives in both halves of the village sought to improve relations by means of drinking parties and gradually accusations of sorcery ceased and relations improved. However, there was still tension which emerged through different explanations of Psyche's death.

After a month, the Arakmbut could see that the prophecy would not be fulfilled in its entirety. The river had indeed increased more than usual for a wet season, but everyone was expecting a vast flood, and when there was no sign of one, they became more sceptical. A few Wakutangeri broke the prohibition on fishing and alternative explanations of the death appeared, demonstrating small but significant discrepancies.

One day a *paron* bird (turkey hen) associated with the Yaromba circled over the camp of the Wakutangeri. When this species appears after a death it signifies that dead person was killed by a snake. People then remembered that before he had died, Psyche had thought that he had been bitten by a snake but had managed to extract all the venom. However, some Arakmbut began to say that he could not have gotten rid of all the venom and that some had congealed in his stomach, because when he lay dying he coughed up 'bitter blood' which is associated with snake bites. Furthermore, the prophecy which Psyche had made before his death was based on the assumption that the river spirits were going to take his nokiren (soul-matter) to Seronwe and that the cataclysm which was to come would centre around the river flooding. No such cataclysm had occurred and so dangerous forest *toto* spirits, whose arrows are seen as snakes by humans, may have been responsible for his death, in which case a part of his nokiren would have been taken into the forest and could be dangerous. With a part of his soul in the forest, the complete ban on all fishing was not so critical.

Whereas both halves of San José agreed that forest spirits had more to do with the death than had been thought, the Kotsimberi had an alternative explanation: that Psyche was not only a great fisher with contacts linking him to the river spirits, but that he was a great hunter too. The species of animal which he hunted best was the white-lipped peccary *(akudnui)*. He had once been on a hunting trip and had killed six animals himself while other hunters had killed only a few. As Psyche had had such good relations with the peccary, after his death, part of his soul had joined them while the other had joined the river spirits. Thus one part of his nokiren would stay in Seronwe and another part would go and live with the peccary in the forest. The spirits of the peccary were dispersed like the beneficial river spirits and so he would do no harm to the community. The Kotsimberi Yaromba consequently reinterpreted the prophecy to preserve the idea that the nokiren (soul) of the dead man would be dispersed among the animals and be beneficial to the community, whereas the Wakutangeri Idnsikambo considered that the part of his nokiren stolen by harmful toto spirits would have dangerous attributes. Thus the Kotsimberi Yaromba considered those aspects of his soul which went to the forest beneficial, while the Wakutangeri Idnsikambo thought that they were potentially harmful. These explanations were emphases in interpreting events according to the context and the political position of the group expressing the explanation in the community.

The Unification

In February, a wayorokeri from Puerto Luz dreamed that Psyche's nokiren had not yet reached Seronwe because he had seen Psyche's first wife walking in the ashes of the burnt house. Other Arakmbut reinforced this view when they heard cries and other strange sounds at the site of his house while passing on the way to a chacra (garden). Two months after the death, the Arakmbut began to prepare their chacras for the following dry season and consequently met more frequently in San José, where they discussed rumours of colonists moving onto gold placers near the community. With these worries, Psyche's death became less of a preoccupation and people slowly began to drift back to San José.

As the Arakmbut moved back to San José to clear their gardens, the rival explanations of the death came to focus on an agreed perspective. The general opinion was that the nokiren of the dead man had stayed in San José for two months because both river and forest spirits had been involved in the death and there had been much celebrating. He was now ready to leave the village and go to Seronwe, from where he would disperse into species associated with both the forest and the river.

Other events at this time indicated a return to the status quo before the death. Immediately after the death of her husband, the widow had assumed a position of importance rare for a woman in an Arakmbut community, holding considerable sway in the Kotsimberi gold camp of Santa Rosa where her words and opinions were treated very much as if they were those of her dead husband. However, when the community became reunited, her prominence declined and she lived in the house of her husband's brother as any other widowed woman.

Gradually, San José restored its former order and life moved on and, as the community became purged of the death, no one mentioned the events of the previous months; the crisis of death had passed and life could go on. By May 1991, the community would have looked to an outsider as if it had returned to normal. However, the death and transfiguration of Psyche was not simply a rite of passage which enabled the community re-establish itself anew. A new political and spiritual situation now existed in San José.

The Significance of the Death

The series of events which took place in San José in 1980 are significant because they illustrate the complex relationship between the invisible and visible worlds, animal species, political rivalries, and change within the community. Although not all the elements of the prophecy occurred after his death, Psyche was correct about the catastrophic social and cultural consequences.

The funeral and subsequent events followed a course not dissimilar to that of the myth of origin Wanamey, which reappears in several forms throughout Arakmbut experience (see Volume 1). Following the first theme of the myth which tells of a cataclysmic flood of fire, Psyche's death itself was a catastrophe for the community and chaos reigned during and immediately after the funeral and the wake. Spirits came into the community which normally remained outside, the river rose, and sorcery was rampant. Social relations became extremely tense and the village could not stand the strain; at this point accusations of sorcery were prominent.

In the second part of the myth, the Harakmbut escape destruction by climbing into the branches of the tree *Wanamey*. After Psyche's death, San José was abandoned and the two halves lived apart downstream, separated from the village. During this period relations gradually improved. Discussions became oriented towards theories as to whether the death was good and beneficial or whether there were some harmful consequences.

The reunification of San José marked the beginning of the 'new epoch' parallel to the final part of the myth, which tells of the founding of Arakmbut communities. During this period, a more moderate balance was restored to life. At this moment a general interpretation explained the death for all the community, marking the improved relationships between the two halves of the community. However, beneath the unity, the vacuum left by Psyche remained an underlying disquiet which regularly re-emerged during moments of crisis in the community and set in motion changes which were to have repercussions over subsequent years.

Whereas all deaths follow this 'mythological' structure to some extent, Psyche's death was different in several ways. In the first place, when someone dies, the Arakmbut leave the community for a night or two, but never for six months. Furthermore, although some households work gold for extended periods downriver, some Arakmbut are always left in the village. However, for Psyche's death, the community was deserted. The activity of harmful spirits for such a period clearly demonstrated that this was a special death.

The prophecy which Psyche made before his death is highly unusual and its contents draw attention to his special status. When the Arakmbut die, they usually go to Seronwe, below the river, where they live separated from daily community life. They occasionally return to people in their dreams and give messages, but their more infamous appearances are to dying relatives in the form of spirits called *wambetoeri* who show the way to the underworld. However, Psyche made clear in his prophecy that he would return to the community not as a harbinger of danger but as a friend who would protect the Arakmbut in the future.

Perhaps connected to this continuing relationship to the community, is the unusual way in which people still refer to him. Dead peoples' names are not usually uttered and they are referred to as little as possible. Although no one would be bold enough to call out the dead man's real name openly (or to publish it, for that matter), he has not been forgotten, and references to him regularly appear in conversations about the history of the community.[5]

The final major difference between Psyche's death and other deaths is that he not only went to Seronwe but also dispersed into species of the river and forest with which he had special relationships during his life. These species are important for the dead shaman's male relatives or friends who have a good chance of becoming proficient as hunters of these species because they are helped by the spirits. This dispersal happens to all great shamans and is a sign of their special relationship with certain animal species.

The differences between Psyche's death and those of other Arakmbut are, on the whole, factors which would provide security

5. Taylor's article on death and memory among the Achuar (1993) is extremely pertinent in this context. Her concept of 'disremembering' a person encapsulates perfectly the Arakmbut notion of dead people being present in afterlife but not as someone with a name. Her observation about forgetting a dead person's face and the shame associated with the capture of a head in a feud is not found among the Harakmbut. Nevertheless, a 'bad' death from a feud, capture by a harmful spirit, or death by sorcery is considered a terrible fate because, as with the Achuar, the person's soul is no longer under their control.

and confidence for the community in the face of such a loss. However, the community has felt concerned about its future ever since he
died. This disquiet revolves around two areas. In the first place, San
José had no replacement for Psyche. Among the Arakmbut, people
with shamanic powers can teach others their knowledge, but this
does not necessarily mean that those learning will emerge as people
with the skills of a wayorokeri (dream shaman). Psyche's brother
knew several curing chants and discussed spiritual matters with him,
but he never gained recognition from either the spirit world or the
Arakmbut community as his 'successor'. San José was left without a
wayorokeri and the people felt themselves vulnerable. Psyche had
provided information, warned of danger, and cured the sick but
now, without him, there was a considerable chance that the sick
would not be cured, conflicts would not be mediated so easily, and
threats from the spirit world and white invaders would increase.
Psyche's death, however, did not lead to a complete break in the
continuity of community life. The wamanoka'eri (curer) and the
practitioners of *ayahuasca* continued to contact the spirit world and
received information, enabling them to discuss and reformulate theories of the spirit world.

The second area which caused concern within the community
was political. A wayorokeri is a peacemaker within a community. As
will be shown later, his reputation rests on being able to find solutions to problems between clans or groups which threaten to split the
community. After Psyche's death, there was no mediating person
recognised by all the Arakmbut of San José who could resolve conflict and aid decision-making. Furthermore, a wayorokeri frequently
provides confidence not only to defend a community against hostile
spirits but also against the invading miners of the gold rush. The
death of Psyche left a gap at the spiritual and political centre of the
community which people still consider to be a weakness in their
defence. The word *nowenda* (centreless), which people used throughout the period of mourning, is a highly appropriate word to describe
the feelings of the community after the shaman's death.

In order to appreciate the importance of Psyche's death, we have
to look at the areas where his influence was most significant in
shamanic and political matters. Through the case study, this chapter
has alluded to many aspects of Arakmbut social and cultural life
together; in subsequent chapters we will unravel several of these.
The next three chapters, for example, will look at Arakmbut relationships with the spirit world in sickness and health in order to draw
out the shamanic qualities necessary for practical survival. Subse-

quent chapters look at the internal social and political workings of community life. A community survives on the basis of an unstable balance between a multiplicity of different forces, both spiritual and social, which are held together by the shamanic and political qualities of specific persons on the basis of relationships between people, the spirit world, and animal species. Out of these relationships arise the possibilities for change.

Chapter 2

SPECIES AND SPIRITS

One morning in November 1991, I scrambled down the steep cliff of San José to the harbour by the river Karene where the Arakmbut tie up their boats. As I took in the spectacular view of the red-brown muddied water racing past the red cliffs and white beaches framed by the dark green forest, I heard a strange echoing sound from the other bank. Scouring the river, I could see nothing. Then I saw an old man (Ireyo) emerge from behind a low pathway around the cliff which had been revealed by the recent drop in the river level. He laughed at my surprise and said that although he had talked to the *waweri* (river spirits), they had not wanted to give him any fish that day. After reflecting on this episode, I thought that maybe I could improve my abysmal fishing record by communicating with the waweri. Two days later, after some instruction from Arakmbut friends, I went downstream and cast my line. As I sat, I began to murmur to the waweri in Arakmbut, explaining my desire to catch a fish. Within thirty seconds a large sabalo *(mamori)* had bitten my hook and I had a fish to offer the household with which I ate.

This incident introduces several of the features discussed in this chapter and illustrates the relationship between the Arakmbut, species of animals, fish, and plants, and the spirit world.[1] The interaction between these forms of existence is most apparent in activities of production and reproduction which provide the Arakmbut with

---

1. Throughout this text I use the term 'species' to cover animals, fish, birds, and plants. The Arakmbut do identify species in a way which is recognisable to non-indigenous classification. However, rather than viewing each species as an individuated labelling device, they see each species in a broader context in relationship to other aspects of the flora and fauna of the area.

the means to live. The visible world of plants, animals, and fish are intimately bound up with the invisible world of spirits. Arakmbut production depends not only on a knowledge and expertise of the potential inherent in the environment, but also on a capacity to communicate with the spirit world to ensure the regular availability of produce and to avoid transgressing boundaries of acceptable behaviour. These boundaries are described in myths and stories from personal experience *(wambachapak)* which contain illustrations of transgressions and their consequences. At the same time they provide bases for an understanding of the way in which the Arakmbut conceptualise and experience the relationship between the visible and invisible worlds.

By looking at this relationship on a daily basis, an understanding of Arakmbut shamanic practices becomes possible. Although from a cursory glance, curers (wamanoka'eri) and dreamers (wayorokeri) constitute Arakmbut 'shamanism', a closer look reveals that all Arakmbut have some aptitude at shamanic experience and techniques. The production of food is the most salient example of the utilisation of links between the domains of human, spirit, and species. Meat *(sisi)* and fish are extremely important for the Arakmbut because they provide life; without meat people would waste away and eventually die.[2] However, meat on its own is not sufficient for survival. Vegetables such as yuca *(tare)* and plantains *(aroi)* or fruit such as papaya *(apoare)* are also necessary to stall hunger during periods when there is no meat.

In order to provide meat for survival, creatures have to be killed and this presents the Arakmbut men with a dilemma. Hunters sometimes comment that they do not like killing animals and yet male prestige is based on practical skill at hunting and fishing because providing meat to a household is the man's responsibility. Women's production responsibilities do not put them in such a predicament, but are no less significant. Women have to ensure that there is a constant supply of vegetables and fruit, especially when there is no meat. Furthermore, when meat is brought into the community, they have to cook it well in order to ensure that no harm comes to the household from the animal's spirit. Uncooked meat can cause illness and even death. All Arakmbut, therefore, have to be able to over-come the potential dangers in dealing with animals. This means understanding the invisible spirit world.

---

2. The Arakmbut emphasise the potency of animal flesh rather than fish, although in practice fish is as important for life as meat.

Souls and Spirits

Soul-matter, referred to by Reichel-Dolmatoff (1971) as 'energy', is an animating principle which gives life. All material bodies in the visible world receive life from this invisible source.[3] The spirits, which have no bodies, are invisible to waking vision and consequently outside of time and space. Humans can only see them by interpreting the forms which are imposed on the spirits from the visible world. By being beyond space and time, free spirits are more knowledgeable than human beings and understand the potential inherent in the universe.

The Arakmbut cosmos consists of a fundamental distinction between the visible world of form and an invisible world of animating soul or spirit. The relationships between these elements constitute different levels of existence which are based on the amount of soul-matter within the body. Inanimate objects such as rocks are predominantly visible and static, and have little or no soul-matter; small plants and insects have a little more, while human beings and animals have souls (nokiren) which are semi-detached and easily transformable out of their bodies. The invisible spirit world consists of unfettered soul-matter which takes on the ephemeral form of the visible world. In this way, it is possible to see that animals (particularly larger ones such as the tapir or the deer) are cosmologically closer to human beings than inanimate objects.

Soul-matter connects all life because the same invisible characteristics animate everything; at the same time, it takes different forms according to certain criteria. A nokiren takes different forms. The term usually refers to the image which soul-matter takes when manifest as the form of a visible body. However, it also has a dispersed aspect which can also be called *wamawere*, which is like a breath or breeze and floats in a dispersed way through the air. Whereas the nokiren is concentrated within the body, the wamawere is dispersed. When I asked about this difference, an Arakmbut elder sketched the following diagram:

3. Establishing an appropriate word for spirit or soul is difficult. The Arakmbut with whom I spoke emphasised that the nokiren is invisible and animating. On the one hand this creates the impression of a force or of energy. On the other

Helberg (pers.comm.) talked to Arakmbut in other communities and found that a consistent feature in discussions on the invisible world was the distinction between concentrated and dispersed. Whereas there are different ways in which the Arakmbut could express this distinction in concrete terms, it is impossible to encounter neat concepts which convey these abstractions.

For example, the Arakmbut word nokiren means literally 'shadow which is in the centre' (Helberg forthcoming). This expresses a form of concentration. Meanwhile the term toto could arise from the particle *-to*-which means 'under' or 'jointly/together' (Helberg 1984:246) which also reflects the notion of concentration. According to Robert Tripp (nd), the extension particle *-chi-* also means 'connected'. Chi- appears in several words referring to sorcery – *chiwembae* (female sorcerer), chindign (chant), *chindignwakeri* (male sorcerer) – and also conveys some of the notion of concentration through the juxtaposition of elements.

In contrast, the verb *e'nopwe* (to think) is, literally, 'not the centre of affections' and refers to the dispersed nature of thought within the person. A person who is depressed or upset is *nowenda*, which means 'centreless'. I have not encountered an analysis of the word wamawere; the ending *'were'* is the consistent feature when used for particular species (*kemewere* – tapir spirit). The particle *-ere* means 'with'or 'close to' and appears in the words *mbere* (steal) and *tere* (cut up), which convey the notion of phenomena being separate but proximate.

Free spirits come in various forms according to their power – which the Arakmbut refer to as 'strength' *(tainda)* – and temperament. For example, harmful spirits (toto) are concentrated and take the form of the nokiren of dead humans or species, while the ndaky-orokeri are more dispersed beneficial spirits which provide the Arakmbut with important information about the potential in the world. However, the world is not divided simply into two and it is possible to encounter benign powerful spirits *(wachipai* and *chongpai)* which are more distant from humans but which keep the ndakyoro-keri informed, and the dispersed and more impersonal spirits, where toto become like wamawere which can harm people while walking in the forest as a breeze or breath of air. Shamanic activities consist of trying to avoid an excess of concentrated spirit (toto) or dispersed spirit (wamawere) and ensuring regular contact with the

---

hand, the invisible world has substance because it is shaped into images. My juxtaposition of 'soul' with 'matter' tries to convey this blending of concepts. The Bororo avoid this by distinguishing the form of a soul *(aroe)* from its animating force *(bope)* (Crocker 1985).

ndakyorokeri. In contrast, sorcerers utilise the imbalance in the world to harm people.

Within the body, the soul also reflects this classification. In each person, the *wanopo* is a point at the base of the spine which is known as 'centre round' and is translated as 'seat of affections'. It is the part of the body where the nokiren comes together causing strong feelings. These can be harmful when the feelings are negative, as with the emotion ochinosik (hatred), which on a human level is connected to sorcery. However, the soul normally has emotions centred in the wanopo which are not out of control such as desire *(e'pak)*.

Within the person, the nokiren takes on a dispersed aspect through thought (e'nopwe). Thought is not associated with the brain for the Arakmbut, which they refer to as *wasiwa* (fat), but it is dispersed throughout the body, and is less emotional and more reflective than the passions centred at the base of the spine. Emotion and thought are therefore states of the nokiren. However, a person can find that the soul becomes too dispersed and a person feels at a loss with grief or depression, hence the term nowenda ('centreless') noted above. Within the nokiren the dispersed aspect of the soul consists of thought while the concentrated parts are feelings and emotions.

Soul-matter exists in a state of flux throughout the invisible world and reacts to events in the visible world. However, every person tries to ensure a balance between thought and emotion. Too much concentration of soul-matter leads to negative emotions, ochinosik (hatred) or *senopo* (meanness or avarice), while too much dispersal leads to weakness or sorrow (nowenda). A healthy person feels good *(ndak)*. This means that the state of the nokiren reflects a balance between concentration and dispersion within the body and this ensures sociality. Any sickness or anti-social behaviour is a sign that the balance has become disrupted either because too much soul dispersal or loss makes the person weak and prone to illness or because too much concentration makes the person dangerously over-emotional, too powerful, and a possible receptacle of sorcery. In the past, young women were prime targets of sorcery accusations, but these ceased after the period in Shintuya.

Soul-matter, whether animating a body or in free-form, thus contains a spectrum of force or power determined by its intensity and recognised by the dispositions and behavioural traits of humans and animal species. The dangers from the spirit world come from uncontrolled soul-matter. This takes the form primarily of concentrated harmful spirits (toto), and, more rarely, dispersed spirits (-were) which shamanic techniques and ritual try to tame.

Humans and Animals

The sensitivity of the Arakmbut and their hunting and cooking practices demonstrates the closeness between humans and animals. As the consequences of over-hunting or undercooking take the form of spirit activity, the relationship between spirit, animal, and human is crucial to understanding the invisible world. Several Arakmbut myths look into this relationship by telling of the intricate connections between humans and animals and how that relationship was broken.

Throughout Arakmbut mythology, animals are treated as if they were human. The story of Keme (the tapir) and Torogn (the opossum) tells of the time when animals and humans began to separate.

Torogn

In the past the difference between Arakmbut and *ohpai* (game animals) was not like it is now. There was a meeting of Arakmbut who wanted to become animals. Animals also wanted to become people.

Keme (the tapir) was making arrows. He made all types of arrows but they were very dangerous. They had barbs and painted feathers, and the bow and point of the arrow were painted with achiote. People were worried and Torogn (the opossum) was annoyed.

Torogn went to Keme's house and prepared to shoot him. Torogn cried out 'Torogn, Torogn!' and Keme went out and saw some *paka* (hollow bamboo casing used for cooking). He thought Torogn was inside one and stamped all over it. Then he gathered the branches and threw them out. But he did not stamp on the paca which had Torogn inside. The next night he heard the song 'Torogn, Torogn'. Torogn had his arrows and shot Keme in the stomach. Keme shouted 'Ayyyaah!' and shat. Keme always defecate when they have been shot. Afterwards, Keme shouted: 'Who has shot me? Torogn, Torogn, Torogn.' Torogn burnt all of Keme. He placed it all in paca. 'I have shot Keme,' he said.

Before, Torogn and Keme spoke like people. They were people like us. The next day another Keme appeared. He said, 'Now that our leader is dead let us change into animals. We must continue to convert ourselves into animals. I am going to turn myself into an animal, I am not going to be like us.' And he said to the deer *(bawi)*, 'Let's make ourselves animals!'

The people decided to look for new coats. Bawi said 'I want the bark of the *tawiresindak* tree as my skin.' Then he put on the red tree bark and it was light so he could run in a straight line. Keme put on a *wakumbuesindak* which is much heavier, and so he moves in circles. Before Keme used to go in groups and were very dangerous, but after the conversion they became solitary animals. Where Keme goes with his thick skin, spines don't hurt him and so he can go through paca without problem.

This myth is a description of the separation between animals and humans. The division is clearly expressed by Keme and Bawi, who decide to transform themselves from humans into animals and live a more solitary existence. The Arakmbut with whom I discussed this myth explained that it tells of a general process whereby all creatures decided whether to be human or animal. This form of differentiation is important when discussing hunting and the treatment of meat because it shows that the animals which a hunter kills are considered to be living beings which have had, and maybe still have, some human characteristics.

A second feature of the story which is of relevance to the Arakmbut is that it tells of the considerable power of certain animals, particularly the tapir. They were not simply a resource for being killed but could be extremely dangerous and dominate both animals and humans. The power play between the animals expressed in the myth of Tororgn shows Keme to be capable of dominating all other creatures, and for this reason he was killed.

Another myth raises similar problems but from a different angle. It concerns the tortoise, Sawe, and parallels certain events in Torogn such as the death of a tapir at the beginning, the distinction between humans and animals, and the dangers certain of species becoming too powerful.

Sawe

A tortoise *(sawe)* managed to obtain poison by killing a tapir (keme). The tapir liked the black dye 'huito' *(o)* and the tortoise came and took a bite. Keme said: 'This is mine. You cannot eat it.' He then uttered a very strong insult: 'Suck my cock!'

So Sawe bit Keme's penis and would not let go.

Keme ran through the forest with Sawe hanging behind. Eventually Keme died. Sawe met an Arakmbut in the forest and told him to take the meat to the house but leave him the *'washakpo'* – but the Arakmbut did not understand the word. No one knew what the word meant and, frustrated, the Arakmbut stormed off, forgetting to take his axe. Sawe ate the shit which tapir always leave when they are killed. Then he looked at the body and in its stomach found a deadly poison. Sawe immediately called all the animals.

All the animals which are poisonous, the jaguar *(petpet)* which has poison under its claws, the snake, and the harpy eagle *(sing)*, which eats monkeys, all said, 'Let's prepare poison.' The snakes (biwi) put it in their teeth and the jaguar put it in his claws so that they could kill Arakmbut.

Matuk (gallinazo – vulture) also did it. 'I will put it in my claws to kill all the young animals,' he said.

The other animals were frightened when they heard this as it would be dangerous. Petpet said: 'I will trick him.' He went to Matuk and said, taking in his claws, 'We have pulled out our nails, why don't you?' Matuk then cut his talons. The Petpet said, 'Look at my claws.' Matuk realised that he had been tricked and cried, rubbing his feet into his head until he became bald. Then Petpet felt sorry for Matuk and said, 'I will hunt for you. I will eat the fresh meat first and leave you the rotten meat to eat later.' It was agreed.

Then a snake called Yeninu (a fearsome looking black snake which can rise on its tail) said, 'I will be the most powerful animal. I will kill all the creatures as I can jump through the air and am most agile.' The other animals were afraid and when he had poison in his teeth they decided to trick him. 'Bite the Singpa tree (peach palm)', they said. Bushmaster and Fer de Lance are all doing this to see how strong we are among the snakes. See who is the strongest'. The Yeninu wanted to be the strongest and so went and bit into the Singpa. The bark is so tough that all his teeth were broken and the snake lost his poison. The Yeninu now is not a poisonous snake but if this had not happened the world would have been left with a very dangerous snake.

This second myth takes place at a time when animals and Arakmbut were still broadly similar creatures. However, unlike the first myth, which tells of the separation between the two, the second points to the main differences between animals and humans. Two main features distinguish animals from humans. First, their languages are difficult to understand and, secondly, they have certain sexual proclivities which are abhorrent to humans. In the story, when Sawe speaks to the Arakmbut he uses the word 'washakpo'. The Arakmbut told me that they have no idea what it means because Sawe could not communicate with humans properly. Another mark of distinction between humans and animals is in their attitude to sex. The act of sucking or biting a penis is considered by the Arakmbut to be animal behaviour and is one of the criteria which distances the animals from humans. In this way, both stories trace the similarities and separation of animals and humans.

The other main theme of the myths is the danger of specific species becoming too powerful. In both cases there are successful attempts by other animals to curtail the potential dangers of certain species. The animals are portrayed with human qualities, concerned about their own power and that of the others. As with human beings, insults, fighting, revenge, and fear are all part of their personal relations.

Both myths begin with the death of Keme, the tapir. The original 'human' Keme lived socially and appear to have been a dangerous people who bullied other animals through access to special weapons such as powerful bows, arrows, and poison. This power is witnessed in the death scenes. Torogn kills Keme out of anger and fear that he will become too powerful, while after the death by Sawe, Keme is the source whereby the animals gain access to the poison which can make them dangerous. The Sawe myth contains an episode which parallels Torogn's fear of Keme's weapons in the first story. Petpet (the jaguar) fears that, with the poison from Keme's stomach, Matuk (the gallinazo – a vulture scavenger) and Yeninu (the black snake) will become too dangerous. The myths tell of the origin of animal power in Keme, and also about how the power has to be dispersed or else it will become too dangerous.

The concentration of power is the main form of classifying the spirit world. The most dangerous beings of the invisible world are those whose concentration of soul-matter is harmful to others, such as toto or humans who practise sorcery. The animals in the stories want to prevent the accumulation of power by distributing the danger. The poison is spread around to the other animals, whereas the power of the Keme, in its concentrated and harmful form, is physically dispersed into the solitary creatures which, in their thick and heavy skins, wander around in lonely circles without causing anyone any harm. In the same way, the most beneficial spirits of the invisible world are those which are most dispersed.

The myths thus point out that the separation of human and animal is not only about species, it is about the attempt to disperse the dangers of concentrated power. They express characteristics connecting and distinguishing human beings, animals, and spirits. Animals and humans have separated over time in behaviour and physical features, but their concerns are similar regarding unlimited power which, if uncontrolled, threatens other creatures with considerable danger. This is the dilemma about eating meat or fish which all Arakmbut face. Killing a creature can lead to retribution from the species. In order to avoid this problem, human beings have to try to transcend the separation with animals and commmunicate with them, particularly those which they eat.

Transcending Separation

For the Arakmbut, as indeed for anyone living in a world of practical knowledge where thought and experience are embedded in each other, boundaries are marked both by separation and by the act of crossing. The Arakmbut need to eat the meat of certain large animals and fish in order to survive and yet they have no way of communicating directly with them. Whereas an Arakmbut can sometimes recognise a bird-song in the forest and understand what it means, it is not possible to enter into discussions with particular creatures. Nevertheless, there is a way of transcending the separation by utilising a knowledge of the universe to enter into the spirit world. To understand this, it is necessary to look in more detail at the Arakmbut universe as a whole.

Arakmbut cosmology consists of the organisation of phenomena into physical domains and the movement of elements between them, linking together and separating the visible and invisible worlds, the physical domains of the earth, animal species, and social distinctions. The Arakmbut universe is divided into three spheres: the sky (*kurudn*); the earth, which is divided into the hak (Arakmbut settlement), wawe (river), and *ndumba* (forest); and the two underworlds, Seronwe below the river and Totoyo below the forest (see Figure 2.1). Whereas the spirits have their origins above and below the earth, humans and animals share the central sphere.

The forest and river domains, which surround human settlements on the surface of the earth, comprise the major lateral divisions outside of the Arakmbut social world of the house and gardens. The relationship on the horizontal level of the universe consists of a concentric relationship where there is a marked separation between humans and animals and between their settlements and the forest and river beyond.

Live creatures cannot travel between adjacent spheres because that is the prerogative of the invisible spirit world; however, human beings in states of awareness arising from dreams and visions can make contact with spirits. The spirits are almost entirely indifferent to the separation of humans and animals because they can transform their images from human to animal with ease, depending on the situation. Spirits can also transcend the boundaries of the settlement and the outside domains of river and forest. For this reason spirits provide the means for human beings to communicate with animals.

Figure 2.1: The Arakmbut universe

Kurudn (sky)		
Kurudneri (sky spirits)		
River birds		Forest birds
Wawe (river)	Hak (community)	Ndumba (forest)
Waweri (river spirits)	Nokiren (human soul)	Ndumberi (forest spirits)
River species	Arakmbut	Forest species
Seronwe (riverine underworld)	Totoyo (forest underworld)	
Pugn (moon) Master of Seronwe	Miokpo (sun) Master of Forest	

At the highest point is the sky which is the most distant domain, higher up than where birds fly. It is the abode of otiose spirits called *kurudneri* who rarely come down to earth. The kurudneri were once human beings who went up into the sky with the culture hero Marinke when he had to flee from the jaguars (see Volume 1, chapter five). However, within living memory, they used to descend during a ritual known as *mbakoykoy*. The Arakmbut would gather in a communal house where they would light fires and sing for the kurudneri sky spirits to descend. The spirits would come down in the form of a small bird (mbakoykoy) and empower a child with the strength of a jaguar to become a fearless war-leader. This ceremony enabled a leader to convert into a jaguar during war. In this way, the sky spirits provided the means for humans to transcend their separation and join with the jaguar.

A more frequent connection between humans and animals comes from the spirits which live in the two underworlds. Seronwe under the river – whose master is the moon *(pugn)* – is mainly the abode of beneficial spirits (ndakyorokeri) with relatively dispersed soul-substance; *Totoyo* under the forest – whose master is Manco who is connected to the sun *(miokpo)* – is the haunt of harmful spirits consisting of concentrated soul-substance. They can travel onto the earth's surface and appear in spirit form in a dream or vision. In addition to names based on their form, these spirits take on the name of their domain of origin and are known either as *waweri* or *ndumberi* from the river or forest respectively. Concentrated spirits are the most dangerous, although they can also cause harm in a dispersed form. Beneficial spririts are usually more dispersed, although otiose wachipai, ayahuasca plant spirits *(chongpai)* and the nameless *apoining,* which are more concentrated, are usually benign. The distinction between beneficial and harmful is thus more about extremes of power and control than about ethical values.

The images which spirits take on can change regularly. They can have human forms as beautiful women (ndakyorokeri) or ugly men (toto) and can also appear as beings with animal characteristics. This is particularly significant because the old mythological relationship where human and animal are undifferentiated still exists in the spirit world. Thus, by means of dreams and visions, it is possible for human beings to use spirits as intermediaries for communication with the separated animal world. The result is that spirits are the ideal intermediaries for human beings to find out about the creatures which live in the forest and river which they want to hunt. This is extremely important for the Arakmbut who are involved in production activities because it is their clearest means of securing a supply of food in safety. Only through a knowledge of the spirit world can the separation between human and animal be transcended and the retributive power of the dead creature assuaged. This capacity, which almost all Arakmbut know, constitutes the most common use of shamanic practices and techniques.

Species and Spirits in Production Activities

Human beings (Arakmbut) come from the hak domain, the human social world which once took the form of a communal house (*maloca*) and now consists of the native community. Gardens (*tamba*) are the extreme boundaries of the hak domain where Arakmbut men convert the forest into cultivated spaces for the women to produce vegetables and fruit.[4] All hunting, fishing, gathering, and clearing activities

---

4. Descola's description of the production methods of the Achuar (1989) traces in superb detail the relationship between domains and activities. The strong rela-

involve leaving the domain of the house and going into the forest or onto the river. These are the areas fraught with danger from which the Arakmbut need spiritual protection through contacts with the invisible world by means of dreams. The result is a complicated series of exchanges between human and non-human via the spirit world.

Two activities which illustrate the varying relationship between natural species, human beings, and the spirit world are the provision of meat and vegetables. In both activities men and women have distinct but complementary responsibilities which become more proficient with age.

The Provision of Meat

Animals all contain meat, some soul-matter (which makes them potentially dangerous to eat), and a species name. They are divided into those species which can be eaten *(mbapndik)* and those which cannot *(mbapwendik)*. Reasons for food prohibitions vary: some creatures cannot be eaten because they are considered poisonous carnivores (jaguars, harpy eagles, and snakes), others because they eat impure substances (vultures), or because they are too small and insignificant (rats and ants). Although there is no single reason for not eating certain species, the explanations all point to features of the animal and its behaviour which can, in many cases, affect the taste of food and cause harm to the consumer.

Meat comes in different shapes and sizes, with distinct dangers. The smallest animal food consists of grubs and small fish which are gathered from forest trees or collected during fishing with barbasco. Women and children mainly carry out these activities. The larger animals such as fish, small birds and monkeys are pursued by men, and are the first creatures a young hunter will look for. Young hunters often avoid eating an animal they have killed because they fear that the spirit of the species will attack then and make them ill.

A hunter builds up experience and knowledge of places which animals frequent, such as the salt licks *(sorok)* or areas where certain edible fruits grow which attract certain species. This information is amassed through personal encounters with animals on forest trails

tionship between gardens and the female part of the Achuar house contrasts with the Arakmbut perspective, which is based more on imagery of male as predator and female as connecting the house and garden as a whole. Indeed, in the past, the garden was physically parallel to the round concentric shape of a communal house (see Volume 1, chapter ten).

and from listening to older hunters telling their stories in the evenings when people chat before their meal. By these means, a hunter acquires the background knowledge necessary to interpret the signs of animals, such as calls, tracks, the areas an animal frequents, periods when its favourite fruits fall, and its sleeping and waking behaviour. Knowledge of different species, combined with skill in stalking prey and shooting accurately, comprise the technical skills necessary to be a good hunter.

Young men are the most liable to forget to behave respectfully to the animal species which they hunt. A particularly pertinent story tells of the fate of young hunters who treat their prey badly and indulge in unnecessary cruelty.

Orognorogntone

A group of young men went on a hunting expedition. They met a large toad called Orognorogntone on the path. The youths laughed at the toad: 'What are you doing here? Get out of our way!' Then they began to hit the toad with their arrows and it began to sweat and blood flowed.

But one youth defended the toad. 'Why are you doing this to the toad? What harm has it done you?' he asked. He found a leaf and covered the bleeding wound.

It was late. The youths made a camp and the young man who had defended the toad went to sleep there. The toad came to him in a dream and said, 'Only you will be saved. The others will be eaten by the animals. When the attack happens you must cover yourself in a *yaro* leaf. All of your body must be covered. Lie down on this spot and they will not eat you but pass over you. They will do nothing to you.'

The young man woke up sweating. He told no one about the dream. Then there came a small monkey *sipin* (black mantled tamarin). The man who had dreamed realised that this was a scout. He shot at the sipin but he missed it and it fled into the forest.

After a few minutes a torrential rainstorm started. First came an *ihpi* or *washa* (common squirrel monkey), then other monkeys such as *hor*, as well as other tree creatures like squirrels. They were close and the youths began to shoot the animals, but the arrows ran out and so they hit at them with their bows. Many monkeys were surrounding them and the dreamer realised what was happening. The youths began to kill the monkeys with their bows.

Some of the monkeys were killed by the youths but the other monkeys did not attack the Arakmbut and retreated. Then all the monkeys climbed the tree and waited until the next day to attack the youths again. The youths made a big fire and cleared around the tree first. The fire below the tree sent up so much smoke that the youths thought the monkeys would fall.

Each large monkey had its *ohpu* – animal guide and leader. When they made the fire the toyori ohpu fell into the fire at the side and was burnt but not killed. Other monkeys fell into the fire and died. Those that died (small monkeys) do not have an ohpu. The ohpu monkeys are *toyori* (red howler monkey), *shiok* (common woolly monkey), *sowe* (black spider monkey) and *kapiwi* (coati). Those without the ohpu are *ihpi* (common squirrel monkey), *okmbu* (night monkey), *toca* (mono toca), *waewembedn* (red tailed squirrel), *sipin*, (black mantle tamarin) *wambign*, and *wawesik* (guayaquil squirrel).

The next day the surviving monkeys descended from the tree, killed the youths and ate them. The youth who helped the toad was afraid and hid in his yaro leaves. He was the only Arakmbut who survived. One monkey, the hor (mono martin), refused to eat human flesh.

This myth tells of a rebellion by the animals against human beings who did not treat them with respect and acts as a warning to potential young hunters who treat killing lightly. The story shows the dire consequences should the relationship between spirits and species ever break down through disrespect. The boy saves the toad who in return saves him. The emphasis of the story is therefore on the beneficial attributes of mutual respect between humans and animal species.

A second aspect of the story is the practical information which it provides with regard to species identification. The list of monkeys and related creatures, such as coati and squirrels, teaches the listener the names for identifying and distinguishing between the different species. Particularly emphasised are the ohpu monkeys, which have prehensile tails and are larger. The Arakmbut ohpu were historical war leaders who, through the mbakoykoy ceremony, received from the otiose sky spirits (kurudneri) the power to transform into a jaguar and kill all enemies. The ohpu monkeys are the same species which Arakmbut are prohibited from eating during pregnancy and immediately after childbirth. The myth describes the immense power of certain animal species and the harm they can inflict if they are not treated well. Animals can rebel against humans and cause enormous devastation.

When an Arakmbut is considered to have gained enough experience as a hunter to provide for a wife and eventual children, he will find that he becomes a desirable candidate for marriage. Adult males are experienced enough to look for all types of edible game animals (ohpai), including the larger species such as tapir (keme), collared peccaries *(mokas),* white-lipped peccaries *(iari/akudnui),* deer (bawi), and countless bird, monkey, and fish species. From adulthood, a man can develop a more sophisticated understanding of hunting and perhaps make new discoveries of animal behaviour which will be of use to other Arakmbut.

His most important information, however, comes in the form of dreams from the spirit world. This is a level of shamanic experience which all Arakmbut men know. Everyone dreams to some extent, but a skilled dreamer can interpret his dreams correctly; when this happens, shamanic attributes become particularly marked and are noted by the rest of the community. The person in this case will be referred to as a dreamer of the particular species with which he communicates.

However, there are dangers in communicating with beneficial spirits; they usually appear as sensual women who easily fall in love with a young man and his family and call them to the underworld to live – causing their death in the visible world. These women (the ndakyorokeri) come from the underworld of Seronwe prior to a hunting trip and tell the hunter where game may be found and how many animals can be taken. A hunter usually only publicises his dream after the hunt when the advice of the spirit has been taken and used well, otherwise failing to bring a promised animal back is not good for his reputation.

If a hunter shows any sign of expecting a catch or assumes he will kill an animal he will fail, and so, if he should meet another villager on his way to the forest, he will avoid saying where he is going and why. Should he tell, the spirits may warn the animals to escape. On the contrary, a hunter must demonstrate humility and a willingness to recognise the part played in his success by the advice of the spirits. Over their lives, men build up reputations as good hunters of certain species through the strong relationship they have established with particular ndakyorokeri spirits and with their increasing knowledge they develop special ties with particular animal species. This is not to say that everyone has their own species with which they are associated, but rather that some hunters have a species or clusters of species to which they have privileged access. However, a hunter has to avoid the temptation of overindulgence when hunting because he may become too attracted to his spirit contacts who may want to carry away his soul, causing sickness and even death.

After a death, such as Psyche's, the nokiren of a hunter with a particularly close relationship to a species will join that species. This takes place in a generic manner by which the soul is dispersed throughout the different animals. The Arakmbut express this as 'going to the species'. In this way species, spirits, and humans are inextricably connected by a train of communications through dreams, hunting practices, consumption, and death which are based on a principle of exchanging meat for soul-substance. In Volume 1, chapter seven, this exchange was described from the perspective of clan continuity where meat moves into the clan line and soul-substance moves out on death. However, the relationship between the spirit advisors and the animals themselves is far from straightforward.

The spirit communicators (ndakyorokeri) which inform hunters of the availability of game have a knowledge of potentiality which embraces space and time. The information comes from animal spirits through the presence of the wachipai spirits, which are known by the Arakmbut in Spanish as 'mother of the animals', although in Arakmbut they are not distinguished by gender. They are also called the 'ohpu of the animals' by some Arakmbut which makes an interesting connection with the Orognorogntone story above.[5] The wachipai have various forms, but most people agree that they normally appear as one of the species or else with the head of the species and the body of a snake. Should a hunter meet a wachipai he will undergo a frightening experience, as happened to one man in San José.

The man said that he had been hunting in the forest and saw a parrot high on a branch. Taking aim, he fired his gun and hit the bird, but instead of the bird flapping and falling, it exploded into many pieces and cascaded all about him. The hunter immediately fainted and passed into a deep sleep where he dreamed of a future where San José was running with the blood of the Arakmbut.

The difference between a wachipai dream and an ordinary dream is that it does not involve interpretation. 'It is the truth and what it says will happen', said the Arakmbut who told of the old man's experience. People rarely encounter a wachipai, but the experience can change lives. Sometimes the spirit tells a person to change his name, or else, as in the case of Psyche, the spirit offers special powers of curing and facilities for communicating with the invisible world. The

5. An interesting parallel also comes from the Wachipaeri. In a story told to me in Shintuya, a man took a chick out of a nest. It was a kokoy bird (like a gavilan) and it taught the man how to kill people with metal knives and a machete. But he did not look after the chick, which became angry and flew away. The man said 'I don't care.' Mbakokoy is the name of the of the Arakmbut ritual which gives power to the ohpu, who can transform into a jaguar and become invincible to enemies. Meanwhile, the kokoy bird is in fact called *watohpu* by the Arakmbut.

experience of meeting a wachipai can set the ground for becoming particularly adept at shamanic skills. In most cases, however, the person is not capable of taking advantage of the offer and cannot remember what he should do to exercise the powers.

The wachipai keeps a close tally of its associated species, takes care that they are not over-killed, and passes on information to and from the spirits of the species, which include aspects of the nokiren of dead Arakmbut shamans which have 'gone to the species' after death. The female spirits know this information and pass it on to the hunters in their dreams. In this way, a complicated set of relationships is formed linking humans, animals, and spirits. In one direction, the hunting potential of the animal species is passed from the spirits of the animals to the ndakyorokeri women via the wachipai. They inform the hunter in his sleep.

Through this spirit communication, the hunter receives messages from the animal world as to the amount of meat he can kill and from where. As a result of this he goes into the forest or to the river, catches his prey, and receives the meat. Fishing practices are almost entirely conceptualised as river spirits offering vegetables from their gardens which appear to us as fish. In the other direction, expert hunters, who have a good knowledge of certain species, pass when they die to Seronwe and from there to the animal spirits themselves. The dual circuit is made up of a meat for soul-substance exchange mediated by knowledge and control by the spirit world.

Figure 2.2: Hunting information in return for meat and soul-matter.

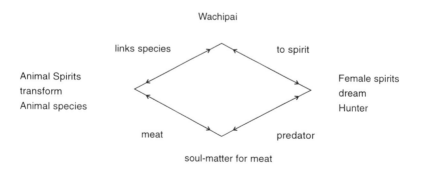

The system can only operate when a hunter respects the animal species he is killing and does not indulge in excess killing or eating. In this way the balanced, complementary relationship between the visible and invisible world can quickly become one of unbalanced danger. However, the provision of meat does not end here. Gender complementarity among the Arakmbut is clearly exemplified by man's responsibility to provide meat and a woman's responsibility to prepare and cook it. Cooking is extremely important and not considered a lowly task by the Arakmbut; indeed, without cooking, meat is not only useless but dangerous. If meat is not cooked until the blood is gone, all those who eat it will risk illness from the spirit of the species.

The significance of Arakmbut cookery is fundamental to the way in which the Arakmbut transform something which is dangerous into something which is safe. The process of creation, for example, is expressed in the myth Wanamey through the imagery of cooking, where burning and immersion in water become controlled by fire into roasting and boiling (see Volume 1, chapter one). Women's cooking methods are primarily boiling and frying; their work is to cleanse the raw meat which the men bring home and make it safe. This is done by getting rid of the animal spirit which disappears in the smoke or steam from the fire.

This is a process of dispersal of the potential retribution of the animal. A similar feature occurs when meat is distributed. The women are responsible for deciding who should share the meat and for carrying out its distribution. Women therefore protect men from the consequences of their hunting activities both invisibly and visibly. From the invisible world the ndakyorokeri inform them of the limits of their activities, while the women of the household ensure that it is cooked and appropriately distributed. In this way the hunter does not become prey to the consequences of his own actions.[6]

The Provision of Plants, Vegetables and Fruit

The importance of women is underlined even further when looking at the provision of plants, vegetables, and fruits for the household. Small fruit is gathered in much the same way as grubs or small fish.

6. See Descola's work on animism (1992). He establishes three ways in which social life and the environment relate among the lowland South American peoples. The first example, from the Desana, consists of a cycling of soul-matter; the second, from the Shuar, is based on the system of the hunter catching prey and risking revenge; the third, from on the Arawak peoples of Peru, consists of mutual predation or dualist exchange. The Arawak example is most similar to the Arakmbut case.

The women and children usually undertake trips into the forest at appropriate seasons to look for *kotsi* (aguaje) or *ho* (peach palm) and throughout the year encounter countless different wild fruits.

Women spend most of their days in the gardens where they learn techniques and knowledge which are as complicated and detailed as those of a male hunter. A young girl usually works with her mother in the garden and, when weeding and planting, develops some knowledge of the main species. An Arakmbut garden (tamba) contains a considerable variety of species, and as Arakmbut women learn to distinguish between them, their gardening competence increases. For example, there are four clearly marked types of yuca, each with its own edible liana, which grow around the bushes; there are fifteen types of plantain and no less than seventeen types of pineapple. As with a man's knowledge of animal species, a woman's garden knowledge increases with experience. Old women also know special chants to help certain crops grow, particularly barbasco, the poison used for fishing. Dreams also relate women to the spirit world with regard to their gardening pursuits, but these are shrouded in mystery.

The preparation of a garden is the responsibility of the men of the household. As with the relationship between animals and humans which cannot be overcome without spirit contact, the settlement and the forest are mutually exclusive domains. The cutting of trees with axes and the burning of the garden prior to planting is a form of predation on the forest, which is left for the women to transform into crops. Although not as dangerous as hunting, clearing untouched forest poses the risk of disturbing dangerous spirits of the area. After this, the women take over the task of tending the garden and nurturing the plants.

A myth raises several points explaining the importance of women and gardening.

Chiokpo

Night came and day dawned, boding well for working in the chacra. In the evening, a woman raised her hands to the stars *(chiokpo)*. 'Stars,' she said, 'help me make my chacra. I am working alone. Please help me.' At that moment there were many stars because she had asked them to help her cultivate the chacra.

On the following day she went to the chacra again to cultivate and work alone. 'I am working alone,' she said on the path. She reached her chacra and a miracle appeared to have happened. Everything was cultivated and cleared where the previous day there had been forest. Everything which had been in the chacra had been thrown out, all which had been harvested was placed in a corner. Everything which had been there, logs, weeds – everything was cleared and well cultivated.

The woman stood there and marvelled, and was a bit worried too. Everything seemed like a dream. She returned to the house and said nothing to anyone, not even to her children, about what had happened. She slept and night came. She slept well and at dawn she went again to the chacra. The woman was afraid because she saw bananas, yuca, and pineapple planted and growing. A young fair-haired man came near and spoke to her. 'Do you remember, woman, that time when you said: 'Help me?' I am he who came to help you plant the chacra.'

And the young man continued 'But look, woman, do not tell anyone and I will always come and work with you.' But that night she told people that the star man had helped her in her chacra. On the following day, she went to the chacra to look at it. The whole chacra had been converted to forest again. For this reason, chacras always grow weeds quickly. If the woman had not told her story, the chacra would have remained cleared.

This story parallels the relationship between men and the spirit world regarding the availability of game in the forest, but there are also some significant differences. The handsome young star man in the story is similar to the beautiful ndakyorokeri spirits, but he does not seem to be a source of support for women in their daily lives as are the beautiful women for the men. Gardening is considered by the Arakmbut to be the hardest of all tasks and the story is clearly a utopian wish. However, Chiokpo has various other levels of meaning. On a practical level, it explains that husbands should cut the forest and prepare the chacras for women or else some attractive young rival might do it instead. From a woman's point of view, on the other hand, the story has another meaning: it warns women against revealing their secrets or else everything could collapse around them. If women do have help from the spirit world through dreams in their chacras, the story makes it quite clear that others should not hear of it.

Superficially, men appear to have a stronger link through their dreams with the spirits. However this is not necessarily the case in practice. Whereas men talk about their spirit relationships with their clan kin, women's spirit contacts are largely personal and they are far more reluctant to discuss them. Nevertheless women communi-

cate with the spirit world through chants to ensure production of barbasco (*kumo*). The women explained that this is because barbasco is
a plant which originates in the forest and needs spiritual encouragement to grow.[7]

From these observations, it is possible to conclude that species
and spirits communicate with men and women in different ways to
provide the continuation of life and preservation of health. Men act
as predators and use their spirit contacts to protect themselves and
their household from harm. Women complement the process by
converting the meat or gardens into food. The system can only be
upheld through respect, modesty, secrecy and the accumulation of
knowledge used with understanding. This last attribute is fundamental for enabling the Arakmbut to control their environment.

Accumulation of Knowledge
and Understanding of Natural Species

In the discussion of hunting and gardening, it became apparent that
learning methods of production is something which takes many
years. Not only is there a difference between men and women, but
the distinction is cross-cut by a growth of knowledge which one
gains through age. This is particularly apparent in questions of
species diversity.

Knowledge and understanding of species and spirits is not available to all Arakmbut equally but depends on experience and age. As
hunters mature or women gain experience in the chacras, they learn
more about the variety of species and the clusters of relationships
between one and another. This knowledge provides them with the
ability to produce and reproduce their means of subsistence. An
informal survey which I carried out in 1992 compared knowledge of
fruit, plant ,and animal species for different age groups of Arakmbut.
Children of three to eight years had knowledge of the fruits which
are usually gathered but little awareness of animals; young hunters
(13-25) knew of the different types of birds they shot and the larger
animals but nothing beyond those they hunted for food; young
women (13-25) knew several species of crops in the chacras but not
the enormous variety which exist; full adults knew a greater variety

7. In his book on garden magic, Brown (1985) discusses the use of orations by
   women. The importance of female chants is more significant for the Aguaruna
   than the Arakmbut. This parallels the contrast noted with Descola's observations
   connecting gardens and the 'female' part of the house among the Achuar.

of species which were not only useful for consumption but for other activities, particularly curing purposes. Women and men also knew more varieties of animals and crops as these were brought from the forest or gardens by their spouses; old people (50+) had an encyclopedic knowledge of hundreds of species from curing chants, personal experience, and information passed down the generations.

Knowledge of species is thus cumulative and is important for all production and reproduction activities in an Arakmbut community as well as for diagnosis and curing. Young people's knowledge covers straightforward production for consumption, but as people become older their knowledge is necessary for other skills such as curing, where a detailed inventory of animals and their behaviour and desires is important technical information. Initially this information takes the form of clusters of data surrounding the name of the species. The name of the species, just as the names of human beings, are important means of identification and communication in the spirit world. However, lists of species names are not sufficient to understand and act within the invisible world because the non-human world operates on the basis of the relationships of countless species which we can refer to as 'biodiversity'. As the Arakmbut grow older they learn the details, which give them the means to produce a wider variety of food for consumption and to practice shamanic curing activities.

Arakmbut knowledge is not, therefore, solely 'intellectual' labelling, but is based on practical experience of the relationship between species. It was clear in gathering species data that people could not name plants and animals without some personal knowledge or experience of the species. Whereas initially Arakmbut knowledge consists of recognising the main species of plants and animals and their characteristics, profound knowledge consists of understanding the relationships between species. For example older people know not only different types of monkey, but the kinds of fruit they like, when they will be fattest in the annual cycle and where they live and sleep. In this way, along with the identification of particular species comes a view of how life appears from the perspective of the species, which broadens knowledge (e'nopwe) to understanding (*e'anopwe*). Understanding the species diversity from different perspectives constitutes a principle of relativity where the world appears differently according to the domain, the species, and the form of soul-substance.

For example, in the account of my fishing expedition, the *mamori* fish are pineapples to the river spirits. In fact, several species of fish are different crops to the spirits. A zungaro is yuca *(tare),* paco is a large pineapple *(wakawa),* and carp-like boquichicos *(ambaru)* are maize *(toket)*. Similarly, different species speak in different languages which sound like distorted forms of Harakmbut. A sowe (black spider monkey) adds *to-* to many Harakmbut words – *ondikwe* becomes *tondikwe*. An anuje *(mapi)* does not call peach palm 'ho' but '*mbaw*' in its own speech.

This knowledge is based on direct experience and a proficiency in understanding dreams and visions. For this reason, an accumulation of this sort of knowledge paves the way for the more complicated shamanic practices which will be reviewed in the next two chapters.

This chapter has looked at the relationship between human beings, animal species, and spirits in production activities which ensure social and cultural reproduction. The key factors consist of overcoming the separation between human and animal and between settlement and forest while preventing the accumulation of spiritual power. This is achieved through the distribution and diversification of dangerous elements. The accumulation of sameness is harmful – an Arakmbut equivalent to western ideas about the benefits of bio-diversity. Whereas men act, in the main, as predators on the world outside of the settlement, women conciliate and ameliorate the danger by cooking and utilising the burnt forest so that they can cultivate and nurture crops for consumption by the household.

The Arakmbut cosmos thus consists of three different sets of relationships between humans, species, and spirits. In the visible world, human beings and animals are as separate as the village settlement is from the forest and river. However, mythologically, spirits, animal species, and human beings were once all aspects of one existence associated with different domains. This is how the invisible world remains. By utilising the invisible world where spirits and species are one, a person can transcend the separation and act as a predator. However, unless the meat is carefully cooked or the garden carefully tended, the food will be bad and people will become sick. This involves constant care and keeping a wary eye on the spirit world.[8]

8. Authors have noted that peoples throughout the indigenous world like the Arakmbut, have a phenomenal knowledge of their environment and utilise its resources with skill. Reichel-Dolmatoff's work among the Desana (1971) presents them as proto-ecologists, utilising the spirit world in the form of energy chains. Others, such as Balée and Posey (1989) remark at how indigenous peoples, such as the Kayapo, manage their environment, to such an extent that most of their territory is utilised or has been utilised for some purpose. In contrast, Colchester (1981) considers that the Yanomami are more responsive to everyday needs such as the desire to produce food in as efficient and labour-saving a way as possible.

To some extent, the Arakmbut demonstrate all these positions. On the one hand, it is clear that the spirit world does have an important influence on con-

The successful hunter or gardener needs to combine knowledge and understanding with technical proficiency. This is knowledge in practice. When I went fishing, I could not have caught the mamori fish simply by asking the river spirits. I needed to be at the river at a time when the waters were almost clear and the fish were making their way back from side streams. In addition to knowing the day to fish, I had to know how to speak to the waweri, to approach them tactfully, to know the fishes' behaviour, and to pull it in. These complicated prerequisites for landing a catch demonstrate the skill of Arakmbut hunters and explain why it has been hard for me to repeat my success.

Knowledge is available to all Arakmbut to some extent and is the initial element of shamanic experience. However, there are certain specialists whose knowledge and efficacy is such that they become recognised as particularly skilful. These are people who could be called 'shamans' because they do not just use their skills for hunting but for the health and welfare of others. They are the subject of the next chapter.

---

trolling the amount of hunting and clearing which takes place. However, this is not to say that the Arakmbut obey these dictates for environmental purposes. The practice is based on a desire to avoid sickness and death rather than any conscious conservation ideology.

The Arakmbut, through their enormous hunting and gardening experience, manage their resources. However, the term 'manage' cannot be seen as a maximizing utilisation of all of their resources. They organise their lives and environment as much as they feel they need to in order to ensure a supply of food. Perhaps, for the Arakmbut, it would be more accurate to say that they control and organise those parts of the environment which they need and use; the rest they leave to the spirit world and for the future.

This approach also has an element of the Yanomami 'opportunism' because the Arakmbut are reluctant to do unnecessary work for production and, given the technology, they would certainly be tempted to kill more animals and try to make life easier. However, the power of the spirit world is so strong that should anyone acting in this way become ill, their errant behaviour would be given as the reason. Furthermore, his fate would be expressed in term of his excessive appetite, rather than the over-exploitation of natural resources.

E'MANOKA'E – CURING

The separation of animal species, invisible spirits, and human beings occurs within Arakmbut cosmology as a means of preventing accumulations of power within the universe which could destroy all forms of life. The actions of the animals in the myth of Torogn displaced life between several spheres and established a cosmos based on divided powers. The effect lessened the intensity of danger and the possible eradication of particular species, but it did not eradicate the threat of death itself for individual persons. Shamanic knowledge and power is about temporarily reconnecting these separated spheres in order to gain access to powers which can restore order.

This approach to shamanic practices is holistic (Chaumeil 1983: 20-21), in that it connects the social and religious and relies on a visionary capacity which draws on both personal and collective experience. Shamanic experience for the Arakmbut is complicated because it blends together several features. Whereas all Arakmbut have some shamanic qualities which help them in their basic production, certain men have the ability to protect the community from hostile spirits (toto) which cause sickness.

The danger of sickness arises from the possibility of death. Arakmbut assume that human beings should live until they are old and then can die a 'good' death, but this is frequently not the case. Bad deaths come from accidents, illnesses, and sorcery attacks, all of which seem random and unfair to the victim's relatives. In order to prevent death, the Arakmbut have a complicated procedure of curing rituals which protect the soul (nokiren) of a sick person from immediate dangers.

This chapter looks in detail at the Arakmbut specialists in curing and the different methods they use to help their patients. The methods consist of ways by which the divided world, which we investigated in the last chapter, is temporarily unified in order to establish communication between the orders and effect the cure. However, these techniques are quite formal and involve not just remembering dreams, but utilising ritual methods to interact with the invisible world.[1]

For the Arakmbut, curing is a clear example of the way in which species, spirits, and human beings relate to ensure the health and continuity of the community. During periods of sickness and death, a person and the community as a whole face life-threatening dangers which can only be combatted by means of shamanic techniques. Shamanic knowledge of curing resides with curers (wamanoka'eri), who are recognised as having the capacity to diagnose and cure certain sicknesses using the chindign curing chants which are learnt over time and sung at the patient. Chindign refers to the special words which are chanted to gain a particular objective. They can be used to cure, to increase growth, or to practise sorcery. They are learnt from others but also contain much knowledge gained from dreams and personal experience.

The skill of a wamanoka'eri rests in identifying the symptoms of an illness from the part of the body where the patient feels pain (e'chiri). According to his analysis, the curer will use an appropriate chindign which is associated with a particular species, usually an animal whose behaviour is related to particular symptoms. A wamanoka'eri learns the chindign from close relatives such as a father, an elder brother, or occasionally a father-in-law. Younger men in San José frequently remark on the difficulty of learning chindign because the words are archaic and sometimes involve talking in an animal language. Furthermore, chindign are not standardised. Each person, on the basis of his dreams or visions, can shape and develop them according to his relationship with the spirit connected with the particular chindign.

The wamanoka'eri with whom I worked knew thirteen different chindign which he had learnt from his father and grandfather. This

---

1. Writers on shamanic activities have covered a broad field of characteristics. A shaman who cures tends to people as an healer to a patient (Lévi-Strauss 1963:169), in addition to protecting the community from sickness, and acting as a conciliator during internal conflicts (Metraux 1949); furthermore, the visionary shamanic capacity to understand the world also makes him a philosopher - both speculative and interpretative (Reichel-Dolmatoff 1971); in all these cases, the shamanic experience is one of the intermediary between the visible and invisible worlds (Harner 1972 & 1973).

seems an average number, although a young man told me that his cousin in Shintuya had made a survey of the number of chindign and found that there were over two hundred in the community. If this is the case then they are spread broadly among the Arakmbut. In San José there are eight recognised wamanoka'eri, but there are two or three others who consider themselves to be curers and whose relatives recognise their skills but who have not as yet convinced the rest of the community that they are proficient.

The power of a wamanoka'eri is paradoxical. An adult Arakmbut male may be physically and spiritually powerful because of the close relationship between his body and soul, yet he may not be the best person to sing a chindign. The efficacy of a chindign comes from many years of curing experience gained by the wamanoka'eri as he learns to adapt personal knowledge to the wisdom received from the shamanic teacher.[2] Chindign consist of long lists of species connecting the animal causing the illness to its habitat and food. This battery of knowledge has to be adapted to each circumstance and involves years of patient observation and understanding of animal behaviour. A mature *wambokerek* (man) rarely has this knowledge, but older men *(watone)* often do. The paradox arises because the young adults have the strength but not the knowledge, while old men have the knowledge and not the strength to defend themselves from the dangers of the spirits they might meet during the curing sessions.

The introduction of ayahuasca, a hallucinogenic banisteriopsis plant, from the lower Madre de Dios to San José has extended the wamanoka'eri's skills more broadly through the community than previously. A younger generation can use ayahuasca as a quicker method to gain contact with the spirit world. In San José, for example, there are eight wamanoka'eri, of whom four use exclusively the old methods and four use a mixture of the old chindign and ayahuasca.

Only men are recognised as wamanoka'eri, but this is not to say that women cannot cure. Whereas men cure illnesses caused by animal spirits through chanting, women have some ability to cure with plants such as herbal infusions for allergies and to use plants to relieve pain. This parallels the woman's role as gatherer of plants and tender of the chacras. The pharmacopeal knowledge of curing plants is not as broad as among the neighbouring Arawak or Panoan peoples, but since the establishment of a traditional medicine project, AMETRA

---

2. In his book on Tsewa garden magic (1985), Brown discusses at length the way in which individual experience is blended with cultural patterns. The result is a practical knowledge which varies from person to person while sharing many common features.

2000, which involved courses based on the practices of neighbouring groups, the importance of plants in curing has increased. Plant cures are seen by the Arakmbut as the equivalent of western medicines – remedies for non-spiritual diseases which can be cured through contact with the body (*waso*). On the other hand, the methods of a wamanoka'eri are fundamental because if an illness which comes from the spirit world is not treated well, death can frequently ensue.

The Importance of Curing Methods

Life (*e'e*) is the constant motion of soul-matter within the body. In a healthy person, these aspects of the soul work in harmony; sickness occurs when a person's soul is invaded by a harmful spirit and becomes too concentrated, or when the soul leaves the body and the person becomes weak. At the point when the soul leaves the body permanently, death occurs. The skill of a shaman is to be able to control these shifts within the parameters of life and restore health to the patient.

Health (*ndak* – 'good') is the control of the relationship between body and soul, which is fundamentally a question of power or strength (tainda). This includes physical strength, which results from a steady supply of meat, but also a spiritual strength, which combines humility and the capacity to assert oneself. Assertion can best be translated as 'matamona' – the ability to frighten enemies, to tell people to do something, or to take responsibility. Health therefore affects not only an individual, but also those with whom the person has regular contact. When sickness takes hold of someone and weakens them, considerable fear can spread through a community. The Arakmbut all feel themselves under spirit attack because sicknesses can spread rapidly. The fears of the Arakmbut in the face of a serious illness are founded on bitter experience of the consequences of epidemics in the 1950s.

Illness has always been connected to death, which means that the history of decimation among the Harakmbut is important in order to understand the current concern for health protection. The death rate among the Harakmbut in the past is difficult to estimate, but 95 percent of the Toyeri, Sapiteri, Kisambaeri, and Arasaeri are calculated to have died in the first three decades of this century as a result of the rubber boom.[3] The Arakmbut did not suffer massacres and slavery

3. These figures are based on Von Hassel (1905), who gives a total of 9,100 for the Sapiteri, Wachipaeri, Toyeri, and Arasaeri after the great decimation of the Harakmbut between 1894 and 1904. By including estimates of these deaths and the hitherto unknown Arakmbut (Amarakaeri), 30,000 dead would not be an

to the same extent as the other groups when they first encountered white people, although they were highly susceptible to illness and lost an estimated 40-50 percent of their population of three thousand during the 1950s.

An old man in San José worked with me to calculate the numbers of people in the Wakutangeri residential group at the time of mission contact. This group appeared in about 1950 as a reformulation of the Yawidnpoteri and Pewingboteri malocas. The Wakutangeri numbered about sixty adults and about forty children, but between 1950 and 1956, when they moved to the Dominican mission of Palotoa, at least thirty adults and many children died from influenza and yellow fever, while several men caught a disease which suddenly blinded them. The initial response of the community was to consider the illnesses as the result of sorcery and, among the Arakmbut as a whole, at least five women were killed during this time because they were thought to be the perpetrators of the deaths. Later, the Arakmbut thought that the deaths were due to the nokiren of dead Taka killed during the rubber boom who wandered through the headwaters of the Ishiriwe river. The death rate in the early 1950s was about five adults per year.

By the time the Arakmbut reached Palotoa in 1956 they had lost about half of their adult population, while others were critically ill. In Palotoa the availability of medicines alleviated the situation somewhat, and the massive number of deaths which took place among the Toyeri in the Kaichihue mission in the late 1930s were not repeated; developments in the use of vaccinations and antibiotics probably contributed to this improvement. Between 1956 and 1958 the death rate decreased to about three deaths a year (about six Wakutangeri died during this time), while after the move to Shintuya in 1957 the decline continued to about two adult deaths annually for the whole community of about three hundred people. On average one person dies per year in San José, although occasionally disaster can strike, such as in 1993 when three Arakmbut died.

The memory of the period in the Ishiriwe lingers on. Illness, once it sets in, worries the community considerably, and people of forty years or older describe the epidemics to those too young to remem-

---

exaggerated figure for the Harakmbut at the turn of the century. Looking at the current Harakmbut population of 1,500, the population decline (95 percent) correlates with Denevan's 1976 figures for lowland South America. From Denevan's estimates we can surmise that disease accounted for about half of the deaths of Harakmbut, with enslavement and murder accounting for the rest.

ber. The importance of curing among the Arakmbut arises from the constant possibility of sickness leading to death. The ability to cure a sick person and save them from death is a valued skill and demonstrates shamanic altruism and selflessness. A person who can cure defends the community from spirit attack but while so doing can expose himself or his family to the risk of an attack by the hostile spirit. In San José, for example, two shamanic practitioners lost children after they had carried out a successful cure. This was explained in terms of revenge by the spirit.

When someone falls ill, an outside spirit element enters the community and threatens life, whether because of an accident, an intent to cause harm, or the misbehaviour of the patient or his relatives. A spirit attack effects the body in one of two ways: the harmful spirit element enters the body encountering the person's own nokiren and causes sickness by concentrating too much soul in the body. Alternatively, the spirit takes away the nokiren, ultimately causing death from weakness and debility. The contrast is therefore between excess or absence of soul-matter.

Curing by Chanting – the Chindign

The information from the spirits used for curing has accumulated from the insights of shamans over centuries and is embedded within the curing rituals. The methods of curing which the Arakmbut use follow from the diagnosis made by a dreamer shaman (wayorokeri) and a curer shaman (wamanoka'eri). Evidence from dreams, coupled with recognition of the symptoms, directs the practitioner towards a curing chant (chindign). The efficacy of the cure is proof of a correct diagnosis.[4]

A wamanoka'eri cures by means of a ritual which involves remembering and repeating the curing chant related to a particular species or series of species. As he chants he uses an object such as a plant (primarily tobacco or nettles) or part of the body of a predator of the species under focus (such as the feathers of a harpy eagle). These objects are bitter or frightening to the harmful toto spirits.

One of the most difficult curing procedures is for snake-bites because the alien spirit enters the whole body and soul of the patient

---

4. The word chindign means both curing chant and sorcery. When I asked about this, I was told that those who want to practice sorcery also use chants (which only the sorcerers know).

by means of the snake poison. Someone with a snake bite is a victim of an attack by toto, whose poison turns into bitter blood which passes throughout the system and is coughed up by the patient. The wamanoka'eri will chant a chindign and blow tobacco over the body, which toto hate, in order to dry out the body and rid it of the poisoned blood. The patient is forbidden to eat or drink for at least four days and several sufferers say that the cure is worse than the original bite.

Illnesses where the nokiren has been lured away by a harmful spirit are usually caused by hunting in excess of the amounts suggested by the beneficial spirits (ndakyorokeri), or else by under-cooking food, thereby ingesting spirit from the dead animal. The illness occurs when the dispersed animal spirits cluster together to form toto and attract the soul away, making the person listless and weak. The chindign are highly appropriate for curing these diseases because they are related to specific species and consist of strategies for chasing away the toto and attracting the nokiren of the patient back to the body.

The chindign consist of lists of species connected to the animal around which the cure is centred and take on a narrative form. The collared peccary (mokas) chindign follows a similar pattern to most narratives. It is highly atmospheric and includes a variety of species associated with the animal causing the illness.[5]

Mokas Chindign

'Hu hu hu hu' say mokas when they eat *kerongtogn* (fruit from a tree).
On the path they walk together *(wandagnte)*
On the path they walk together (wandagnte)
On the path they walk together (wandagnte)
There is *menkeromba* (a bird)
Through the mud *(masamimbi)* they walk together.
On the path *(dagn)* they see *chupit* (a bird friendly to mokas).
Chupit, chupit. A little one.
They see *ekhomba* (a leaf which cures sickness).

---

5. Throughout this book there are lists in Arakmbut of species which I have been unable to identify. Only a few people knew all these species, and they were not overeager to spend time working out more than their general classificatory relevance to the chindign concerned. We agreed that I would keep the words in the original, so that at a future date they can be identified by an ethno-taxonomist when the Arakmbut wish it. Not revealing the identity of the species also preserves the chindign from being misused by outsiders. I should emphasise that Arakmbut rarely discuss chindign, and I was only told about them when it was certain that I understood their efficacy.

'We we we' (a noise mokas make when they walk in a group).

They eat the seeds of the *weomba* (a sweet fruit).

They walk in a large group.

They walk on the path of the peach palm *(homba wandagnte)*.

They walk in large groups (wandagnte).

They pass *koragnba* (a fruit parrots like)

When mokas are sick they eat *sopi* (worms or grubs).

Mokas walk on.

They pass the *kondapironda* (fruit they like).

They pass by the base of the *waya* (palm tree) *(wayatapo)*.

They pass the base of the *pio* tree (which drops a fruit they like).

They go in a group and eat fruits wherever they find them.

Mokas sing 'we we we' and go round the sides of the path.

They eat at the areas where there are fruits *(supitnba)*.

Wakuru pirotombate – the soul (of the sick person) goes with the mokas, hovering in the air. The soul of the sick person hovers in the air.

Wakirignayo – where it is misty – the mokas take the sick soul.

They go by the *masonara* ('aguajales' – watery areas where aguaje palms grow).

They pass the *mantoro* (achiote).

Where there are many fruits the mokas go in a group *(ayataponda ombatiwehpo)*.

They pass *mawentapo* (the mouth of the stream).

They go. They pass by. They eat fruit.

Where they go all fruits are there. Red fruit *(wambedntapo)*, other fruits *(tombednkerotapo)*.

They meet their friend *topobaudnihpi* (squirrel-like creature which eats the fruit *tombednkerogndogn*).

Mokas are seated there and they are chewing lianas.

'Hu hu hu' they sing as they enter the *mberedn* (a place they go looking for the fruit).

Kodnapiritapo mbuwadningchipi – they are sitting below the tree eating its fruit.

They eat below the *towandign* and *koragnipikntapo tapichipi* (at the base of the tree eating the fruit seeds).

They are seated in a circle and in the centre is the soul of the sick man.

The mokas go round in a circle on the ground.

They walk in groups together.

'Hu hu hu' they say as they walk round in a circle.

They go around on the ground in a circle.

'Hu Hu Hu' they say as they go round.

Ndo akedni – I am going ahead.

Ndo wanokway akkudnpo – I am going to enter the circle. The soul is there and I am going to fight for it to the end.

'Ku ku ku' Run away, mokas!

I want to enter the mokas circle to take the soul of the sick person. We are like flies attached to the sick person.

It is possible to go where the mokas are eating.

By blowing on the sick person I want to grasp the soul of the dead person (*ndo wandokpurmbu wandokmbawadapo*) to save him.

Ndo akden I will be in front curing and then the mokas will pass by us eating fruits from trees.

This chindign follows the mokas spirits into the forest, pointing out the fruits and places which the animals like. The detailed knowledge of the species is important and cannot simply be learned by rote because each one has to be known and understood in a full context. An Arakmbut curer explained that he 'sees' the journey into the forest to find the soul as in a dream (the sense sounds rather like the phrase 'in his mind's eye'). He explained that he 'sees' the whole scene in front of him as he chants, which is why an effective shaman needs a broad experience of the environment and species of the forest and river.

The soul of the curer hovers about a foot above the ground and floats through the misty forest passing the same route which the mokas take, looking carefully at the species and the places where they like to stop and rest. A group of mokas have abducted the soul of the sick person and the curer has to get it back to the community. The first task is to follow the trail of the mokas until he finds them in the circle with the soul in the centre. Most chants at this point frighten the spirits away by referring to a jaguar, harpy eagle, or other predator. In this case, the curer suddenly shouts and 'sticks like a fly' to the soul of the sick person, waiting patiently until the mokas move on without noticing that the curer still holds the nokiren. After that the two souls return to the community and the patient is expected to improve.

Toto hate anything which tastes bitter or which stings when touched. The shaman induces a harmful spirit to leave the patient by the application of certain bitter substances such as chili and garlic which are placed around the sick person. Sometimes a shaman will beat the body with isanga *(macherik)* nettles which cause the toto pain, while tobacco is used for nearly all illnesses. Tobacco is a substance which frightens harmful spirits and protects sick people. Smoking strong tobacco, such as that taken from solid blocks of tobacco grown and cured regionally, makes the cure more efficacious.

The following list of species and symptoms includes the activity which should take place concurrently with the chindign:

1. *kayare* (picuro) use macherik: for pains in the legs, arms, and chest;
2. mokas (collared peccary) blow over patient: for vomiting and fever;
3. *bi'ign* (fish) blow and put tobacco in mouth: for sore stomachs and diarrhoea;
4. sowe (black spider monkey) tobacco: for convulsions, hands clenched, and teeth chattering;
5. mapi (agouti) blow on macherik and hit affected area: for children crying and adult with pains;
6. mamori (sabalo fish) use tobacco for stomach ache, diarrhoea, and vomiting.

The application of tobacco involves the use of blowing and sucking which are the main methods of physical contact with the body of the sick person. To blow is *e'chipoa* and to suck *e'mbuiyuk*; breath is a sign of life and, like smoke, contains the beneficial or harmful elements of that with which it has just had contact, thus deriving its nature from contiguity. Blowing by a healthy wamanoka'eri will impart some of the power of the curer's nokiren to the patient, which itself will have had some contact with beneficial spirits. Blowing tobacco is a means of putting bitter substances into the body in order to expel the toto from the patient's nokiren. Wet, bitter substances such as rum or pisco are sometimes blown over a sick person and other 'bitter' liquids such as lemon juice can also be used.

A shaman will also suck the body of the patient to draw out any harmful elements there might be within. The sucking is very strong and anything found will be spat out. I have no knowledge of anything tangible being drawn from the body of a sick person but any harmful element is sucked out in the shaman's sputum and deposited away from the patient. Arakmbut shamans do not appear to indulge in manipulation or deception of the patient. There were no 'supernatural' happenings in the curing sessions I observed and nothing occurred which was not clear and apparent to everyone present. Shamanism among the Arakmbut is a mixture of skills and techniques which anyone can grasp but only few can do well. A wamanoka'eri need perform no tricks because a shaman is not expected to do the impossible.

One evening I witnessed a curing session for a sick child who was crying uncontrollably and would not go with anyone other than its mother. An old man who was classificatory father of the woman diagnosed that an oriole *(purak)* was responsible and agreed to perform the chindign for small birds. The father of the girl gave the old man a fan of harpy eagle feathers (sing), and he started his oration in an accent which was almost impossible for those present to understand. The chant consisted of several verses which listed species and habitats of the bird. At the end of each verse, the wamanoka'eri placed the feathers to his lips, blew on them and he brushed them against the baby's face, head, body, arms, and legs. He began the chant again and repeated the motions. After the fourth blow onto the feathers he appeared to start the chant again but suddenly stopped. The father then brushed the baby with tobacco leaves. Throughout the curing ritual, the atmosphere was very relaxed, even light-hearted; the family spoke and some even joked. The following morning the mother said that the baby was definitely better.

The mbakoy chindign (small bird chant) which helps children who cry too much was chosen for the cure. The wamanoka'eri used the feather of a harpy eagle (sing) on the patient because it is a predator of small birds who flee in terror when they hear its call. The chindign starts with a 'pipipit!', which is a call of small birds, and then changes to 'kororogn', which is the noise small birds make when they are flying away from a sing in the forest. The wamanoka'eri agreed to tape the chindign and provided a list of the main species, although most of them were not identifiable.

The chindign can be used for illnesses of the following birds: *hutuk, sirokwedn, keyedn, ohpet, mantak, sowsow, sakwis, burakoy, wakoy-ereh, weke, singku, mapitokoy, mao, kohkoh, wanekeinari, torognpo, to'ign, ndumberita'gn, ndumberimako, waoecheri, makei, peyapeya, wanus, pite, pitewambedn, wiey, yokiyok, toktokwa, wambedntoktok, wandak purak, purak wasik, suruping, paiping, onsue, we'ak, koyokoyo, wike, mbegnko, toweya, kurukuru wambite, sia', daudn, saki, wioe, wiwi, wiu, suh, pik, siro, siu,* and *beras.*

These birds eat the following fruit, which are mentioned in the chindign: *pama, chaweri, tongkopai, wepet, tapibedn, kuporo, tapamai, achaweri, pin* and *wakmbednbedn.*

The birds sleep in the following places: *sorokheiyo* (a hole in the earth), *wiwimba* and *korimbayo* (in bamboo scrub), and *oweyo* (in dry

branches of big trees). These birds all live in big trees, are comparatively small, and do not live on islands; they are mainly forest birds.

Their main predator is the sing, especially: *biopising, singkuwi,
machichkaikai* (also known as *keregnsing*), *wiuwiusing, mekodntosing.*

The chindign does not name all the birds but goes with the bird
spirits into the forest where it names the fruits they like to eat and
refers to their homes where they make their nests. Once the bird
spirits are lulled into a sense of security, the curer calls out 'kororogn!' and the name of the different sing species while brushing the
child with the harpy eagle fan. The bird spirits rush away in terror,
leaving the nokiren of the baby alone in its body or free to return.

Explanations for an illness follow a pattern determined by the
presence or efficacy of a cure. Whenever a cure cannot be found,
sorcery is given as the reason; when a cure seems possible, the cause
is attributed to the patient, who has annoyed a spirit by transgressing
some convention, usually involving hunting or sexual relations;
finally, when the patient has either died or recovered and the situation has to a large extent been socially or medically resolved, the
explanation refers to an accidental encounter with a toto.

The example of curing using the mbakoy chindign described
above was largely informal and concerned an illness which was not
life-threatening but still distressing for the child and mother. For this
reason, only the immediate family were involved while the curer was
a close relative of the mother and lived next door. The curing session
was relaxed and I was able to watch alongside because I was eating
with the household at the time. If the problem were more serious,
concern would spread throughout the village with visitors coming
regularly from other households to watch the curing, and various
wamanoka'eri would compare diagnoses and try different chindign.

The curing ritual performed by the wamanoka'eri is an attempt to
bring together the different orders in the Arakmbut cosmos. The
chindign communicate with the invisible spirit world, enabling the
curer to pass into it by uttering the names of the species and the
chants. The curer does not enter into a discussion with the spirits
who have entered the body or taken the soul of the patient, but travels with them, unobtrusively. The experience is not a sleeping dream
but a heightened state of awareness of the spirit world.

The chindign identify closely with the species. The chant uses different methods to produce effects in the invisible world: words from
the animals' languages put them at ease, detailed descriptions of the
species' habitat and behaviour enable them to travel together, while
the bitter substances or, for example, the sing feather can suddenly

make the spirits afraid and leave the patient's nokiren alone. The wamanoka'eri is acting in the visible world and by uttering the words and notes of the chindign he can penetrate the division between human beings and the invisible world and make contact with the spirits.

The result is that the chindign and the curing materials both bring the wamanoka'eri into the invisible world and identify him intimately with the species. This draws together the three orders of species, spirit, and human, which are normally divided. At this moment, by acting in the visible world as a human, the wamanoka'eri is simultaneously acting in the invisible world with spirits and animals. Thus the curing ritual is not really metaphorical, which would still allow for a gap between the orders, but rather an instantaneous fusion of different worlds.

Modern Curing – Ayahuasca

When an illness in San José is considered to be more serious or long-term, wamanoka'eri use ayahuasca. This system of curing is complementary to the old system of chindign. Ayahuasca was introduced to San José during the mid 1970s by some young Idnsikambo men. They had lived in the mission of El Pilar near Maldonado for a year or so after their education in Quillabamba. While in El Pilar they met a locally renowned ayahuascero (practitioner of ayahuasca), a Shipibo whose family first came from the Ucayali during the time of the rubber boom, and he taught the use of ayahuasca. In a year the Arakmbut had learned the techniques well enough to be practitioners in curing and had saved enough money from gold work to pay for their tuition.[6]

The Arakmbut men went from El Pilar to San José via Boca Inambari and gradually established a position in the village for their ability to use ayahuasca, which is now a regular aspect of curing

6. Although Carlos Junquera (1978) discusses an Arakmbut shaman who cured by taking ayahuasca, this probably refers to the mission of El Pilar around the time when ayahuasca had been introduced. Ayahuasca was not in Puerto Luz and only marginally in San José at the time that I first arrived (1980). The article refers to 'celestial' travels which sounds more like a Shipibo view of the cosmos than Arakmbut. Since the death of the shaman in San José (who never used hallucinogens), ayahuasca has increased considerably as a curing method. Ayahuasca has not changed the Arakmbut view of the spirit world, and if anything has had a reinforcing effect. Junquera's subsequent work on Harakmbut shamanism is entirely influenced by the Yagua material (Chaumeil 1983).

practices in the community. The practitioners have taught others in the community their knowledge and in return are learning chindign from older relatives in a complementary exchange of new and old curing techniques.

Ayahuasca sessions take place in San José every few months in order to see the spirits or the future, to find lost property, or, most importantly, to cure. The practitioners are approached by relatives of a sick person when traditional methods have not had much success and they organise the sessions for a specific evening. Alternatively, influential persons in the community may call for ayahuasca to be used when a problem faces the community (such as a company seeking gold on traditional Arakmbut land) and the hallucinogen is considered to be an appropriate means for seeking advice from the spirit world. At the end of each session the spirits suggest a time for the next meeting.

Ayahuasca is gathered from the trees by the organiser of the session and his close relatives, and they have the responsibility to make the preparations. The vines are taken back to the house where the men pound them with stones and blow tobacco over the mashed pulp, which is taken to the kitchen and boiled for several hours. A night with little moon is best for a session. The participants should not eat anything prior to taking the drug and gather in the kitchen of the person requesting the session after dark. The ayahuasca is taken off the fire and the practitioner scoops up some of the liquid in a cup over which he blows tobacco. He then announces and describes the spirits which they wish to see and sets out the problem to be solved.

Everyone sits in a circle and a cup is passed round, each person drinking three cups, unless he is a novice, in which case he can only take one. For the first few sessions a participant will have no visions and at most will see only bright lights. The rest, however, take their three glasses while the ayahuascero chants a specific repetitive rhythm calling for the chongpai (the word for both ayahuasca and anaconda). Chongpai is an interesting spirit because it is powerful, and is thus concentrated, but it is largely beneficial if treated correctly and a person shows it no fear (e'mepuk). Within Arakmbut cosmology, the chongpai shares many characteristics with the wachipai, mentioned in the previous chapter. Both are powerful and benign, if treated well; both are connected to snakes and inform shamans, either directly or through the ndakyorokeri, of events in the spirit world.

The participants in the ayahuasca session wait for about fifteen minutes with their eyes closed. As the chongpai arrives, the practitioner announces it and silence reigns. The ayahuasca ritual is explicitly divided into three stages, not including the preparation and initial drinking of the hallucinogen.

Stage 1: The arrival of the chongpai

The chongpai arrives from outside the hut or else emerges from the noses of the participants in the form of an anaconda. The anaconda is a manifestation of the spirit of the ayahuasca which approaches and wraps itself around everyone at the same time, with its head next to their ears. Here it either rests and helps the participant to concentrate or whispers advice about the subsequent events in the session. The chongpai is protector and advisor and while it is there, no harm can come to anyone taking ayahuasca, unless they show fear, for fear distracts and the vision may become blurred or even lost, subjecting the participant to great danger. When this stage has ended, the chongpai disappears, but it has not gone and will continue to remain present at the session.

Stage 2: The arrival of the toto (harmful spirits)

At this point the toto appear. In a curing session they may take away the sick man's soul and everyone will have to move in harmony to drag it back. Toto come in their human forms either tall, white, and thin or, more usually, short and black with long fingernails. The participants in the session must fight with these toto. This constitutes the most vigorous part of the proceedings. Shots are fired and some men pick up sticks to chase the toto, while others are helped by the ndakyorokeri who appear as beautiful women spirits who lie on beds of flowers and try to lure the toto away from the sick person. Sometimes the visions can be a distraction, though, and there are reports of people becoming so involved with visions of helicopters and outboard motors that they forget why they are taking ayahuasca at all. With success, however, the toto are frightened away and the nokiren of the sick person is restored to normal. The patient usually takes ayahuasca with the rest of the participants.

Stage 3: The Doctors

Then the doctors enter. They appear as medical doctors with suits, ties, and shoes; they carry briefcases and have stethoscopes around their necks. They enter and carry out an examination of the sick person and then they advise the participants what to do. For example, they may say that the toto will return in a few days and the patient will die, or else that he or she will live, whereupon they prescribe how often there should be sessions in order to keep the sick person in good health.

After this the session ends and the practitioner must sum up what has happened. The Arakmbut say that this is a summary and not an interpretation because all the participants will have seen the same thing. If the session is not about curing it will be much shorter, but usually it will last from about nine or ten at night until three or four in the morning.

Ayahuasca visions are shared and all communication takes place through perception of the invisible world. An Arakmbut explained this to me using the analogy of telepathy, and added that the Brazilian football team play as if they were in an ayahuasca session, because they never seem to communicate to each other what they are doing, yet they work together as a team.

In many respects ayahuasca sessions integrate well into Arakmbut ideas of curing and the spirit world and have, over the past twenty years, become a part of their shamanic repertoire.[7] The visions seen with ayahuasca are the same as those in the state of wayorok, and the spirits which appear are the same as those in the traditional pantheon such as toto, ndakyorokeri, waweri (river spirits), and ndumberi (forest spirits). The diagnosis of an illness or post-mortem of a deceased person consist of interpretations of events in the light of Arakmbut cosmology. After a successful cure the explanation normally includes a reference to an accidental encounter with a toto or else some misdemeanour in hunting or cooking. The successful diagnosis is proven by the patient's recovery and so the system always works.

7. The Harakmbut are not the only peoples to have adopted the practice of using ayahuasca. The Ese'eja have a similar experience and have only started to take it within living memory (Gareth Burr pers. comm.). Among other Harakmbut peoples the hallucinogenic plant toe *(hayapa)* has been noted among the Wachipaeri and Sapiteri (Califano & Fernández Distel 1982), but according to Bennet (1991), who studied curing among both the Matsigenka and the Wachipaeri, the Matsigenka use it practically every night (p.202), whereas the Wachipaeri use it much less frequently (p.229).

Evidence from Panoan speakers (Kensinger among the Cashinahua 1973), Siskind among the Sharanahua (1973c), and Morin among the Shipibo (1973) shows that these peoples have regularly taken ayahuasca not only for curing but also to find out more about the invisible spirit world. The same has been reported for Arawak speakers by Weiss among the Asháninka (1975) and Bennet among the Matsigenka (op.cit.:194).

It would therefore seem that ayahuasca has entered the Madre de Dios via the Arawak- and Panoan-speaking peoples, probably with the addition of some influence from the highland practitioners. Over the last few decades this has become incorporated into the shamanic practices of the Ese'eja and most Harakmbut peoples.

If the patient dies then the cause was beyond the scope of the curer and was due to sorcery or to a species unknown to a wamanoka'eri. By means of the dead person's final dreams or the scattering of balsa ashes on the grave to detect marks of the responsible spirits, Arakmbut wamanoka'eri can ascertain a cause of death. However, all of these explanations have a marked political dimension which means that no one explanation will satisfy everyone in the community.

Ayahuasca is more flexible than chindign for curing in that the practitioners deal directly with the spirit world without needing to resort to specific orations. Whereas one might think that with the increase in ayahuasca, the traditional chindign forms of curing would become redundant, this has not occurred. On the contrary, there is an underlying acceptance by the practitioners that the ability to perform a chindign is extremely important, and ayahuasca practitioners themselves spend much time learning the chants from others in their household or close family.

Curing by ayahuasca operates differently than curing by chindign. Whereas the chindign enter the invisible world through the repetition of ritual chants, names, and actions which bridge the gap between species, human beings, and spirits, ayahuasca has the effect of enabling all participants at the session who are actively engaged in the curing to enter the invisible world of the spirits. The practitioner guides the session and, through a song and occasional words and phrases, prepares the participants and explains to them what is happening.

The chongpai, doctors, and toto are all spirits but also appear as species and human beings simultaneously. The participants are therefore taken into the invisible world where the three orders, which are usually separate, are fused together for the purposes of the cure. Those involved in the session can therefore act within the invisible world and affect the harmful spirits directly.

Some of the old Arakmbut shamans consider that ayahuasca is an easy option for young people who are not prepared to spend the time learning how to cure and communicate with the spirit world through experience and without the advantages of hallucinogens. However, the effect of a cure utilises the same principles of finding a technique to break into the timeless invisible world of potency where animals, humans, and spirits all interact. While in 1980 ayahuasca was treated by Psyche and the shaman from the Pukiri as a rival technique, it has now been incorporated into Arakmbut curing methods.

The most effective way of communicating with the spirit world is through dreams. This is a skill which develops through life and which varies considerably between Arakmbut. On the other hand, the wamanoka'eri is able to enter into the invisible world to cure by chanting. His relationship with the spirits is by no means as sophisticated as the wayorokeri – the dream shamans not only learn about the cosmos but have the capacity to change the way in which it is interpreted by the Arakmbut.

Chapter 420

DREAMS AND THE SOURCE
OF KNOWLEDGE

D reams provide an entrance into the invisible world of the spirits
by enabling a person's soul to leave the body and travel freely.
The invisible world is as real for the Arakmbut as the visible world.[1]
The first glimpse I had into the form of this 'reality' took place after I
had been in San José for about six months. One day, after I had admin-
istered some medicines to an old man who had been bleeding pro-
fusely, I returned to my hut and lay down. In a few minutes I realised
that I had the ability to float on air. I hovered a few feet above the bed
and turned over so that my arms were outstretched, then flew across
the village to the old man's hut. As I flew, I could feel the breeze and
the brush of leaves on my face and sparks flew from my fingers into his
hut. As I returned I concentrated by looking through my closed eye-
lids to prevent me from falling. On reaching my bed I rejoined my
sleeping body. The next day the old man had completely recovered.

This intense experience shook me considerably. The only explanation was that this was a 'vivid dream', because I had taken no hallucinogens; the sense of entry into the invisible world was exceedingly
strong. Rationalising this experience of an invisible world into the
non-indigenous terms of my own personal life obscures rather than
illustrates the Arakmbut notion of dream (wayorok), but the example
gives some idea of its intensity.

---

1. This is different from, for example, the Shuar, who consider the invisible world
    the reality (Harner 1972:134). Brown (1987:37) disagrees with this position and
    thinks that the discussion is not between reality and non-reality. Tedlock (1987:4)
    says that to talk of reality implies that we are talking about a common notion of
    reality, when this may not be the case.

Through the discussions arising from the experience, I began to understand that whereas in the visible world possibility is framed by time and space, in the invisible world these boundaries are transcended. In the realm of spirit one can see into the future or the past, call back a lost soul, and communicate with all-knowing spirits. The invisible existence of the spirits is one of 'potentiality' or, as Brown (1987:157) puts it: 'The Aguaruna think of dreams as experiences that reveal emergent possibilities or likelihoods, events that are developing but which are not yet accomplished facts.' This world of potentiality is where shamans communicate with the spirits in their dreams.

Through my dream, I caught a glimpse of a world which, for the Arakmbut, contains knowledge and understanding of all the possible events which could happen and which have ever happened. However, the shamanic skill is in managing to interpret the information encountered in the dream experience. During my periods in the community, oral and visual manifestations of the spirit world took place on several occasions. These events can be explained away or left a mystery, but I found that the most useful approach was a suspension of disbelief which constituted an act of scepticism concerning my own presuppositions; this enabled me to talk with the Arakmbut and take the first faltering steps towards understanding shamanic qualities.

Arakmbut shamanic dreams are 'ecstatic experiences' in the sense that the nokiren leaves the body (Eliade 1951:4). During an Arakmbut dream, the sleeper often plays an active part in the events and can travel outside of his or her body as if in a conscious state. The Arakmbut shamans who have mastered this technique have the capacity to dream at will on any subject they choose, and not only to understand a message, but to participate in a discussion on the issue with the spirits. People do not necessarily dream every night but everyone dreams occasionally, and the contact with the invisible world which occurs helps discriminate between the multiplicity of causes behind everyday events.

Dreaming among the Arakmbut is not uniform and varies enormously according to the control exercised over the dream by the dreamer. Some people can be passive spectators in a dream, rather as if they were at a film show; others can listen to messages from the invisible world; and those whose dream techniques are particularly impressive can participate freely in spirit activities.

Another aspect of Arakmbut dreaming is that it is not only a subjective experience. The invisible spirit world can appear the same to several people simultaneously, provided they have the capacity to understand and interpret correctly what they see and do. A hardened materialist may say that the invisible world only exists to the extent that it could hit you on the head. The Arakmbut insist that people can be attacked by spirits and suffer physically as a result.

The Arakmbut capacity to dream consists of a continuum whereby the dreamer becomes increasingly more agile. A young, inexperienced person has to be careful with spirits because they cannot yet control dreams. A child's nokiren can wander around at night but risks exposure to the harmful influence of waweri of the river, while a young person learning to hunt may make contact with the invisible world in dreams but will understand very little.

A young *wambo* will gradually begin to dream of the beautiful ndakyorokeri spirits who come and tell him where he can catch prey and possibly tempt him with the possibility of sexual relations. With maturity, a man can begin to understand messages from the invisible world, although they are not able to initiate communication. Women also dream, but whether they dream of beautiful young men or not they are reluctant to say.

Fully mature men with some shamanic qualities can, with time, gain the skill of communicating directly to a spirit. This is an important technique because it means that they can communicate in the invisible world as in the visible world. Most men and women can master this technique to a limited extent, but the capacity varies. The introduction of the hallucinogen ayahuasca in San José over the last twenty years has enabled many men and women to communicate with the spirits who otherwise would have found it difficult. Although older shamans such as Psyche initially considered that these short cuts led to inaccurate forms of communication and not to real dialogue, others in the community felt that the old men were trying to retain their exclusive access to the invisible world. The shamans never took a strong line on the matter, however, and in spite of some occasional conflict, the practice increased. Interestingly enough, twenty years later, the young men who introduced ayahuasca are learning the older techniques because they consider them to be more effective.

For the wayorokeri, the real skill of learning how to talk to spirits could not be bought or even taught but grew from many years of experience. The spirits themselves decide when to come and inform a person that he has been chosen as a vehicle for communicating with the rest of the community. Arakmbut shamanic techniques are based on qualities derived from dreaming which are available to all people, yet they are practised with differing degrees of skill. The shamanic knowledge among the Arakmbut takes spirit communication through dreaming to specialised levels which are beyond basic contacts with the invisible world.

Wayorokeri – the Dream Shaman

A wayorokeri is a shaman whose dreaming techniques enable him to step far into the invisible world and travel to different spirit helpers, seeking advice and looking into the past, present, and future. The wayorokeri takes advantage of the world of potentiality to see what might happen in the future and interpret from the visible world the possible ways in which the invisible world will influence events.

The Arakmbut have no formal shamanic training or initiation apart from learning the chindign and interpreting dreams. However, an 'initiation', if it can be called this, is occasionally conferred on a person by the spirits themselves. Psyche became a wayorokeri after his experience communicating with the river spirits, who told him that they would come to him in dreams to help him cure and support the community. This experience was similar to Arakmbut accounts of meeting a wachipai. In a dream arising from the wachipai, the dreamer is sometimes told that he will have the power to be a wayorokeri in the future. If, after an encounter with a wachipai, the Arakmbut tells of the dream or forgets it, the message will not come to fruition.

However, an initiation by the spirits is not sufficient for someone to be recognised as a wayorokeri, for in spite of their spiritual experience in the forest or river, if their efficacy as a curer or prophet is not recognised by other members of the community, then the spirit contact is considered to have been a mistake. Several stories illustrate the special relationship which can arise between a wayorokeri and certain species which advise, support and protect him. The following example is the myth of the caiman *(mama)* and the species' relationship with a wayorokeri who, through various experiences, gains power and insight from the species.

Mama

A man went hunting and found footprints of a caiman near a lake by a stream. He found mama, took them by the neck, and killed one, then another. When you find a mama it does not move and to kill it with your hands you break its neck and it dies.

After killing it, the man cooked the mama. 'With what can I eat this meat?' said the man. He went up the bank of an island where *wiwimba* (bamboo) normally grows. Even though there was no chacra, the mama offered him yuca. [The audience comments that this is amazing.]

The man was thirsty and went into the wiwimba again and found sugar cane *(apik),* which quenched his thirst.

It was dangerous at night, but the day dawned safely and he continued his trip to where he was going to pass the next night. There he saw two more mama. He killed them and continued. He made his camp in an *okpi* (a massive pile of driftwood) where tree trunks had piled up. When he wanted to eat ripe plantains *(aroi)* he went to look for them and found them. He also found sugar cane. He made a place in the driftwood to rest.

A jaguar was calling 'bu! bu! bu!' as the man was resting in the driftwood. 'Perhaps it will come here,' he thought. The jaguar was coming closer. He could hear the noise of its paws on the pebbles: 'ochuk, ochuk, hoo, hogn.' The jaguar was looking for the footprints of the man but he was safe inside the driftwood. But the jaguar pulled branches out from the driftwood one by one and suddenly the man appeared and shouted 'waa a a !' at the jaguar, which fled down the beach in fear. The man then took up a firebrand and went to the river. The jaguar saw him and followed him to the bank. In the middle of the stream there was a big tree where the man went to hide. Dawn came and the jaguar had gone.

On the following day he went on and found another mama. It was a big mama. After cooking it he found everything he wanted – sugar cane, tare (yuca), aroi (plantains). Again he made his camp in the driftwood for the night. He was tired early and made his bed in the driftwood where he entered. He heard thunder and decided that he would return to his house on the following day.

Suddenly he felt something cold touching him. It was a snake (biwi) passing over his body. It was a huge snake which passed right over his body. He stopped breathing and lay still as if dead. But he could not hold his breath too long and tried to breathe. The snake stopped and lay on him when he took a breath so again he held his breath and lay 'dead'. When the tail passed he began to breath again.

Then he heard a 'bu bu bu bu boo!' It sounded like a trumpeter bird *(suru).* Taka (non-Arakmbut people who are potential enemies) imitate the suru in the same way that they imitate a partridge when they come by. The Taka were coming closer. He stayed quiet. They had discovered his footprints. 'The prints go no further. Let us go on,' said the Taka. The Taka went by. The man could hear them upstream. Then they returned and passed by the place where he was lying and went on in the other direction down the river. Then dawn came and the man returned to his community, pleased to get home. He was a wayorokeri of mama, and the caimans gave him what he needed and helped him when in danger.

This story describes several factors connecting the wayorokeri to the caiman. The hunter knows the behaviour of the mama, from tracking to killing it with his bare hands, and he clearly has a special relationship with the spirit because he kills four in a period of three days, which could easily expose him to punishment for overhunting. This is a story of a successful wayorokeri. Thanks to the help from the caiman spirits he is never without food: plantains, sugar cane, and yuca appear in abundance when the hunter is hungry, and during the evenings he sleeps in the okpi driftwood piles which are usually places where caimans sleep. An Arakmbut hunter would normally consider drift wood to be a highly dangerous place to stay.

Three dangers beset the hunter – the jaguar, the snake, and the Taka – and as each approaches he is lying in the driftwood, which provides not only a sleeping place but also a refuge. These dangers are three of the most frequent perils which concern an Arakmbut hunter. The first two are the most dangerous animals, while the Taka are dangerous humans. The wayorokeri has knowledge based on his contact with the mama which provides him with protection from dangers which beset Arakmbut hunters. This myth accounts for the benefits accruing to a successful wayorokeri. However, a dreamer does not always handle the spirit world so providentially. A less successful wayorokeri runs the risk of being tempted into taking advantage of his skills, and he faces dangers if he loses control of his powers or overplays his relationship with the spirits.

Another myth tells of a wayorokeri who suffers as a result of succumbing to temptation.

Keme

One day, a day that was good for hunting, a man who killed only keme (tapir) went following footprints. He went to look for keme, but there was thick forest so he crouched down. From there he looked in front and saw a beautiful woman. He was frightened at seeing a woman.

'Why have you come?' asked the woman, who was a keme woman.

'I have come for you,' said the man.

The girl said to him, 'Let's get married.'

They talked for a while, and then the keme woman said, 'Let's go to my family.'

The man accepted and they both went to the keme family. The arrived and met her family where there was a lake. There lived the keme family. The girl said to the man, 'Close your eyes'.

He closed his eyes and saw a beautiful house. They entered and she gave him a seat, but the man did not see a seat, only a tortoise. For the keme, however, the tortoise appeared as a seat.

The keme girl called her husband to meet his brother-in-law. The man had his bow and arrow and saw his brother-in-law bathing in the water. He pointed his arrow and shot him, because the brother-in-law seemed like a keme to the man. Twice he shot him, and he died in the water. The man returned to his house where his wife was and said, 'I have shot a keme.'

'Be careful you don't shoot my brother,' the keme wife said, but on seeing her brother dead she burst into tears. She returned to the house in a while and said to her husband, 'Why have you shot my brother?'

'I have not shot your brother. I have shot keme,' said the man and he went to bring the body in to eat.

But the girl said to her husband, 'I don't want to see his face because it is my brother.'

The man did not accept this and left the head on the body.

The girl was very angry. She stopped bringing water, and she broke all the bamboo tubes she had gathered for the meat and went off. She was still crying for her brother. The man followed, thinking to shoot her but he did not. The keme girl went on crying for her brother. The man followed her to another watershed and crossed two more but he could not catch her. The prints went into a huge lake where she wanted him to follow but he did not follow because he was afraid. By the lake were guayava trees and other fruits. There was a large purak (oriole) nest in a high tree. The man saw it but could not reach the nest because it was so high.

The man returned to his house sad. He died a week later. His penis had rotted because he had had sexual relations with an animal.

This story explains that being a wayorokeri does not simply mean being able to dream effectively but involves entering into a highly relativistic invisible spirit world. From the perspective of the keme, things do not appear as they do for the Arakmbut, and the wayoro-keri enters a house where tortoises are used as seats because they are logs to a tapir. The relativity also means that, to the keme woman, her brother was a person, whereas to the hunter he was another tapir ready for shooting. Initially the hunter did not recognise the tapir as a person, and furthermore he had no permission to kill it. The result was a fundamental transgression: in his ignorance, he could not tell the difference between meat granted by the spirit world and hunting for the sake of it. He thereby committed murder.

At the same time that he refused to recognise the keme brother-in-law as a person, he suffered the consequences of his inability to appreciate relativity. The young woman is a form of ndakyorokeri who is prepared to help the hunter and has sexual relations with him. As long as he recognises her as a woman there is no problem, but when he ignores her advice and treats her brother as an animal, then his relationship with her becomes animal-like too. The sexual relations he had with the keme spirit woman become relations with an animal, and his penis rots as a result. Thus a wayorokeri has to be particularly careful and knowledgeable or else he could suffer a dreadful fate.

A powerful wayorokeri is not only good at curing but uses his visionary skills of prediction for the benefit of the community. For example, in San José, Psyche was able to say who would recover from illnesses and who was likely to die, to help people find missing objects and, on a broader front, to warn the community if harmful spirits were lurking in any place and in certain circumstances to control the weather. This protection can continue after death. When returning to San José in February 1992, the arduous journey by land and river was particularly tense because of death threats I had received from colonists because of my research into indigenous rights. Throughout the trip, whether travelling by road or river, a white heron *(ereknda kapiro)* regularly preceded the lorry or canoe. When I mentioned this in San José, several people said that this had probably been Psyche's spirit shielding us from the heavy floods which were inundating the Madre de Dios and from the colonists.

However a wayorokeri can also be dangerous because, in order to benefit a community, he sometimes uses his powers to attack others. This can give rise to accusations of sorcery or, if the shaman has died, to the view that his spirit has harmed the living. A wayorokeri can sometimes take the form of a dangerous animal to harm the Arakmbut. When a member of San José lost all his pigs, he said that a dead wayorokeri who had contacts with the jaguar had converted himself into a jaguar to cause the destruction. In a similar way, between 1990 and 1992 there was an increase in the number of snakes around San José, which was attributed to the death of a wayorokeri of the armadillo *(aramburu)* who, missing his close relatives, came to the Karene area in spirit and brought the snakes with him.[2]

In this way, a wayorokeri can be dangerous or beneficial depending on where he lives and with whom he associates. Usually a wayorokeri from within the community is beneficial but one from another community is potentially harmful (an ambiguity already noted with the meaning of the word chindign, meaning both curing chant and sorcery). The wayorokeri is the most skilled of the Arakmbut in communicating with the invisible world, but he has to take care that his powers are publicly seen to be used for general benefit rather than for personal gain, or suspicions of sorcery will inevitably arise.

Wayorokeri are not infallible and do make errors of judgement and misdiagnoses. These are discussed and debated within and between households in each community. Although wayorokeri have considerable influence, it should not be thought that people automatically agree with everything they say, particularly if their proposal involves some inconvenience, such as dietary restrictions, a curtailment on the use of ayahuasca, or an inexplicably negative prognosis. Usually people listen to a shaman's advice and decide on the extent to which they want to take it, often continuing to do what they want. If things go wrong the shaman was correct; if nothing happens, it is noted for future reference.

Shamanic Knowledge and its Sources

All shamanic knowledge comes from the invisible world and can ultimately be traced to collective or personal experiences with the spirits. Some of the information is received wisdom which comes in the form of myths, stories, songs, chindign, and general comments on the structure of the universe. However, this information is refined considerably through revealed knowledge arising from shamanic encounters of wayorokeri with spirits and also the experience of particular events.

1. Received information

Myths, songs, and stories are learned by children from an early age through repetition within the house and also from the occasional

---

2. This connection comes from the fact that snakes often share the burrow of an armadillo, so people see armadillos going into the burrow and a snake coming out. Sometimes a hunter can find a snake inside the hole.

public performances to entertain the community during the full moon or at a fiesta. The chindign, on the other hand, are more diffi- cult and must be learned over time. Curing knowledge among the wamanoka'eri is greatly valued in San José, and the initial preference is to transfer knowledge within the household and between members of the same clan. However, if no member of the close family wishes to become a curer, an old man may help another young man who is more distantly related if he shows interest and aptitude. The instruc- tion patterns of the eight wamanoka'eri in San José is as follows:

1. Idnsikambo FB to Idnsikambo BS. These two work together as a team. The old man has the knowledge and the younger man the power.
2. Idnsikambo elder brother to Idnsikambo younger brother. Both are practitioners of ayahuasca and recognised as wamanoka'eri, but the elder brother teaches the younger the chindign.
3. Yaromba father to Yaromba son. The father is persevering, but the son complains that he cannot remember the chindign and finds them difficult.
4. Yaromba old single man to Idnsikambo grandson (closest rela- tive's eldest son). The young man's mother is a Yaromba and has a warm relationship with the old man.
5. Yaromba father-in-law to son-in-law who respects the old ways more than his son.
   Three do not pass on their information as they are not yet ex- pert enough.

The wamanoka'eri prefer to inform their children or brothers first, unless they have no direct family or their children or brothers have no interest. This means that the information predominantly passes down through clan lines, but in fact it can also pass obliquely through the community across affinal lines. I have noticed that those who pass their information across clan lines tend to be more open and prepared to offer their knowledge free of charge.[3]

2. Revealed information

Various people, and wayorokeri in particular, have the skill and flex- ibility to change their philosophy and cosmological insights accord-

---

3. Some of the old men consider chindign to be their only source of income and charge for curing. This compensates for the fact that they are too old to do ardu- ous gold work for any long period.

ing to the messages they receive from the invisible world. A wayoro-keri receives much respect from his own community through the efficacy of his predictions and cures, with the result that his perspective of the world is quickly incorporated into the worldview of the community. A wayorokeri such as Psyche, who could predict and change events, consequently had an enormous influence on the community's interpretation of the cosmos, as he constantly provided them with new ideas and inspiration from his dreams and visions. Even though his opinions were not always accepted, particularly by other clans, his inspiration was recognised by all.

For this reason the cosmology of the Arakmbut is not fixed and rigid. A general framework exists about which most people are in agreement, but personal interpretations refine the global view into a more dynamic view which changes according to the perspective of people with vision. However unless the interpreters have standing and recognition within the community, their points of view will hold no weight. The relationship between the visionary shaman and the spirit world thus takes place on a personal level and the insights gained from dreams and reflection can, in certain circumstances, spread through the community.

3. Revealed and received knowledge arising from specific events

Illness and death act as catalysts for philosophical thought because they necessitate practical reasoning to diagnose, cure, and explain. During these periods people, particularly the wayorokeri and wama-noka'eri, dream or discuss the causes of the illness. New forms of behavioural patterns regarding hunting methods and cooking can emerge as a result of someone falling ill, even allowing for the fact that precedent is important in terms of curing and cosmological ideas.

If someone wants to illustrate the possible effects of the waweri river spirits, for example, they will point to someone's illness and analyze the symptoms: how the sounds were heard at night calling the sick person to the water; the rush of water the patient could hear inside the ears. Maybe this symptom has not been encountered before, but it adds to the general knowledge of those spirits. Knowledge is therefore cumulative, arising from the pragmatic effects of curing in addition to revelations in dreams. Events such as sickness and death can introduce new experiences to a community and can lead to infusions of information from the invisible to the visible world. Cosmology can therefore change emphasis according to the historical realities which the community faces. For example the waweri are more dangerous now than when Psyche was alive in 1980, and his death has brought to the fore their harmful rather than their benign attributes. On the other hand, when Psyche prophesied that he would return to help the community, this demonstrated that some souls of the dead can be beneficial – not something which people had encountered before in the community – and this opinion is still accepted.

Visions from ayahuasca sessions also provide scope for cosmological change. The old thin white toto are becoming replaced by short fat black demons cast in a Christian mould; in 1992, someone saw a vision of a paradise without scarcity but in the sky rather than in the underworld. These discussions are still hypotheses and have not produced any conclusion at the community level because San José no longer has a wayorokeri to comment on the new information; however, they do demonstrate that within ayahuasca rituals there are possibilities of cosmological reinterpretation.

Curing practices involve different degrees of expertise which are related to the possibilities of changes in cosmological interpretation or shamanic techniques. The crisis moments of illness or death are opportunities for adding new insights into the Arakmbut understanding of the universe. However, the capacity for change depends on the type of illness and the curer involved. A person who is physically ill with a minor ailment can be cured by medicines from outside, whether from a pharmacy or from plants. The knowledge necessary for this form of curing can be learned and is respected and appreciated by a community, but it is not as complex or dangerous as shamanic practices. Once the medicines have been bought or the plants gathered, certain people know how to make the infusions or give the injections, but they are not considered specialists. These people carry out instructions as they were taught.

The illnesses cured by the wamanoka'cri, either by means of chindign or ayahuasca usually have symptoms which are readily observable and about which practitioners have specific experience. Those who do not have unlimited access to the invisible world are not sufficiently flexible in their knowledge to propose any significant changes to Arakmbut cosmology. They are the people who listen to other people's interpretations and act accordingly.

Illnesses where symptoms are vague and shifting are more difficult to cure and need a wayorokeri's insight from the invisible world through his dreams. The wayorokeri, who are also always wamanoka'eri, supplement their basic knowledge with revealed information which not only enables them to adjust their chindign but also to provide clear interpretations of the events. The wayorokeri are therefore a powerful spiritual force among the Arakmbut because their dreams can transform understanding through their dialogue with spirits, and consequently influence a household group, a clan, or even a community in how they see the invisible world.

The influence of the wayorokeri takes place within the framework of Arakmbut cosmology. However, in no cases of revelation have I come across an example of a whole category of spirits appearing or disappearing because of the dream of a wayorokeri. Changes are more a matter of detail and take place within the overall framework of spirits and their possible intervention in the visible world. Any large-scale shifts in Arakmbut cosmology are gradual and cumulative.

These three aspects of knowledge can be illustrated by several versions of a mokas chindign which I collected from three Yaromba men in San José. The first two originated from the Wakutangeri maloca and the third from the Kukambatoeri. Although they share similar tones and similar processes of curing, the differences in detail are considerable.

Table 4.1 shows the differences between the three versions given to me by Yaromba wamanoka'eri from the perspective of the species used in the chants. Of 28 species mentioned, seven are common to more than one of the chindign. This sample of three could have been expected to be similar in that they come from members of the same clan in the same community. However, several reasons can account for the differences. The teachers of the chindign were different; this is certainly the case for Versions 1 and 3, although 1 and 2 may have had the same source (and they have an extra species in common). Another reason for the differences is that chindign vary according to the personal experiences of the wayorokeri who learned them from the spirits and, furthermore, the circumstances of the curing may necessitate learning different attributes which accrue to the species under surveillance. The result is that a wamanoka'eri has a store of different species which he brings out according to the circumstances and these consequently give substantial scope for improvisation in each version. The chindign thus demonstrate how the three sources of knowledge mentioned above – the received version of the chindign, the personal additions which a skilful wamanoka'eri can add to the chindign, and the shifts in interpretation which take place according to the circumstances of the curing – exist together.

These three contexts are fundamental for understanding the relationship between the Arakmbut and the different perspectives of

Table 4.1: Comparison of differences in curing chants of the Mokas

	Version 1	Version 2	Version 3
Birds	chupit		
		hirengpo	
		purung	
		mako	
		mokpayomba	
Fruits	koragn	koragn	
	kodna	kodna	
	waya		
	pio		
	sup		
	mantoro		
	tomenkero		
	wambedn		
	toko	toko	
	towanda		
	tapi chipi		
		yoromba	
		mbaset	
		ponaro	ponaro
		kotsi	kotsi
		atodn	
			metamera
			mendo
			embachiusu
Trees	kerongtong		
	menkeromba	menker	
	ho		ho
	ekhomba		
	biu		

their cosmology. Myths, songs, and stories have the same levels of interpretation as chindign, although the details in a chindign are specific to the context of the cure. These degrees of received and revealed knowledge correlate with the different attributes of contact with the invisible world through dreaming – received messages, sending and receiving messages without discussion, and the full freedom to participate in the invisible world.

In the first case the person learning the chindign imitates the curing in the same way as the dreamer observes the spirit world. Later a person can learn the chindign by passing messages to the spirit world and receiving them but cannot enter into dialogue in order to gain revealed information. It is possible to change the chindign by learning from other wamanoka'eri, but the curer does not actively create with the spirit world. The most skilled point of curing is when a wa-yorokeri can work the chindign to fit any circumstance and, using his contacts with the spirit world, can develop and improve his efficacy.

In this way, a wayorokeri can use his powers of contact with the spirit world and his visionary revelations to reinterpret, redefine, and refine knowledge. This process is responsibile for a wide variety of details in Arakmbut oral culture, while the most plausible of these interpretations convince a group, community, and even the Arakmbut as a whole into changing their perspectives and views of the world.

The Acceptance of Shamanic Views in the Community

Shamanic knowledge passes through the community by means of a complicated process combining received and revealed information which crystallises around certain features of Arakmbut social organ-isation. In 1980, each patrilineal clan had relationships with certain species which seemed to give an advantage to their hunters and curers when dealing with these animals. The correlations (see Gray 1983) led me to the conclusion that each clan was oriented to the river or forest and that certain species of these domains gave pref-erential treatment to members of those clans. For example, Psyche, a Yaromba, was in close contact with the river spirits (waweri), whereas the Idnsikambo seemed better at hunting forest animals such as the tapir. Interpretations of illnesses, causes of death, and hunting patterns seemed to be related to the clans (Gray 1983). How-ever, in 1986, the Yaromba told me that since Psyche had died they no longer had a close connection with the river spirits, while more recently, in 1991, clan correlations were far less apparent, and shared perspectives were connected more to members of the same house-hold and *wambet* (the cognatic-style alliance arranging category) of a married couple.

Fuentes (1982) concluded that Arakmbut individuals make con-nections with certain species and that these broaden to cover house-hold and/or clan relations. However, the process whereby this occurs involves several factors which bring into focus personal and collective experience. For example, in a clan context, Arakmbut could equally say about the opinions of someone with influence: 'such and such a person thinks this' as 'the Yaromba think this'. Even though there may be Yaromba who disagree, the chances are that members of the same clan will publicly back up the position of a

powerful member. In this way a personal experience can be projected onto and taken up by the clan as a whole. The same process
can take place within household and wambet groups.

Death provides another way in which personal contacts with a
spirit affect close relatives and clan members of the deceased. After
the death of a good hunter, particularly a wayorokeri, his nokiren
usually disperses and goes to join those spirits with which he was
associated when alive. Although a wayorokeri supports all members
of his community as a whole, members of his household and clan
have closer contact with him. The net result is that the clan can continue to relate to certain species rather than to others if the spirit of
the dead person is helping. However this is still the de facto result of
personal contacts rather than of a permanent grid-like structure linking the visible and invisible worlds together.

The personal connections between shamans and the rest of the
community are reinforced through the realisation of expectations.
As the community learns with which species clans or household
members are in contact, shared experience and advice from the
spirits direct hunters from the same groups to look for similar
species. Gradually expectations arise whereby particular people, and
thus particular clans, are assumed to be better at hunting certain
species than others. Another way in which the numbers of animals
caught may tally with the clan or family of a hunter arises from the
extent to which he is allowed to kill. A man whose clan or household
has a special relationship with the spirits of a species has a higher
'quota' than others. For example, in 1981 I saw an Idnsikambo on a
peccary hunt bringing home less meat than he might for fear of
annoying the spirits, whereas a Yaromba was able to bring more
without any risks because Psyche was close to the peccaries.[4]

The names of the clans, combined with mythological associations
and historical contacts between ancestors and spirits, all provide sets
of possible correlations between hunters, spirits, and animal species.
In practice, however, these shift and change according to the experiences of shamans. Any hunter may obviously catch whatever species
he can, providing that he kills in moderation and according to the
guidelines set out by the spirits. These assumptions and expectations

4. In his article 'Meat is Meat', Vickers (1978), arguing against Siskind (1973 a & b),
   says that the distinction between a better hunter and a worse one is often minimal, because when game is plentiful anyone should be able to bring in a good
   quota of meat. The hunting expectations among the Arakmbut are means for
   distinguishing good hunters from the less skilled because the best hunters bring
   in meat of species which have a close relationship with their particular clan.

are placed within an ideological framework which effectively relates practice to the general mythological and shamanic knowledge.[5]

Connections between personal knowledge and collective knowledge can spread from clan or household to the whole community if it is considered particularly sound. This happened with Psyche to the extent that many of the details in my fieldwork in San José between 1979-1981 were based on his view of the Arakmbut universe. When these were taken further afield, however, differences in detail became apparent. Since 1983 my results have been widely available in Peru and researchers, such as Helberg (pers. comm.), have taken my findings from San José to other communities. In general, the responses confirmed my findings: distinctions between the visible and invisible world, between forest and river, between dispersed and concentrated soul-substance, seem to be shared by all the Arakmbut.

However when we look at details of myths and songs we can see differences. The Shintuya versions of Wanamey and Marinke (Helberg pers. comm.) are considerably different to the San José versions. Yet a version of Marinke told to Califano in the 1960s is practically identical to one told to me in 1980 (Califano 1978b). The result is that it is extremely hard to predict similarities and differences between communities' ways of thinking about the universe, as much depends on the historical conditions at any one time.

Contacts with the Invisible World

This chapter has drawn together several contexts in which relations with the invisible spirits vary according to the experience of the practitioner. Putting aside the situation of children and youths who enter the invisible world without being aware of the capacity of communications, we are left with three dimensions of expertise: dreaming, knowledge, and curing. The Arakmbut do not divide their skills into levels, but they distinguish between the capacities in several ways.

The basic form of communication with the spirit world is a form of passive relationship in which an Arakmbut receives messages but

5. Von Brandenstein (1971) says that, in looking at section systems of Australia, theory and practice are equal aspects of a 'totemism' which is based on certain opposed elements for classification and extended to cover the whole universe. I am reluctant to call the Arakmbut clans 'totemic' because the Arakmbut do not have one framework in which every spirit, species, and person has its allotted place. One of the characteristics of Arakmbut classification is its malleability and flexibility.

cannot send them. For example, dreams are ways of conceptualising and seeing spirits and even hearing them, but the dreamer cannot discuss or ask questions. The knowledge which a person has of the invisible world comes from what he or she has learned from Arakmbut elders and so the capacity to interpret dreams is limited. A person with a passive relationship to the spirits has a limited curing capacity and can help mainly physical ailments.

With experience an Arakmbut person can communicate more openly with spirits, but the relationship is not one of free interaction. For example, a dreamer can receive messages from the ndakyoro-keri and speak, but there is no dialogue. Some of the information which the dreamer receives can be used as knowledge and it is possible to gain some insights to complement the curing chants learned from older relatives. A person with these skills would be considered a wamanoka'eri and will use chindign and ayahuasca ritually to communicate with the invisible world and cure.

The most active Arakmbut relationship comes from the dreamer wayorokeri shamans, who can communicate and discuss detailed events and interpretations with members of the spirit world. Their personal experience enables them to extend their knowledge from their contacts and their efficacy in curing and interpretation provides them with an influence which spreads throughout the household, clan, and community. The knowledge of a shaman of this capacity usually comes from direct contact with spirits. Through spirit contacts, it is possible to make difficult diagnoses and to predict the effect of a cure shifting and changing direction according to the circumstances.

In general terms, the last three chapters have covered, respectively, these three aspects of shamanic techniques. Those used by everyone in production practices relate to the most basic level of communication with the spirit world, while the curing of the wamanoka'eri involves ritualised contact; the wayorokeri, on the other hand, can interact freely with invisible beings.[6]

6. Both Santos (1991) and Crocker (1985) discuss a division of shamanic and priestly activities among the Amuesha and the Bororo. It is possible to see the wamanoka'eri as fulfilling the curing 'life-force' aspects of shamanic practices and the wayorokeri as more priestly 'securing control of the universe'. However, this should not be seen as a strict division of labour such as that which occurs among the Amuesha and the Bororo. Arakmbut shamanic skills are cumulative. For example, a wayorokeri has the knowledge and spirit contacts to be a good hunter and also an effective curer. However, the more expert a person is in shamanic activities, the less political and self-interested he should become. In this context, it is possible to see the wayorokeri as more involved with broad philosophical questions and perhaps therefore more 'priestly'.

Arakmbut cosmology is based on certain relatively changeless principles which alter only according to emphases accumulating from the interpretations of dreams and shamanic practices. Change is not automatically accepted by communities, so the broader principles remain constant while the details shift. Similarly, the capacity of a dreamer to influence change depends on his expertise. The effect is one of relativity and creativity as Arakmbut from the visible world and the spirits from the invisible affect each other, shifting and transforming as time passes.

Arakmbut relations with the invisible world involve a varying capacity to control the causality which operates between what is seen and what is not seen by transcending the limitations of the visible. Dreams, visions and rituals are ways in which the visible world can create causes with invisible effects in order to counteract the invisible causes which can harm the visible world. Nevertheless, the implications of an illness and communication with the spirit world have effects not only on interpretations of the universe, but also on practical social and personal relations between people. In the wake of Psyche's death, there was a major upheaval of San José. The next chapter looks at the social and political implications of shamanic activity and at how it relates not just to cultural shifts in the meaning of the cosmology, but to social change among the Arakmbut.

THE POLITICS OF
SHAMANIC CURING

A n illness or death not only has consequences on the shamanic
plane, but can affect a community socially and politically. The
effects of the curing interpretations and diagnoses of a wamanoka'eri
(curer) or a wayorokeri (dreamer) can range from food prohibitions
and limits on hunting to inconvenient precautions over general
behaviour. Different interest groups within the community which
stand to be affected may well disagree with the diagnoses of an illness because of constrictions on the production capacity that will
affect them. These tensions can be even more exacerbated if death
results, giving rise to possible conflict, not only within the household
but in the community as a whole. The recriminations can lead to
serious divisions within the village.

The political implications of curing draw together different
themes of this work. Whereas cosmological relations arising from
shamanic practices during sickness and death can provide new interpretations through dreams and curing techniques, the political consequences of different ideological positions within the community
reflect the state of relationships between groups at any one time.

The following is a case study of a curing ritual which took place in
1980. It is presented here largely in the form of a diary which I kept
at the time in order to record the chronological shifts of interpretation which led to the eventual cure. The description provides an
example of how a serious illness connects the wayorokeri, the
wamanoka'eri, and the practitioners of ayahuasca and western medicines, and, furthermore, how the effects on the community were not
only spiritual but political. The successful outcome, when western

medicines seemed to do no good, was a tribute to the curing system of the Arakmbut which should not go unrecognised.

The curing took place in San José only six months before Psyche's death. At that time the community was divided into the two residential groups: the Wakutangeri, including the influential Idnsikambo clan, and the Kotsimberi, with the prominent Yaromba clan.[1] The purpose of the case study is to trace the multi-dimensional nature of sickness and curing and to demonstrate how power from the spirit world connects with the political arena.

Arakmbut Curing

May–June 1980

The sick man was an Idnsikambo from the Wakutangeri part of San José, twenty-eight years old and married with two children. His parents were dead but he had a stepfather. His father had been a close relation of the main Wakutangeri Idnsikambo households in San José whose adult men were at that time the political leaders of the community. Their position was founded on respect for their experience in ayahuasca curing, their gold washing techniques (such as the use of motor pumps), and their secondary school education, which provided them with the capacity for dealing with non-indigenous outsiders.

As he was of the generation below these uncles he could not share their position, but even so, in the corner of the village where he lived with his Wandigpana in-laws he was respected as a good hunter and had a particularly good relationship with spirits of the tapir (kemewere). He frequently dreamed of beautiful tapir women who showed him where to hunt and he shared his knowledge and ability as far as he could with his Idnsikambo relatives. He did not have the defiant manner of a man weighed down with political responsibilities and he was well liked in the community as a whole.

28 May 1980

The man began to complain of severe headaches and took some aspirin for relief. He continued with his work that day, but in spite of repeated doses of aspirin, he felt worse by the evening.

1. During the last fourteen years there has been a political transformation within San José, which is the subject of analysis in later chapters. The rivalries between clans which are articulated here could nowadays as easily be expressed in terms of the alliance category wambet, with its cognatic implications relating to different households or residential groups.

29 May

He tried to go to the gold work area but felt too sick. In spite of taking more aspirin, he did not improve.

30 May

The patient stayed in bed all day, saying that his headache was so bad that he could not move and that he was beginning to feel chest pains. His stepfather (a wamanoka'eri) did some curing using chindign in the evening but it did not have much effect. Then the family asked Psyche, the wayorokeri, from the Kotsimberi part of the village to come and cure him. He carried out some initial tobacco treatment on the patient which involved blowing and sucking, but could produce no diagnosis on the basis of the symptoms. His conclusion was that there was no spirit attack involved and that the patient would recover.

31 May

Psyche did not initially consider the illness to be particularly serious, but the Idnsikambo from the sick man's part of the village were still concerned and decided to go to Puerto Luz to get some tobacco grown there by an Idnsikambo shaman. At the same time the Dominican priest resident in Puerto Luz gave the San José deputation some antibiotics which were never used but kept for a 'rainy day'. The tobacco was blown over the patient and he said that he felt a bit better.

2 June

The patient seemed to be getting better although his headache persisted. Several Arakmbut began to get worried because a young girl had died on the previous night, and all through the morning a wake took place for her. The sick man had already been moved to his mother-in-law's kitchen in the Kotsimberi part of the village where the drinking was going on. At various intervals visitors would come from the wake to visit the patient, scratch their heads and suggest a dire outcome for him and a low chance of recovery because of contagion arising from the girl's death. Even so, during the morning the sick man appeared to rally.

At midday, however, events took a new turn as a report flew around the village that the sick man had died. The Wakutangeri villagers rushed over to find him alive but worse than earlier in the day. By now the community became convinced that he was going to die: he had nearly died at midday but that night he was sure to go for ever.

The first clear explanations as to why he was going to die now began to appear, with sorcery as the cause. The Yaromba Kotsimberi considered that the perpetrators were Taka (non-Arakmbut) ayahuasca practitioners from the Upper Madre de Dios who had hated the people of San José since the time they were all in Shintuya mission together. The Idnsikambo Wakutangeri, on the other hand, thought that Taka from the Pukiri river were responsible because they had reputedly killed Arakmbut a few years back but they did not know how the sorcery had been done. Both of these accusations pointed at non-Arakmbut living outside the community.

3 June

The Idnsikambo felt that the traditional curing methods were not working and decided to take the matter into their own hands in order to save the man's life before day broke. They had already brewed some ayahuasca and in the early hours of 3 June there was a session in the kitchen nearby while the rest of the villagers sat outside waiting. The first stage of the proceedings went quietly but the fight with the toto was fierce, with shots fired and shouting. A participant said afterwards that the anaconda had wrapped itself around him and whispered that the spirit of the white-lipped peccary (akudnui or iari) was the cause. They had all heard sounds of a peccary. The patient began to foam at the mouth just like a dying peccary, while his teeth chattered and his chest heaved, showing that the spirit was a harmful toto spirit which had entered the soul(nokiren) of a peccary, using it as an intermediary to attack the sick man. People remembered that a few weeks before, the patient had killed too many peccary and had not distributed them. As a result, the nokiren of the sick man had been carried off by the toto and the Idnsikambo who had taken the ayahuasca fought with the toto and retrieved it. The patient was better in the morning and through the ayahuasca the practitioners had established that he would not necessarily die.

The Yaromba shaman (Psyche) was somewhat sceptical of all this: he had never thought that the patient would die anyway, as there had been no fear on his face. He was in touch with the spirits of the peccary and they were not involved, or if they were it was in a very minor way. Furthermore, he had had a dream of a bright light shining down a broad path through the forest, which meant that the patient would survive. The Idnsikambo were not in frequent contact with the spirit of the peccary and he felt that their diagnosis and cure by ayahuasca was probably not a correct interpretation of what was going on. He considered that the ayahuasca session was useful only because it confirmed his conviction that the patient would not die. The Idnsikambo did not see the matter in this light. They said that

Psyche was a shaman skilled in curing peccary illnesses and that the Yaromba, who were good at hunting peccary, feared that there would have to be a curb on their hunting if that spirit was proven to be the cause.

4 June

Everyone went round to see the patient the next day. His stepfather, an Idnsikambo, was chanting curing songs which were said to be for peccary diseases, even though he was not able to cure peccary illnesses as well as the Yaromba shaman could. As he sang he sucked and spat out the impurities still in his stepson's body.

5 and 6 June

During these days the patient remained calm, but he could eat nothing and was becoming progressively weaker. His parents-in-law were allied to the Yaromba, and together they sought a curing method other than the ayahuasca of the Idnsikambo. They decided to bring in an old Sapiteri shaman from the river Pukiri who was in contact with different species from Psyche, mainly of the forest, and who could decide whether the Idnsikambo methods were best. The Idnsikambo did not think much of this shaman and considered him to be a bit dangerous. The shaman in turn thought that all ayahuasca practitioners were charlatans. Thus, bringing the Sapiteri shaman was an attempt by the Yaromba to re-establish their abilities in the face of the Idnsikambo ayahuasca curing.

7 June

This morning the patient took another turn for the worse. The old Sapiteri shaman was in the hut and chanted songs against the power of toto, sometimes chanting in the kitchen where the sick man lay, at other times entering the neighbouring hut and singing through the slatted walls. At the same time the stepfather continued his own quiet chanting and all the men blew tobacco over the patient.

Then Psyche appeared and there was silence. He said that in the night he dreamed that the patient would die that day. The peccary was not to blame but another species which he had no means of curing, but he would do all he could to help. Everyone left the hut and the shaman beat the patient with isanga nettles, hitting the trunk of his body first and then his head.

By midday it looked as though the sick man could hold out no longer, because he had already seen the spirits of his dead relatives (wambetoeri) coming to take him away. As many people as could fit packed into the kitchen where he lay and some checked his pulse. Meanwhile the Idnsikambo men began to look extremely upset and the sick man's father's sister took a stick to the walls in order to frighten the dangerous toto. The patient, who appeared to be dying, pointed to a corner of the hut and some of the men grabbed arrows and threw in the direction he indicated, also stabbing at the ground where the toto might be. The patient's wife, who until now had kept a low profile, took out some of his clothes and burned them, while others destroyed his documents and broke his possessions. The sick man then collapsed into a sort of trance, his eyes rolled so that they were almost entirely white, his tongue flickered, and he became incontinent. Some of the older men took a long stick and laid it next to his body, measuring him for his grave. The wife of the Yaromba shaman then came in and held up the lifeless man, hitting his body and screaming for his soul to come back. His pulse was so slow that it was barely perceptible. He was at the moment of death.

Everyone in the hut froze. Then slowly the Idnsikambo men began to weep and the women shrieked their mourning cries. And yet the patient was still breathing. Minutes passed and he still lived; he even moved his head slightly. The uncles went out to find a root to make an infusion while the Sapiteri shaman came to the front of the group around the patient and sang with all his might for the nokiren to return to the body (waso). He called for someone to make a necklace of chili, and for fires to be lit in the kitchen to burn chili leaves and isanga nettles so that the bitter substance would cleanse the area with the smoke. By the evening the patient, still weak, was sitting up and beginning to talk slowly.

The shaman from Pukiri and the Yaromba shaman from San José now discussed the patient and agreed that the cause of the illness was not a peccary but a tapir. While the patient improved slowly, people went to his house in the Wakutangeri part of San José and looked for any sign which the tapir had left there as to why he had been attacked. Throughout the night the community was afraid. People living on their own moved into huts where there was company.

8 June

The sick man had a quieter night than most of the other terrified members of the community. The Yaromba and the Idnsikambo now had two similar but different theories: the Yaromba claimed that the cause of the illness was the tapir with the peccary as a subsidiary toto, whereas the Idnsikambo said that the peccary had been the main cause with the tapir as a subsidiary. The reason for this difference was pragmatic: after an illness, there often has to be a curb on killing certain species. The Idnsikambo, particularly the sick man, were in closer contact with the spirits of the tapir, and the clan seemed to hunt them in larger quantities, while the Yaromba had a better reputation with regard to the peccary. The Idnsikambo preferred to blame the 'Yaromba' species and the Yaromba preferred to blame the 'Idnsikambo' species.

During the day the patient was quiet and regularly received chanting treatment from his relatives and the Sapiteri shaman. The Yaromba shaman admitted that he was not so skilled at curing illnesses caused by the tapir and that was why he had done nothing earlier in the crisis.

9 June

The Idnsikambo decided to hold another ayahuasca session and collected some of the vine and prepared it for the next day.

10 June

In the afternoon the Idnsikambo prepared themselves for the ayahuasca session and used pisco (a bitter Peruvian spirit – painda) to spray over the patient's body. This seemed to revive him somewhat. Meanwhile, other members of the community began to dismantle his house, where they felt toto might be lurking. They burned the wood but kept the nails, as they could be useful for other construction work.

In the evening there was another ayahuasca session led by the Idnsikambo, which managed to chase the remaining toto away. There was even a humorous element, as they later told of one of the participants who had shouted at the height of the chase to leave the little fat female toto for him as he could not run so fast. The laughter was a contrast to the earlier fear.

11 June

The sick man felt much better and began to take food. Over the following days he continued to improve gradually.

Conflicting explanations as to the cause of the illness and the reason for the cure exacerbated clan conflicts throughout the village during the patient's recovery. Although open conflict was avoided, there was clear tension, and people sought audiences to set forth their claims. The problems covered each area of the process. At the beginning, the Idnsikambo thought that if sorcery was involved it could have come from the Pukiri and the Yaromba from the Upper Madre de Dios. When the Idnsikambo brought tobacco from a shaman in Puerto Luz, the Yaromba brought a shaman from the Pukiri. Meanwhile, Psyche, although a Yaromba, remained above the conflict, trying to be reassuring and calm.

When animal species were thought to be the problem, the Idnsikambo (including the patient himself) considered that the cause of the illness was toto using the peccary as an intermediary to attack the sick man's nokiren because he had overhunted the animal. He had been cured by the ayahuasca sessions when he had shown symptoms of peccary attack and his nokiren had been retrieved from the toto as they were chased away. In this way his household would not be too affected by hunting prohibitions, as the Yaromba hunted more peccary than the Idnsikambo and their new ayahuasca curing had been shown to be successful.

The Yaromba (and the Sapiteri shaman) considered that the illness was the result of the tapir being used as an intermediary by the toto. He had been attacked because he had hunted too many tapirs, and had been cured thanks to the traditional skill of the two shamans who had known the correct songs and had acted in the proper way; the ayahuasca had done nothing. In this way the patient would have to bear the inconveniences of prohibition on tapir for a period and their old curing methods were once again proven. The Yaromba considered that the Sapiteri shaman, who knew about the tapirs, had been key in the curing.

Two different explanations of an event in a village might be a problem, but as the patient gradually recovered, another explanation appeared which satisfied everyone. It was said that the patient had accidentally come across a leaf or an 'evil eye' in the forest, which was the wild toto from the depth of virgin jungle. The spirit had attacked him, and the curing had been a mixture of old and new; ayahuasca could work well in conjunction with the old ways.

The illness was not 'normal' because the patient was young and active and was not expected to die. The concern within the community arose at the point at which his life appeared to be in danger. This is not to say that all illnesses and deaths are not important, but some have more political implications than others. For example, when the young girl died on 1 June, the community was shocked and upset, and all participated in the wake.

People feared for the safety of the young and weak (including the sick man), in case the spirit of the girl wanted companions and might lure others to the same fate. However, her death had been expected because she had been sickly. The Idnsikambo patient, on the contrary, had been strong and active.

Taking into account that this illness was a case study of a 'large-scale' illness, it draws to attention features which would normally be less apparent in more common examples.

The Effect of Personal Relations on the Patient

The pressures surrounding the patient as a person before and during the illness are an important factor in curing. Two aspects of this are the position of the sick man in the community and the role of visitors. The psychological effect of shamanic curing is important to understand and has been discussed in the past by Lévi-Strauss (1963:183). The attention given to the patient by members of the community and their intense desire for him to live gave him much needed confidence and strength to resist the illness. The patient began to improve noticeably when he saw distress on the faces of all members of the community at his bedside and he became the focal point of the village as social and cultural life centred around him. The attention of the whole commu nity is an important aspect of the cure, demonstrating that it is not just a personal relationship between the curer and patient which leads to recovery but that health concerns the whole relationship between a person and his peers. Sickness affects everyone.

The illness described above is in clear contrast to a small illness which is inconvenient but not deadly, such as a child crying too much, which only affects the immediate household. In the case described above, the prospect of death affected the whole community and many people were so worried that they did not work during the worst period of the illness and all the Arakmbut diverted their energies into concern for the well-being and survival of the patient.

Visitors came frequently to the bedside of the sick man and openly speculated about his condition. People did not consider it wrong to tell him that he was going to die, discuss when it might hap pen or pass rumours of his impending death around in the community throughout the illness, frequently causing a rush of people to his hut to see what was happening. Visitors suggested and reinforced the ways in which the patient felt he should behave, and the different theories as to which were the most prominent symptoms might have emerged from these discussions.

Visitors also discussed at length different interpretations of what was happening and commented on the efficacy of the shaman, connecting the diagnosis of each curer to improvements or deteriorations in the condition of the patient. The discussions, which were largely informal, consisted of the acceptance or rejection of a particular theory as to the cause of the sickness, thus making the cure not just a psychological adjustment of the patient connected to his physical improvement, but also a recognition from the community as a whole that he has been cured.

This case was particularly memorable, and twelve years later people still discussed the illness and how the patient had been brought back from the point of death by traditional practices. Psyche is credited with having seen from the beginning that he would not die, and this is given as an example of the power of his dreaming (even though at one point he had doubts). The illness itself seemed to bring the patient a certain spiritual power, and since he was sick he has made several songs about his illness which are his own personal commentary on the experience.

Three Songs by the Patient

a. You are my *enchipo* (brother-in-law). We always behave well to each other. We share things. I almost died recently but now I am well.
b. In the future I am going to die. You, brother, will die too, I suppose. When I am alive, I cannot go on living for ever. I could die at any time.
c. I don't want to die because I do not want to leave my children alone. If I had no children I could easily die and willingly go to the spirits.

At social events for at least six months after the illness and beyond, the patient drew attention to his sickness and his songs demonstrate a sense of the experience of death. He acquired more respect in the community and people consider him to have potential to be a wamanoka'eri curer. His stepfather has been teaching him his chindign so that the sick man can use his spiritual strength to cure in the future. The illness itself has been a form of 'initiation', because he was sufficiently strong to resist the spirits and manifest his potency.

Social Aspects of the Curing

The curing of the illness followed a pattern of explanations which is repeated in practically every case of sickness or death among the

Arakmbut. These reasons reflect not only the causes of the illness but express the political situation of the community at any one moment. The first reason for an illness or death always seems to be sorcery. During the first part of the illness, when sorcery was mentioned, the community was united in holding a common enemy responsible, and accused sorcerers from non-Arakmbut communities. Unfortunately, sorcery is almost impossible to cure because of the concentrated power used against the victim. In the context of the case study, two methods were mentioned in retrospect. The first method is used when a sorcerer can find some part of the victim's body such as hair, nails, or the leftovers of food such as bones or other waste, which can be used in conjunction with a harmful chindign. The second method is to make a distillation of tobacco or ayahuasca which is converted into a powerful potion and deposited on the person or in his food. The chindign spell made over the potion can have delayed action, with the result that a person can be bewitched but the sickness may not materialise for several years. The initial reaction to an illness with which no one can cope is therefore to blame an enemy.

The second reaction puts the blame on the sick person or a member of his or her family for having transgressed the social conventions surrounding hunting and the preparation of meat. The curing involves diagnosing which animal species is or are responsible and performing the appropriate curing ritual. The problem here is that, whichever species are responsible, there will be a curtailment in hunting quotas, in which case people will hope that no species with which they have built up a relationship is to blame. This is when tensions can arise in a community. Several interpretations as to which species are responsible for an illness, and hence which clan or household will have to curtail its hunting practices, usually emerge. The prohibitions in the example above were quite severe on the patient but they became less intense the greater the social distance from his household, wambet, and clan. No one wants to have to curtail hunting because meat is crucial for growth of the household and fundamental to a man or woman's chances of receiving respect. Furthermore, the community considers important the distribution of meat to members of the wambet and, where possible, to more distant relatives, and so cutting down hunting can prevent a household and the clan as a whole from demonstrating its generosity in response to the desires of the rest of the community. In the next chapters it will become apparent how important desire and generosity are for political prestige within an Arakmbut community.

The differences in explanations of an illness can take on a political flavour which could split the community into factions. However, there is an in-built social device for preventing such a breakdown of the community whereby a shaman is proficient at curing illnesses which have been caused by species with which he has a special relationship. The last chapter demonstrated how shamanic skills are often related to a wider social unit such as the household, the wambet, or even the clan. A shaman's species are not only those which he can hunt but also those whose illnesses he can cure. When he achieves a cure, the shaman may have to accept a curtailment on hunting the animals with which he and his relatives have a special hunting relationship. However, by blaming a rival clan or household's species which he is less skilled at curing, the shaman forfeits the opportunity to demonstrate his skill, thereby gaining prestige and recognition. As the diagnosis is only proven after the cure, a shaman does better to recognise symptoms with which he can cope, or else, as happened with Psyche, accept that another shaman in the community, or outside, is better qualified to deal with the problem.

Presuming that the patient is cured, the shaman and his clan win the shamanic battle and receive credit for the success and respect for their spiritual knowledge. However, his clan may find its hunting limited, which will affect the political ability to demonstrate generosity to one's household network or wambet with meat. The result is that the shamanic and political factors which give rise to prestige in the community are distributed between different interest groups.

Another way of ensuring that there is no conflict within the community is to secure a third type of explanation which sees the illness as a result of an unavoidable incident such as an accidental attack by a harmful toto involving neither the machinations of a sorcerer nor the transgressions of anyone in the community. The sickness is considered to have been an unavoidable accident, and consequently people should always be careful when outside of the community in the forest or on the river. The effect is to dissolve social conflicts both outside and within the community and the illness is laid to rest.

Politics and Shamanism

If these two methods of calming the crisis after an illness or death do not occur, there can be several consequences. Should a shaman's diagnosis lay the blame for an illness on a rival clan's species, thereby pleasing his own fellow members at the expense of the future hunting practices of the other, then every illness could split the community into at least two warring factions, each blaming the other for the illness. A shaman who promotes division is seen as self-ish and dangerous rather than as a unifying influence. If he shows too much interest in internal political divisions he will be accused of manipulating the spirit world with the intention of disrupting the community; this would be tantamount to sorcery.

A selfish shaman who enters into the internal conflict of a com-munity risks being accused of using his ties with the invisible world for his own advantage. He should never become emotionally in-volved with the information he receives from the spirit world, still less should he use the messages from the spirit world for personal gain. The only time he can use these powers is in defence of the com-munity as a whole when under physical attack or facing sorcery. The affective part of the nokiren is the concentrated part at the base of the spine (wanopo), and for a shaman to appear selfish would be to expose this aspect of his soul to the spirit world and possibly attract concentrated spirits such as toto to his aid. This is dangerous and harms other people in the same way as sorcery.

A shaman's prestige within a community rests on his remaining above politics, even though his attempts to be apolitical are 'political' because he is not only curing sickness but also trying to establish interpretations which will not split the community. When relations within the community break down, one party usually moves away, as occurred in 1986, when a conflict over sickness and marriage in San José became so intense that sorcery accusations arose and a large household left for another community. A split is often con-nected with sorcery accusations internal to the community, which is a sign that the political situation has reached crisis point. In the past this meant death for women accused of sorcery; now a split means serious physical fighting between the households and clans of the accused and usually bitter recriminations on both sides. Sorcery is thus a manifestation of tensions in a community such as control over resources or competition over finding a marriage partner.

During the period of the case study, the political and shamanic conflict became acute. At the moment when the Yaromba and Idnsikambo both had their possible causes and remedies, the com-munity looked as if it was split. However, there was a difference. The Idnsikambo took a risk with the ayahuasca because the method was new to the community, and if they succeeded they would have both held political and shamanic sway and bared themselves to charges of sorcery. Although they did not let this occur, some murmurs of the potential for sorcery in ayahuasca arose during subsequent months at emotional moments in community festivities.

On the other hand, Psyche avoided mixing political and shamanic activities. He admitted that he could not cure the illness of a tapir (thereby risking his prestige), yet he allied himself with the Sapiteri shaman, who was considered to have contributed to the cure. Furthermore, in retrospect, the community remembered Psyche's reassurance and his initial dream that the patient would not die. Over the next twelve years, since the illness, Idnsikambo ayahuasca practitioners have increasingly shifted from the political to the shamanic sphere and are gradually learning the techniques of a wamanoka'eri. Indeed, they could become future wayorokeri.

This account illustrates how illness and curing affect personal, social, political, and spiritual aspects of Arakmbut life. The patient and household have their lives thrown into turmoil once the illness seems serious, and if the sickness spreads to others, the whole community can be under threat from the spirit world. However, the immediate household of a sick person is most under threat because people who eat together and share the same meat run the greatest risk of the presence of the spirits which cause the illness.

Shamanic activities are important in relating personal knowledge to species and spirits, but as sickness affects the community as a whole, the process of acceptance or rejection of hypotheses leads the Arakmbut to fight politically over interpretations of their cosmology. Furthermore, the political situation in a community comes to the fore over conflicting diagnoses for an illness or a death. This gives rise to sorcery, misdemeanour, or accident as alternative explanations reflecting the political relations within the community a particular moment in history.

Illness or death, consequently, threatens not only a person but the whole fabric of the community. Tensions which exist between interest groups, clans, or people can quickly erupt into divisions which can threaten the well-being of the community. Conflict is not seen as positive to social life, and the Arakmbut do all they can to avoid unnecessary or serious differences between households and clans. A good shaman can thus cure without exacerbating the rivalries between people but by smoothing them over through a blending of political and shamanic prestige evenly distributed throughout the community between the different social units, or else by finding a harmless explanation such as an accident. The concentrated emotional and spiritual tension is thus dispersed.

This conclusion, however, should not give the impression that the Arakmbut world is ultimately an ordered system, with illness or death as the chaos trying to enter and the shaman acting as the interpreter who can restore order and health once again. This does not reflect an Arakmbut perspective, in which chaos is part of the universe and is as much a part of existence as order. The community represents the central point of the Arakmbut cosmos and the further one goes away from the village, the ordered world becomes less apparent and the unknown areas more dangerous. The threats which come from the invisible world are spirit forces from the river or the forest, originating in places where human beings never normally reach such as holes in the ground, deep inside lakes, or places under the river. The power or energy which comes from the invisible world provides life to the visible world and so has to be immanent, but in an uncontrolled, concentrated form the effect is destructive. Shamanic practices seek to control this power through the utilisation and expansion of knowledge while at the same time smoothing over any political consequences within the community.[2]

Power (tainda) is both shamanic and political. Power is a difficult concept to discuss because it can too easily be misunderstood as a tangible commodity. The Arakmbut see strength or force in a physical and spiritual sense as a tight relationship between soul and body. This strength provides a person with authority (matamona). Power is thus a relationship rather than a thing – in the first place it links the visible and invisible world through people and in the second it relates to the relationship between people themselves. The use of names *(wandik)* provides the link between the invisible power of the spirit world and the visible world, so that much shamanic activity consists of knowing the correct terms or names for species and understanding how they relate. The chindign consist of lists of species names which provide a sense of order on top of the spirit chaos which threatens the patient. The power of the name lies not only in the word itself but the connotations it holds throughout the invisible spirit world.

At the same time, to collapse knowledge and power into each other denies the fact that knowledge is not open to everyone equally. Shamans build up their power by relating conceptual categories and practical activities in ways which are recognised as being particularly efficacious. The shaman's mediating role between the visible and invisible worlds is parallelled by his work in keeping the peace within the community. In this way he helps to keep order in an

2. Bloch (1992) discusses this concept of power from the outside in the context of prey becoming hunters. This occurs among the Arakmbut most clearly in the context of spirit revenge on hunters who have overkilled.

unbalanced and chaotic universe, and receives respect and prestige because he has successfully repressed his political desires in favour of social harmony. The respect he receives is connected to the success of the curing, and consequently the shaman gains recognition as an altruistic positive influence for the community.

Thus the efficacy of knowledge in curing and predicting consequences of certain actions are not sufficient to ensure a positive reputation, and the shaman has to fulfil social requirements in terms of maintaining the uneasy balance within community social life. This implies that Arakmbut knowledge can change and challenge political interests because it operates within a social context, thereby seeing knowledge as separate from political power.

Knowledge and power thus take on two forms for the Arakmbut. They are both intangible aspects of the spirit world as well as a capacity in human beings to understand and act on the visible world. Thus, on the one hand, power arises out of the shaman's knowledge of the relationship between the visible and invisible worlds, while on the other hand, shamanic knowledge and spirit power can become vehicles for political interests. With the first there is the shaman's own desire for recognition, while the second leads to social conflicts of interpretation within the community. The Arakmbut have no fixed relationship between knowledge and power because, whereas the name connects the power of the invisible world to the material substance of the visible, by judicious usage it can have practical effects in curing. At the same time, the social implications of the curing and its interpretation have another power relationship connected to the political social order.[3]

The order of the world is not something outside of people or projected onto a formless universe, it comes through the use of the

3. This contrasting relationship between power and knowledge reflects two influential perspectives in twentieth century social philosophy. Michel Foucault considered that 'Power and knowledge directly imply one another ... There is no power relation without the correlative constitution of a field of knowledge' (cited in Turner 1985:204). This position sees knowledge and power as aspects of the same phenomenon; from a shamanic perspective, this refers to the power of the word and control through access to the invisible world. However, there is another position in philosophy which separates power from knowledge. This is the approach of Jurgen Habermas, who sees knowledge as independent of power structures and consequently emancipatory (McCarthy 1985:95). From this perspective, a shaman or political leader can use knowledge to change the political life of a community; this is manifest among the Arakmbut by the way in which different factions argue over the implications of curing diagnoses. Thus for the Arakmbut the two perspectives as to the relationship between knowledge and power co-exist simultaneously.

name itself. However, meaning is not only its use in a Wittgenstein-ian sense, but also the practical and physical effects of its utterance in terms of curing, community politics, and the social standing of the shaman. In previous chapters on shamanic techniques, we have seen that practical effects can only be obtained through knowledge. Intel-lectual differences of opinion and the interpretation of names have consequences outside of the word. The name, its physical utterance, and its connotations constitute a field of knowledge and understand-ing which neither corresponds to fixed definitions nor fits into neatly coherent structures: the invisible world intervenes constantly to question such rigid organisation. In this chapter, the political ele-ment has opened up a new dimension to shamanic activity because of the social implications which arise from different interpretations of Arakmbut cosmology.

An Arakmbut shaman combines spiritual and political activities but in many respects he is 'anti-political' in that he subsumes his interests to his altruism for community harmony. It is now time to look more closely at the political world of the Arakmbut to investi-gate in detail the social dynamism of community life.

Chapter 6

THE SOCIAL PATH FROM
DESIRE TO POWER

Just as Arakmbut shamanic practices involve understanding a multiplicity of perspectives, political activity is no less complicated. In the invisible world, each perspective is connected to a species or spirit. A tortoise appears as a log seat to a tapir; a heron is a chicken in Seronwe, while fish appear as plants to the waweri river spirits. Human beings have a view of the cosmos which is not necessarily shared by the other orders in the universe, and only through shamanic dreams can the Arakmbut break the bonds of the visible world and see themselves from outside. These different perspectives provide dreamers with the capacity to step outside of Arakmbut space/time and begin to appreciate how possibility and potentiality are embedded in the invisible world known to spirits but not to waking people.

Arakmbut social organisation also contains a variety of perspectives which differ from the position of each person. Structural principles such as clan, gender, age, and residence can be interpreted and used in markedly different ways from one person to the next. Each person's social activity takes place in a context which utilises several of these structural principles as tools in the creation and assertion of identity. As this increases in intensity, so its political importance becomes more apparent.

The last chapter discussed the double sense of 'power' among the Arakmbut as a relationship between the invisible and visible worlds through shamanic knowledge and between people through political action. Just as shamans have to understand the different perspectives in the spirit world in order to be efficacious, they also have to understand the conflicting views within Arakmbut socio-political organisation. If they do not, they will fail to reassure the community and no will longer promote social harmony, which could expose them to the criticism that they have a vested interest in community political rivalries. In contrast, a political leader is less concerned with spiritual community mediation than with the material welfare of his clan and close relatives, providing that he can avoid attracting envy and hostility from rivals.

However, in practice, both shamanic and political qualities involve seeing life relativistically, and the interests of spiritual and political leaders frequently coincide. One difference between shamanic and political leaders is age. Political leaders are usually adults with growing children; they are not old enough to be fully knowledgeable about shamanic activities, even though they will have some rudimentary understanding. The older men, whose children have grown up, are most respected for their shamanic skills. Sometimes this leads to a division of labour in cases where the knowledge of the older men and the strength of the younger adults can work together. This was apparent in the previous chapter's case study, in which the older shamans advised the younger political leaders. Nowadays, fifteen years on, several of those younger leaders are themselves becoming experienced in shamanic techniques.

The overlapping dimensions of political and shamanic life are apparent throughout the Amazon. In some cases (such as the Piaroa), shamanic power is dominant, whereas in others (such as the Shavante), the political power is pre-eminent (Santos Granero 1986). Furthermore, in some cases, such as the Cashinahua (Erikson 1988), shamanic and political leadership are separated and clear-cut by means of a moiety division. The Arakmbut lie between these contrasts. While shamanic and political realms are not as sharply distinct as the Cashinahua, they cannot be reduced from one to the other as in the previous cases. For the Arakmbut, political and shamanic activities are based in social life and are bound up with notions of production and access to resources.

The relationship between political life and production has been somewhat difficult to pin down in Amazonia. The approaches of Clastres (1977) and Kracke (1978) emphasise not so much power on the basis of access to resources as respect for certain qualities such as generosity, oratory, and physical prowess. On the other hand, others see Amazonian life as based on an access to resources which embraces both visible and invisible worlds (Descola 1989). The Arakmbut would not necessarily see these positions as alternatives. Political qualities which give rise to prestige and power are not attributes of a person's essence, but are the manifestations of social relationships expressed through the state of each person's soul in relation to daily encounters. A respected person is someone who is adept at production activities (hunting for men and cultivation for women), which, as we have seen in chapter two, cannot be successful without some support from the invisible spirit world.

The next three chapters in this book look at Arakmbut political life from three connected angles. This chapter reviews the relationship between social organisation and resources in order to outline the boundaries of the political economy, and investigates the concept of e'pak (desire) which is a dynamic factor of production. The next chapter looks at the qualities which provide an Arakmbut person with prestige in socio-political life based on the principle of generosity *(e'yok)*. The following chapter looks at the process of decision-making in an Arakmbut community in order to see how influence is created and used. By juxtaposing this information with the description of shamanic activities discussed above, it is possible to see how political and shamanic life interact on a daily basis and how this provides the context for change in the community.

Earlier in this book, shamanic practices were divided into production activities, which affect everyone, curing activities, at which some people are adept, and dreaming, which is a skill used by only a few. A similar view can be taken of political life. All Arakmbut are related to each other in many ways, and this provides a repertoire of social identities which are expressed in daily life. Almost all Arakmbut daily life concerns production and distribution of resources. Even when the community is relaxing at a drinking party, the host is demonstrating his successful gold production.

All the Arakmbut live because of the resources which stem from their territory *(wandari)*. Life (e'e) is ensured by means of food *(aypo)* which can be obtained directly from the forest or river and grown in the gardens. Life is prolonged by reproducing the household, and this means seeking a marriage partner *(watoe)*. In addition to basic production, the Arakmbut mine gold *(wakupe)* on their territory. Gold provides resources which cannot be found on Arakmbut land such as bought foods, prestige goods, capital goods, and beer for distribution at fiestas.

Resources can be divided into food, gold, and people. Access to resources is controlled by various means. As was noted in Chapter 2, the forest, river, and garden resources are watched over by the spirit world. The Arakmbut all need some degree of shamanic expertise to ensure that their production activities are successful and that they do not expose themselves or their households to unnecessary risk. Spirits are not involved in access to gold, and since 1975, the Arakmbut have increasingly been negotiating with non-indigenous colonists for access to the beaches on their territory for mining. Access to spouses, both for women and men, involves competition within the community and can be best achieved by demonstrating capacity in food and gold production.

Although it is tempting to view Arakmbut political economy as a struggle between all the adult members of the community over resources, with power as the goal, this would be too simplistic. Attaining political power is not the principal aim of every Arakmbut person; well-being and the quality of life does not always mean controlling other people. Most of the villagers in San José are like the old man who told me that all he wanted was a quiet life, working in the gardens, panning gold, hunting, and enjoying fiestas at the weekends. Although some may have ambitions to be community president, this brings neither power nor prestige, and often precisely the opposite.

A general observation of Arakmbut politics is that people would like to have enough food to eat, beer to drink, spouses to marry, and children to rear, and at the same time be respected for their talents and skills including shamanic practices, speech-making, singing, telling jokes, hunting, gardening, cooking, child-bearing, and fighting. To reduce all this to power is to overload the notion.

A more general Arakmbut term, which is logically prior to shamanic and political power, is e'pak which means 'to desire', in the sense of want and love.[1] Desire covers material goods, position, and respect in the community as well as affection for other people, and is that aspect of a person which 'reaches out' to others. The root 'pak' is a particle which verbalises substantives and provides them with motion. Pak is thus the sociality of the transcendental person, and is a broader category than power or strength (tainda). Politics is therefore, on a personal level, about desire, its achievement and control.

Pak is also used to refer to someone who is liked. This reciprocation of the verb in a social sense would perhaps be best translated as 'prestige'. Prestige arises from the capacity of certain Arakmbut to satisfy the desires of others. This means demonstrating generosity by giving (e'yok). Giving distributes resources throughout the community and is a means of expressing personal qualities and skills. There

---

1. Unlike the Amuesha (Santos Granero 1991), the Arakmbut do not distinguish love from desire in general.

is potentially limitless prestige within an Arakmbut community, and gaining it need not involve intense competition (this is not to say that there is not an agonistic component to prestige, however). Furthermore, prestige is a comparatively egalitarian concept, because it can be gained by excelling at many different activities.

The starting point for looking at Arakmbut politics is the dynamic of desire, which draws the person into contact with others through the identification, production, and distribution of resources. This interaction constantly shifts focus and enables him or her to transcend any uniform view of the world into one of multiple perspectives. The corollary of this is that desire in one direction often means separation from people in another. The result is that each person creates a political space out of the potentialities inherent in the social context in which he or she lives. Within the constrictions established by the social organisation, the person is a free agent.[2] As people share their desires and enter into similar socio-political frameworks, personal desire for prestige becomes more concentrated into notions of power.

Power is an objectification of the strength (tainda) which consists of the relationship between every person's waso (body) and nokiren (soul). In the spirit world, power is apparent in shamanic activities: dreaming and knowledge enable a person with the right qualities to defend the Arakmbut from invisible dangers. In the visible world, power can be seen socially through the political solidarity of household, clan, and community during periods of weakness (such as sickness) or of conflict (such as competition for community influence). However power is really about the ability to control (matamona) resources and, in certain circumstances, people.

The constitution of the Arakmbut person is important in this context because this transcendental aspect of motion is built into its structure. The physical property of the body separates a person from all others, whereas the soul is a dynamic, invisible substance which is constantly seeking contact outside; yet the soul is tied to the body by the name (wandik) which 'participates' (in a Levy-Bruhlian sense) in the individuality of the body and the universality of the nokiren. The effect is a total contrast to the occidental view of the soul as the unique and essential aspect of a person because, for the Arakmbut, whereas the body gives a distinct form to a person, the nokiren reaches out in dreams to others – not just humans but also species and spirits. The

2. The Matsigenka have this capacity to construct a socio-political space around them (Dan Rosengren pers. comm.)

name is extremely important for providing the boundaries of existence and as a person changes, so does his or her name.

In a social dimension, groups and categories operate in a similar fashion to names. Every Arakmbut person is a member of several social groups and categories which are identified by the superimposed principles of gender, age, residence, alliance, and descent (see Volume 1, Part 1). The names of the groups and categories provide criteria for defining recruitment and thereby placing a contextual framework around the multiplicity of possible social identities available to each person. However, no one is isolated, and each of the groups and categories are to a greater or lesser extent shared by other Arakmbut, thereby creating clusters of overlapping perspectives, drawing people together and distinguishing them. According to the context, a person uses different aspects of his or her identity to make sense of the world and to act within a particular social situation. Sometimes these aspects can appear contradictory to an outsider, such as when a person is a 'Peruvian' in one context, or an 'Arakmbut', a 'woman', or a 'member of the Yaromba clan' in another.

In this way, it is impossible to separate Arakmbut production from political and shamanic spheres of activity, while at the same time it is important to understand the flexible and interpretative aspects of social organisation which arise from the relationship of the principles of 'desire' and 'generosity' which connect production, social identity, political organisation, and shamanic practices.

Resources and Relativity – Outside the Community

Whereas the categories which make up Arakmbut social organisation initially appear consistent, in practice they are malleable. The word Arakmbut means 'people', but the meaning varies according to which people are being contrasted. The broadest meaning of Arakmbut refers to all indigenous peoples ('indígenas') or specifically to the peoples of the Peruvian rainforest ('nativos' or 'paises'/ 'paisanos'). In contrast, 'Amiko' consists of three main categories: 'Peruanos', which covers the authorities and colonists (themselves subdivided into 'Blancos' and 'Wahaipi' – highlanders); 'Gringos' (non-Spanish foreigners, mainly anthropologists) and 'Espanoles' (priests). However, in practice the division varies according to context.

In July 1995 I returned to San José for a brief visit and was told about the mobilisation of the Peruvian armed forces against Ecuador over a national boundary conflict the previous April. Fears that the state's territory was to be invaded caused several young men in San José who had been in the military as conscripts to offer themselves to fight for Peru. They said that their country was under threat and that they would join the armed forces. However, the international conflict calmed down before they signed up. Yet during the same period, San José was in conflict with the illegal colonist settlement of Boca Pukiri. This land invasion is one of the greatest threats to the community, potentially affecting the forests and gold placers surrounding the village. They recounted this invasion as 'Peruvians' coming to invade their indigenous territory and plunder their resources. In the first context the Arakmbut are Peruvian, in another they are clearly distinguished from the state. The distinction arose in the context of defining their territory in the face of external threats.

When asserting their indigenous identity, the Arakmbut ally themselves with their Federación Nativa de Madre de Dios y Sus Afluentes (FENAMAD), which consists of all the indigenous peoples of the Madre de Dios. However, FENAMAD itself consists of nineteen different indigenous peoples, some of whom are treated with suspicion to the extent that the Arakmbut will set themselves against the 'other peoples' *(nogn Arakmbut)* such as the Shipibo, Ese'eja, or Matsigenka, and sometimes even other Harakmbut peoples such as the Wachipaeri, Sapiteri, or Arasaeri. The shifting alliances between the Arakmbut, the other Harakmbut peoples, and the more distant 'other peoples' is apparent in the context of resource access.

FENAMAD's strength is in its reputation as a defender of indigenous rights against colonists. Thus, whenever there is a problem with local invaders or gold companies, as occurs in Boca Pukiri, the Arakmbut of San José are strongly supportive of FENAMAD and assert their rights as indigenous peoples. In 1993, however, the Harakmbut formed their own Consejo Harakmbut (COHAR) despite initial opposition from FENAMAD (see Volume 3, chapter six). COHAR contested the distribution of external resources within FENAMAD in the form of projects: the Harakmbut of the upper Madre de Dios felt that they were losing out to other indigenous peoples in the lower Madre de Dios. In this case, the Harakmbut combined forces and relations with FENAMAD became strained. The relationship improved, however, in February 1995, when COHAR and FENAMAD agreed to work together on health and land defence programmes.

Within COHAR, the unity in the face of FENAMAD is also fragile, because the different Harakmbut peoples themselves have long histories of conflict and alliance. For example, the Arakmbut refer to other Harakmbut peoples as 'Taka' and fear them for their powers of sorcery. They particularly fear the Wachipaeri and, according to Bennet (1991: 172), the feeling is mutual. In the past, conflict was particularly strong within the Harakmbut peoples over access to metal tools, but nowadays, fear of death is more apparent.

Politics among the Arakmbut consists of ever-shifting alliances and, from a community perspective, external relations can overcome or exacerbate divisions. For example, the two Arakmbut communities on the Karene, San José and Puerto Luz, come from two Arakmbut sub-groups – Wandakweri and Kipodneri respectively. In April 1992, the two communities successfully invaded the trading post of Boca Colorado and sacked the mayor's office. They removed the materials which had been promised them for new schools but which they had learned were being sold off (see Volume 3, chapter two). However, during the same period, there was a conflict between the communities: San José was seeking access to caña brava, which grows on Puerto Luz' lands, for their arrows. Puerto Luz was reluctant to allow San José to take the canes as they feared there would not be enough for their own use. In contexts like this, relations can shift from good-natured co-operation into hostile rivalry, quickly justified by a long memory of incidents reflecting the gamut of possible relations.

When conflicts arise between the communities, they will frequently ally themselves to different non-indigenous patrons who, understanding the political implications of the situation, encourage the division for their own interests. The same differentiation takes place within communities, particularly when conflicts arise between obligations to colonists and internal loyalties. For example, in 1981, two men from San José were trying to expand their gold workings and needed to buy motor pumps, but as they could not afford to buy new ones, both bought second-hand pumps from local rival colonists. When the younger Yaromba could not pay his debt, the other older Idnsikambo scoffed at his alliance with an untrustworthy outsider while he himself had a solid relationship with the trustworthy rival colonist. Meanwhile, the young Yaromba criticised the older Idnsikambo for allying himself with a man who was working close to San José's placers and who obviously intended to take over the gold mines of San José in the future. Both criticisms of the respective colonists proved correct, but the thrust of the criticism was aimed less at the colonists than at the poor judgement of the indigenous rival.

A particularly problematic feature of relations with colonists which occurs in all Arakmbut communities is the god-parental system of 'compadrazgo'. This institution is not Arakmbut but is important in Peru as a means of political patronage. Parents invite another person (almost entirely non-Arakmbut) to be godfather/godmother ('padrino'/ 'madrino') to their children and consequently form a quasi-religious connection with them. The parents become 'compadres' and 'comadres', which involves obligations such as gift giving where possible and a strong moral prohibition on entering into direct or indirect conflict. For this reason, if a community enters into conflict with a local colonist, those Arakmbut with 'compadrazgo' connections to the colonist will abstain, thereby weakening the indigenous position and exacerbating internal division (Rummenhöller 1987).

The divisions between and within communities reflect the internal fault lines of the political system, covering three main possibilities: friendship and co-operation; abstention and lack of desire to enter the conflict; and hostility. Friendship in one direction usually means, by implication, hostility or abstention in another so that when members of San José are in alliance against outsiders, they emphasise their Arakmbut identity, but should divisions arise, both parties will criticise the rival, complaining that they have betrayed the Arakmbut through 'compadrazgo' or some financial arrangement. Relationships with people outside the community therefore reflect differences within the community.

This review of the shifting relationships outside of the community illustrates the intricate relationship between access to resources, social identity, and political relationships. This is not to say that resource competition determines identity or any particular set of political relationships. Rather, conflict and alliance are bound up with production and resource allocation as well as with the means of obtaining them – spirits and non-indigenous outsiders. Thus, a person in San José can be Peruvian, indigenous, Harakmbut, Arakmbut, Wandakweri, or Wakutangeri (maloca names for San José) depending on the sociopolitical context and the claim being made for certain resources.

Resources and Relativity – Inside the Community

'Native community' is the term which defines the Amazonian indigenous peoples of Peru in relation to state law (Ley 22175 is the Law of Native Communities). Like the other indigenous organisations of Peru, FENAMAD operates on a principle of representation from each native community in the Madre de Dios and makes its decisions at a Congress held every three years. The Arakmbut have always lived in collective settlements rather than the dispersed homesteads found among the Asháninka or Aguaruna, and so the transition from communal house to village consisted of a change from a spatial concept stemming from the house to the notion of a community consisting of a cluster of individual houses (Volume 1, chapter twelve). The territory of a community is known as wandari, and this provides the spatial context for people staking claims to resources.

The community is the most stable residential grouping among the Arakmbut, and most people remain in the same village for most of their lives and use its name as their prime form of identification in a local and regional context. An Arakmbut community makes decisions and takes defensive action in the face of external threats, and although internal factions sometimes divide the community, a unified front is presented to the outside.

The residential pattern within each community consists of houses (hak) and kitchens where each household sleeps, cooks, eats, and socialises. Households try to live as near as possible to friends and allies with whom they co-operate at gold work, hunting, and relaxation. Whereas in the pre-1950s period, the maloca occupied the position of 'the House', encapsulating under one roof the overlying elements of the social organisation (S. Hugh-Jones 1993), since the formation of communities the house has become the sleeping quarters of nuclear or extended families, with the kitchen, a separate building, serving in addition, those relatives who are not an entirely self-sufficient production unit.[3] Unlike the Kayapó, the Arakmbut do not have a conceptual notion of 'House' which transcends households (Lea 1992), but rather have clusters of houses which relate on the basis of spatial and social proximity (Rosengren 1987:141).

The household is the main production unit and usually consists of a husband who is responsible for bringing in meat and a wife who is responsible for a series of gardens (tamba). The Arakmbut do not identify themselves as members of particular households, and the internal business of each one is left as autonomous as possible. In spite of the increasing shortage of meat and the occasional flood which destroys gardens, the household remains a largely self-sustaining body and does not play a direct part in the political climate of the community.

The household is the most common locus of the relationship between men and women in Arakmbut communities. The impor-

3. The Arakmbut do not have a word for 'family' and use the Spanish 'familia' to refer to clan, wambet, or household according to the context. In order to avoid confusion I have distinguished between these different social units.

tance of the women within the household and their muted position in politics seem to be connected. The myth of Chiokpo, recounted in chapter two, explains that a woman benefits in the long term by maintaining discretion about spiritual matters; the same attitude is taken on social and political matters. Women speak far less than men in public meetings, and all the qualities of political and spiritual activities are directed towards men. Thus women are absent from discussions of Arakmbut politics, and it is assumed by outsiders either that they have no influence or that they reserve their opinions for the confinement of their own household.

This perspective is correct to the extent that a researcher asking a woman directly for a political opinion or for comment on the spirit world would have great difficulty in eliciting a response, yet during casual conversations in the house, the kitchen, and in informal groups throughout the community, women are vociferous, have clear opinions, and in moral and political questions are strongly principled.[4] The household is the responsibility of women and, like women, does not feature assertively in political matters. Nevertheless, all socio-political existence in Arakmbut communities consist of arrangements between households, and in defining these relationships, women play central roles in making major decisions concerning the exchange of resources external to the household such as meat and arranging marriages. Furthermore, women gain prestige from their knowledge of gardening, their capacity to produce crops such as barbasco (kumo), and their ability to manage the household efficiently.

Women's paradoxically muted (Ardener 1975) but significant participation in community life beyond the household varies according to the political climate in the community. This ranges from periods when the patrilineal clans are in dominance and the asymmetrical, unequal aspects of the gender relationship come to the fore, constraining women into holding back their opinions for fear of being thought 'gossips', in contrast to times when the wambet affinal relations are more prominent and women, who are key bonding factors in the alliances, become more open and influential.

The political organisation of an Arakmbut community consists of the way in which some principles of social organisation are emphasised at the expense of others, and particularly significant in this respect is the choice of household neighbours. House position there-

---

4. In her work on Arakmbut women, Aikman (n.d.) demonstrates the frustrations which some feel through the asymmetric and constricted aspects of their lives. At the same time, many are strong, hold influence, and in some contexts control aspects of community life.

fore largely reflects the political layout of a community, although as the buildings are renewed every five years or more, there will not be a complete match. For this reason, when making a political analysis of a community, the future building intentions of a householder provide important insights into the current political preoccupations of the Arakmbut.

No household is a completely independent unit and in order to survive a household must co-operate with its neighbours. Men from neighbouring households, related through clan or affinity, will help each other to drag canoes, make houses, and, above all, work gold; women will work together in their gardens if they are relatives or close neighbours. The collaboration between households is the primary means to shift production beyond subsistence and gives men the opportunity to build up prestige.

Whereas the household is the focal point for women, the patrilineal clan is the primary focus of identity for men. The seven clans, Yaromba, Idnsikambo, Wandigpana, Singperi, Masenawa, Embieri, and Saweron, are unevenly spread throughout the five Arakmbut communities. The first five clans are the most numerous, while the Saweron and Embieri are few and are frequently considered connected in 'kinship' with the Idnsikambo. The clans provide a classificatory network which connects all of the Arakmbut. At the same time, alliances between members of clans usually take place between neighbouring households where groups of siblings living near to each other.

In each Arakmbut community various factors allow some clans more influence than others and this constitutes an informal, but significant sense of hierarchy between the clans. In spite of Arakmbut clan patrilineality, women are extremely important in these factors: numerical predominance and sibling groups living close to each other involve both men and women, while dependent in-laws working for bride service and personal qualities necessitate the presence of women to attract a spouse to a household. Only the clan ideologies, such as hunting expectations or shamanic expertise, do not involve women. All these factors can be significant in Arakmbut community political organisation.

The death of Psyche and the earlier curing both took place in 1980, when San José was divided into two residential groups, the Kotsimberi and Wakutangeri, which were dominated respectively by the Idnsikambo and Yaromba clans in two alliance blocks.[5] Each

5. The Arakmbut clans are not sections as found among the Panoan peoples to the east of the Madre de Dios. For a discussion of the presence of sections among the Cashinahua and Sharanahua see Kensinger (1977:235) and Torralba (1981:43-4).

block was formed by a group of two sibling cores which developed alliances with other neighbours through clan and affinal ties. Alliances within the blocks were based on certain political features. In the first place, no clan ever entered into a direct conflict in which any of its members actively supported the opposition; the choice was to support the initiative of the most influential clan members or abstain. Numerically dominant clans were the central focus of intra-village rivalries, while subordinate clans formed intra-block alliances. This means that when there are conflicts within the community, such as those in 1980, the clans support or abstain, leaving a de facto division into two blocks.

The conflicts in the 1980s centred around resource acquisition. In the case of the sickness in the last chapter, the clans fought over diagnoses of the illnesses because they did not want their hunting to be curtailed. Each male Arakmbut has connections with hunted species, which are mediated by the experience of clan elders. Thus although a hunter primarily brings in his meat for his household, any excess has to be distributed and this contributes to his prestige and that of his wife. Thus the prohibition on killing certain species can have repercussions for the members of certain clans.

The imbalance between men and women is another reason for clan conflict. Male Arakmbut fiercely compete to marry suitable wives in the community. This can lead to internal competition within a clan for spouses, but once a group has agreed internally on who is a suitable spouse, negotiations begin in earnest. If, after a proposal, the reply is negative, the result can be severe internal conflict within a community. The situation is even worse when a married couple undergoes problems. Clan alliances can quickly become involved and the fighting stretched out over several years. This occurred in San José and the conflict lasted from 1981 to 1986. Puerto Luz is currently in the middle of a similar conflict which has so far lasted for over four years.

I have called these 'blocks' and not 'moieties' as there is no prescribed exchange between the groups (c.f. Kensinger 1977), nor any ceremonial exchange as among some Gê groups (c.f. Maybury-Lewis 1974:Chapter IV). Nevertheless, it should be noted that the neighbouring Ese'eja have a clan moiety system which, as with the Panoan groups, distinguishes chieftainly from shamanic qualities. Here I have used the word 'block' in the same way as Barth (1965:104): as an alignment of small groups to form a broader political organisation. However, it is worth noting that the presence of sections and moieties in the area provide some room for looking at the possible contexts in which quadripartite and dualistic perspectives of social organisation can arise (see Conclusion).

The political rivalries between clan blocks constitute different interpretations and opinions of significant events in community life, such as cases of sickness and death (as exemplified in the case studies), negotiations, the break-up of marriages, and different strategies for working gold. Occasionally relations become so strained that violence breaks out, particularly at fiestas, when the consumption of alcohol can add to the volatile atmosphere.

Nevertheless, rivalries between clans are often subsumed by a desire to preserve community unity, in which case the dominant clans patch up their agonistic relations by alliances, which take such forms as building houses closer to each other, marriage ties, and cooperation in production activities. This has the effect of weakening the alliances and solidarity within each block, whereupon the subordinate clans increase their contacts with the other block and sometimes other communities.

Thus when trying to picture the political identity of an Arakmbut person we have to take into account clan membership and its current relationship with the other clans in the community. The overall pattern is one of flux, as clan political alliances wax and wane in relation to changing conditions in the community. The social organisation of an Arakmbut community is therefore an uneasy balance between the household and clan, with women and men emphasising different social units through their production activities. Conflict arises when these production activities are put into jeopardy and this leads to an assertion of identity and power.

Clan and residential groups are not the only features of social organisation. The Arakmbut are connected on the basis of the relationship categories. The Arakmbut relationship terminology is constructed on the principle of symmetrical prescription on the basis of distinctions of genealogical level, gender, age, and parallel/cross relatives (see Volume 1, chapter four), whereby each person classifies the whole of the Arakmbut social world according to his or her perspective; even same sex siblings, who apply most of the terms similarly, distinguish older relatives *(tone)* from younger *(sipo)*. The terminology provides the basic categories for an Arakmbut person to define all relatives living in a community, and, when travelling outside the community, enables rapid classification of kin and affines.

Most Arakmbut know the relationship terms and clan affiliation of everyone in their community. Adult women are particularly knowledgeable, to the extent that most can classify all members of the five Arakmbut communities with appropriate terms. However, it is also clear that most people can be related to each other by several different genealogical routes. When meeting for the first time, two people will approve a mutually acceptable correct term with which to address each other. The decision depends on the different genealogical relationships between the parties and they have to decide which of the possible connections they will emphasise – whether through father, mother, in-laws, or grandparents.

The choice of term is important because the classification draws people of adjacent generations into three groups: kin, affine, and those in between. The relationship terminology is the main classificatory scheme for distinguishing affines among the Arakmbut, but it is also the prime means, depending on the circumstances, of disguising affinity. Affinal relations who are direct relatives through marriage retain the terms because they demonstrate a sign of affection and respect, yet in several contexts, affinity is disguised by the terminology:

1. A person who is a cross relative is rarely considered an affine until a marriage takes place which makes them direct in-laws through their respective households.
2. If, however, the potential affine is also a close friend, the two people will continue to call each other by the term for brother, father, or sister after marriage, provided that the affinity is not direct.
3. If an outsider comes to the community who is related distantly, then the term for brother and sister with an age qualification will suffice to define the connection with the person, because it is not polite to address a stranger as an affine.

According to the circumstances, affinity can be redefined; I heard two men talking at a fiesta and as they agreed and disagreed they called each other *egn* (brother) or *en* (brother in law) depending on whether the conversation was light and amusing or whether serious issues and conflicts were discussed. The application of the terminology is the most extreme form of social relativity among the Arakmbut, and it is also the most flexible form of classification, enabling them to distinguish affinity in the exogamic context of the clan or to bridge any divisions of affinity within the wambet.

The Arakmbut recognise affinity because it is the basis of the relationship between the patrilineal clans. At the same time, there are several contexts where affinity is suppressed. This operates as a means to smooth the potential gaps and conflicts which can occur between the responsibilities of a household where a married couple comes from different clans and a political system where clan conflict is a strong feature. The Arakmbut have the ego-centred alliance category called a wambet which expresses the process of disguising affinity over time.

A wambet includes the close kin of a person's father and mother but not those of one's wife, which means that, like the clan, the wambet is, de facto, exogamous.[6] When a child is born, his or her wambet includes both parents. In this way what from the perspective of a married couple is an alliance-arranging category is, from the perspective of a child, a cognatic category. The effect is a social category which transcends the clan and reveals the importance of women in broader political alliances.

In practice, Arakmbut tend to choose their wambet from within a relatively close spatial proximity, including as far as possible those with whom a person has the most positive contacts. Those who collaborate in work (both clanspersons and affines) are often those who are interested in the welfare of their relatives' children and their future marital arrangements.

6. Helberg (1993) contains an excellent and detailed study of Harakmbut relationship terminology and a discussion of the words 'onyu' and 'wambet'. His material, based on a study in Shintuya, is broadly similar to mine, apart from some lexical details. However two differences are interesting: the term 'onyu' is not used in Shinutya and 'wambet' refers to the clan.

   'Onyu', in San José and Barranco Chico is not so much a label for a clan (as I initially thought) but a descriptive term referring to its 'purity'. In Shintuya, Helberg finds that 'wambet' is used to refer to the clans and, if this is the case, it is not the cognatic-style unit about which I was told in San José. On the other hand, Helberg says that cognation exists in Shintuya but it is called 'ndoedn Arakmbut' (my people) – a term used for clan in San José.

   Two conclusions can be drawn from this. In the first place the clan and cognatic-style distinction exists in Shintuya and this is more important than the labels given to them. A hypothesis for this is that in Shintuya, where Wachipaeri and Arakmbut live in the same community, the social organisation is slightly different to that of San José. The Wachipaeri have a weak clan system and therefore, those households with a mixed Wachipaeri/Arakmbut marriage in their ancestry would only have one clan in their wambet. Furthermore, on the basis of Helberg's data in Shintuya (see chapter nine), the Shintuya Arakmbut emphase the clan more strongly than in San José.

   The second point is that the term 'onyu' means 'pure', while a wambet in San José draws together father and mother's relatives. In Puerto Luz, Thomas Moore (pers. comm.) found wambet used to refer to a household group, (which might include wife's relatives). The wambet is in this case a localised group of relatives. The common element in Shintuya, San José, Barranco Chico and Puerto Luz, is that the wambet is a specific localised application of the terminology or the clan system. In Puerto Luz it would appear to be exclusively the terminology, in Shintuya exclusively the clan while in San José, Barranco Chico and Boca Inambari, the wambet brings the two into line. Thus, the distinctions which I have found in San José appear in various forms throughout the other Arakmbut communities, but with different emphases. These are analysed in chapter nine.

Whereas clan groups are emphasised in an Arakmbut community in which sibling cores in close proximity concentrate political influence, wambet alliances build up through friendships, affinal relations, and women's close ties. For example, after a marriage, a husband will usually move to his wife's household to work with his father-in-law for several years and during this time the wife's mother helps her daughter to establish her gardens and feed her offspring. If the mother and daughter tie is close and a strong friendship grows with the new son-in-law, after the couple move out, they will continue to live close to the wife's parents. On the birth of children, these close affinal groups become the wambet of the new generation.

Furthermore, a man or woman with close wambet relatives may choose to live near to them and to form an alliance which cross-cuts the sibling relationships of clan politics and may eventually be joined by a tie of affinity. A single man with few relatives, or one who has fallen out with his siblings, may live as a single person and will seek out friends and relatives of his wambet with whom he can co-operate. Unmarried mothers usually stay in their parents' household, while widows rapidly acquire a new spouse, even elderly ones.

Whereas clan alliances build into solidarity blocks within the community, wambet alliances cross clan divisions, are more numerous, and concern only a few households. Rather than agnatic ties which spread throughout the community, wambet alliances are based on a variety of criteria such as mother's relatives, friendship, and affinity, all of which are sealed through the flexible use of the category and through contiguous house sites. When violence breaks out between clan blocks, the fight quickly extends to cover other villagers who provide political support to their kinsmen; however, conflicts between wambet are more contained because the alliances are constructed on the linkage of personal ego-based categories and not broad-based groups such as clans.

The difference between a political system based on a wambet style category and a clan based on a group loyalties has repercussions which spread throughout Arakmbut social organisation. A clan emphasis leads to a concentrated number of clans in a block formation, operating through a balance of power, tottering uneasily between conflict and solidarity, while a wambet-based system consists of smaller groups created out of the possible members of the category, dispersed throughout the community in clusters of about ten people. Rather than a clan-based community made up of two groups of rivals, the community consists instead of as many as twelve small units operating comparatively independently.

The internal political relationships within an Arakmbut community connect residence, clan, and wambet patterns and illustrate how Arakmbut relativity not only encompasses agonistic relations and perspectives held by interest groups, but also consists of potential for changes in emphasis between different aspects of the social organisation. Each person participates in the variety of elements in the social organisation by transcending the personal isolation of the body, soul, and name which, through the motivation of desire for people, goods, and prestige, draws groups together at the expense of others, thereby constituting the political system among the Arakmbut.

The household and wambet units are based on the assertion and negotiation of control over resources, in particular hunting, gardens, and spouses. A community which operates on these terms is largely self-sufficient and not too agonistic. However, where there are disagreements about resources, larger alliance units take shape and these are formed around the clan. For this reason, community conflict is more apparent when clan antagonism comes to the fore.

This brief survey of Arakmbut social principles has demonstrated the flexible features of residence, descent, and affinity which are cross-cut by gender and age/generation. These set the boundaries of the political space for dynamic interpretation and manipulation of the 'system'. At the same time, they are the building blocks for Arakmbut identity, which is not simply a statement of social position, but a claim to status and resources. The dynamism arises out of the relativity because each Arakmbut person has room to create and control his or her identity in relation to other Arakmbut. This does not mean, however, that the Arakmbut social and political life is a free-for-all. There are clearly constraining factors which limit social manoeuvrability. Furthermore some people have more freedom than others, and this differentiation becomes especially apparent when looking at the politics of power.

The principles described above are not simply co-ordinates through which a person moves during his or her lifetime but constitute a set of possible strategies of interpretation or assertion of any perspective of Arakmbut social life. These become consolidated through negotiation with other people and, as with shamanic ideas, are accepted or otherwise by their practical efficacy. Rather than conceptualising each Arakmbut caught within the web of a social structure, the effect is a series of potential relationships which can be articulated in several ways, according to priorities established by each person within the context of current community power relations.

Each person thus takes up multiple social spaces which present a gravitational pull to or repulsion from other people according to the principles of social organisation. On this basis each person's perspective on life is relative in space and time to everyone else (Gray 1984). However, relativity in this context is more than a series of unconnected interpretations because, through communication, the perspectives are reinforced, changed, and directed into overlapping views which constitute shared experience.

Each person's range of different perspectives overlaps onto those of others and is thus reinforced through constant communication and negotiation, whereby clusters of viewpoints provide dense areas of mutually acceptable orientation to the world. It is impossible to say whether the personal perspective influences the collective or whether the collective reinforces the personal because both processes operate simultaneously. Only by accepting the relativity of each person's participation in Arakmbut political life according to a flexible interpretation of categories and the varying degrees of collective density and ego-centred interpretation can the Durkheimian 'social fact' shed the uniform force which it is meant to exert over the individual. The 'social fact' is not a constant, but varies in intensity according to the historical activities of persons who articulate the current manifestations of structural principles.

This flexible view of Arakmbut social life as a process illustrates that political activity is the extension of social activity, in that as people interact and take account of other's points of view they also reflect on their own perspectives on life. Some people, particularly women, defend their viewpoints by keeping them hidden, whereas others modify their positions or assert their interests. This process draws social interaction into political relations and comprises the point at which the relativistic position described here overlaps with the Arakmbut view of process.

Although the Arakmbut would not necessarily describe their social world as based on principles of relativity, they would recognise the need for people to break out of their personal concerns and frustrations in order to discuss, negotiate, and share opinions with other members of the community. Earlier in this chapter the particle pak was introduced to cover the notion of 'desire' and the linguistic dynamism of converting a noun to a verb which refers to the transcendental aspect of the person, reinforcing old or forging new relationships with others. These social relationships become more intense when people desire objects, spouses, or recognition of proficiency in certain skills and, at this point, social relations take on political features because prestige and perhaps ultimately power or strength (tainda) are needed to achieve these goals and to assert a particular view of Arakmbut society. Male prestige is most obvious to an outsider because certain men are constantly referred to by the others in order to justify their positions. The muted aspect of the women does not mean that they are without prestige: their management of all planting activities, their responsibility for cooking, and their crucial influence in meat distribution and marriage alliance are recognised by both men and other women alike. Nevertheless, prestigious women are not as apparent to outsiders as the men.

All social activity relates ultimately to some use of resources whether gold, food production, or, occasionally, support from outside. Where production is not competitive, within the household or wambet, social relations are not intense. Prestige arises from the exchange of gold or meat which has been over-produced and shared or generously distributed to others in the community.

However, restricted access for men to meat, wives, and sometimes gold beaches can give rise to internal disputes in the community which frequently take the form of clan conflict. As emotions become stronger, violence can erupt and political rivalries become power struggles. Relations outside of the community are even more fraught with danger, as competition with colonists for the fruits of Arakmbut territory give rise to a permanent power struggle.

The path from desire to power leads through sociality and the need to gain prestige through generosity. The claims to resources made through social assertions of identity are intricately connected with the spirit world because the beneficial and harmful spirits regulate access to the resources. As assertions become more public, male politics becomes more apparent and women's more muted, but both sexes are responsible for gaining access to the resources, producing, consuming, and distributing them. In this way, a person who is able to produce sufficient quantities of gold or food to distribute to others without encountering sickness, clearly has positive relationships with the spirit world.

When looking at shamanic and political leaders among the Arakmbut, the women come out of focus because of their position in the household, and men appear more prominently. A characteristic of shamans is that they are older and more experienced than political leaders. They are always good hunters and can bring in more game than other men without suffering the consequences. Psyche was often described as entering the community after a hunt, laden with animals, birds, and fish. A shaman also has the reputation, noted in the previous chapter, of being a reconciliatory influence in the community. Apart from the spiritual contacts which provide him with authority and influence, there are also social reasons for a shaman's capacity to intercede. Wayorokeri are elderly men who have not passed into the decline of old age but are still at the height of their powers. However, they are not as physically strong as the young adults who are mainly the political leaders. As people become older, their network of affinity broadens as more of their close relatives marry into other households and clans. The shaman is, therefore, an elderly man with affinal contacts throughout the community which he can call on at any moment to make the peace. In this way, we can see that the distinction between a political leader and a shamanic leader is as much to do with the experience and strength which come with age than with specific qualities which are exclusively the prerogative of one or the other.

This chapter has looked at the multi-dimensional elements of Arakmbut socio-political life, the relativity of perspectives, the quest to satisfy desire, and the consistent struggle to claim resources and transform them into goods for household and community consumption. Through human relationships, the social world of the Arakmbut emerges, shifts, transforms and reinforces itself – whether in the context of clan, wambet, or community. Each person has his or her perspective of Arakmbut social life, through sharing and comparing rather than as an isolated being. For example, women will share certain perspectives of Arakmbut life but as members of different clans, or of different generations, they will see things differently. According to the context, people will agree or differ and in this way collective representations merge, dissolve, or intensify as a matter of course.

When the community is under threat, all members share the desire to defend themselves. This struggle is almost always one for territory or external resources. However, at the same time, clan members may be competing over resources and a husband and wife protecting their children's reputation in a conflict between households. In practice, social categories, relativity, and solidarity are all independent variables which defy any reductionist analysis because of the simultaneous multiplicity of daily life linking the identity of the people to those of the person. Thus, by combining the Arakmbut notion of 'desire' as the dynamism which operates within the relativity of the social formation with the competition and co-operation over resources, a sense emerges of the shifting boundaries of acceptable behaviour and consequently of each person's liberty.

Defining the contents of a category in action is complicated but this chapter has tried to point out the manifold elements operating when people live together in the same community. The next chapter looks at the attempts to satisfy desire through generosity and the political organisation which is constructed on this principle.

Chapter 7

GENEROSITY AND GIVING

Arakmbut social life is based on the transcendental principle of e'pak (to desire), the meaning of which stretches from general acquisitiveness to affection and respect. This principle generates social relations, thereby constantly recreating the socio-political organisation through daily activities and providing the context for evaluation and recognition of personal qualities. However, desire in itself is not sufficient to account for the ways the Arakmbut recognise different qualities in people, which embrace affection, prestige, and power.

People only gain respect to the extent that they are capable of satisfying the desires of others; this is expressed by the Arakmbut in terms of the corollary principle to e'pak – e'yok (to give). The term e'pak has been translated as 'desire' to embrace as broad a semantic field as possible, and, similarly, e'yok means 'generosity', which covers a wide variety of material and non-material phenomena.[1] This chapter investigates the different qualities in Arakmbut life which generate respect.

Prestige and respect are the objects of Arakmbut desire, and are gained through generosity to other people. The terms ndak, or *wandaknda* (good, healthy, fine), referring to a person, or *urunda* (wonderful), referring to the act of generosity, provide a positive evaluation, whereas *ndakwe*, or *ndakwenda* (bad, unhealthy) refers to a mean person (senopo). The advantages of prestige are that the

---

1. In the way that Appadurai (1986) considers that the value of a commodity relates exchange to political factors, so the Arakmbut example demonstrates that political activity is a constant movement between personal qualities, social categories, and groups through the exchange of ideas and goods.

prestigious are liked, and the Arakmbut listen (*e'pe'e*) to what they say, which ensures that they have influence in the community.

Respect and prestige are available to all members of the Arakmbut community whether female or male, old or young, depending on the context and the resources available. For example, children's prestige is not widely spread throughout the community and is limited to the sphere of the household or the groups in which children participate.

Children gain prestige primarily among their peers, and to a lesser extent from parents, for carrying out activities which will be of use to them as adults: boys for acts of daring, for skill in killing small animals, or for knowing how to make a balsa raft; girls for their quick grasp of garden work and wild plant identification and for their skill at food preparation. In both cases, the prestige is given providing that other children in a group share the benefits of their skills, such as meat from hunting or fruits from gathering. In the parental context, children receive prestige for their support in household activities and for looking after siblings, which provides their mother with time to carry out production activities.

As a person becomes older, responsibility grows beyond the household and the fruits of generosity are more widely distributed to neighbours and close relatives. For adults, the gender distinction is more marked than at any other period of the life cycle, and consequently the spheres of activity for recognising qualities arising from generosity are different for men and women. For men, this is predominantly centred around meat distribution and gold through an arena of political activity stretching outwards from the household and work group to the house cluster and the community at large. For women, the specialisation of crops allows those who are well established to share products which not every woman grows, such as peanuts, sweet potato, papa del monte, or barbasco, among close relatives and neighbours. The women's field of generosity focuses with more intensity on the household and on those female neighbours with whom they work.[2]

The generosity of old age is demonstrated by both men and women in the distribution of knowledge. This takes the form of teaching younger people the skills needed to make contact with the spirit world so that production activities can be regulated and health

2. The use of spatial terms in a gender context should avoid seeing women as somehow relegated to the periphery of social life. Rather than being peripheral, the position adopted here is that women are at the centre of Arakmbut life and consequently more distant from outsiders at the periphery of their social organisation. Indeed, as will be explored later, the perspective of seeing men as constantly dominant largely arises out of the anthropologist's marginal point of view.

ensured through curing chants or other knowledge. Generosity is therefore not simply one type of activity which gives rise to a political structure but a quality which can be recognised by anyone, according to their skills and their access to resources. All of these aspects of generosity will be explored in more detail below.

Generosity and the Recognition of Personal Qualities

Generosity (e'yok – to give) is the primary attribute of a respected person and is the only way of counteracting accusations of selfishness and meanness which arise from holding back material goods or knowledge, giving rise to jealousy in others. To distribute is to satisfy the desires of others. For this reason, e'pak and e'yok are parallel concepts. Desire is the transcendence of the soul reaching out to others, and generosity is the satisfaction of this. There is no need to respond to generosity immediately because prestige itself is the 'return' of the gift, creating an exchange (Sahlins 1974).

Generosity is not only manifest in material goods, but is a general principle of distributing goods and knowledge throughout a community. On a personal level it creates a certain state within the nokiren (soul). In chapter two the soul was described as being divided into the more concentrated emotional part, based in the 'seat of affections' (wanopo), and the more dispersed intellectual part (e'nopwe). Those persons who concentrate goods and ideas on themselves concentrate their soul-matter, which attracts dangerous spirits either to attack them or to use them as vehicles to harm others. To be generous, on the other hand, disperses the concentration of attention and desire, thereby releasing pent-up emotions. This explains the double meaning of the word senopo, which blends meanness and selfishness. This word is a grave insult among the Arakmbut. Generosity, therefore, like desire, has personal and social aspects which, through the state of the nokiren, make statements about the relationship between the body, the soul, and the name.

Generosity and Concern

Responsibility is an important quality of an adult Arakmbut and appears as concern, worry, and signs of depression at the consequences of threats to the household, clan, wambet, or community. Depression and concern (nowenda) are signs of caring about others and so a serious countenance is an important sign of a political leader. Anyone who makes a decision which affects another (matamona) should ensure that their decision arises out of altruistic concern rather than self-interest. Arakmbut political life consists of making decisions which are constantly under scrutiny and, if anything goes wrong as a consequence, the person responsible will accordingly suffer a lack of prestige.

A woman's responsibilities are the produce of the chacras which provide food and fish poison for the household and neighbours, as well as reproducing the clan line by giving birth to children. Men are responsible for the welfare of the household through the provision of meat and gold. These responsibilities are so important that they are the reasons most frequently given by men for not taking on positions of importance within the community, the municipality, or the local indigenous organisation. Responsibility for both men and women begins with the household, and prestige increases as concern spreads to broader social units, such as the clan, the community, or indigenous peoples. A person who is conscientious and cares about his or her household is respected and can become influential in the community. However, men are more visible in the political organisation of a community than women because they are responsible for external relations and consequently appear first to outsiders. This includes defence.

The Arakmbut respect physical strength (tainda), which is not only the capacity to do hard physical work, expected of all men and women in their daily tasks, but also, in the case of men, the ability to fight (*e'munka*) in order to hold off physical attack and to defend oneself and those for whom he is responsible. However, respect only arises in certain contexts. In the past, killing an enemy was rewarded with honour, but nowadays the strength of physical violence is less respected if it is in attack. A man should defend his or his relatives' honour, but at the right moment and without excessive emotion. The generosity factor comes into play here according to whether the person uses his or her strength to help others, or simply for the pleasure of imposing his or her will. The Arakmbut feel highly ambivalent toward strong men who use their strength and power to assert themselves (see the Mayeri jaguar song later in this chapter).

Generosity and Production

1. Hunting and the Distribution of Meat

A good hunter is someone with beneficial relations with the spirit world and is recognised for his skills at bringing in prey. However, prestige can only result from a generous distribution of meat throughout the cluster of neighbouring households, and, whenever possible, beyond. A household with a dependent son-in-law can increase its meat production and augment its potential for distribution. A man becomes desirable to a woman not only for his looks but for his capacity to bring in meat for the household; indeed, the chin-doi meat presented prior to marriage is an assurance that the future husband of a young woman is either a good hunter or has good hunters in his clan and therefore has good 'prospects'.

The internal economy of the community is based largely on meat distribution, on the assumption that some will return in exchange when it is available. However, the amount of meat presented to other households is not usually more than enough for a meal or two, and therefore no kitchen survives on the fruits of distribution. Furthermore, the decrease in game in Arakmbut community lands since the gold rush began in 1979 makes meat distribution considerably less than that reported from other parts of the Amazon.[3]

The motivation to distribute meat arises not only from the desire to be generous but from the fear that eating too much of one's own meat will lead to a concentrated influence of the species within the body and cause illness. There is, therefore, not only a 'pull' factor to distribute in order to gain prestige but a 'push' factor arising from the dangers of keeping meat. The expression of generosity is not simply altruism but expedient household organisation in the face of the consequences of anti-social selfishness.

When a hunter brings a large amount of meat into the kitchen, such as a tapir, the men organise the jointing and the women boil and prepare the innards. However, the wife of the hunter is responsible for cutting up the carcasses of most other animals brought in from the forest. She chops the meat into pieces and divides it into small piles. If the amount is limited, then the meat goes to the immediate clan or affinal neighbours, but with larger animals, she will confer with her husband about which pieces should go to whom according to size and quality. In the final analysis, meat distribution rests almost entirely in the hands of a competent wife, and she or her daughter distribute the meat from house to house. The generosity of meat distribution is not, therefore, simply a question of a man hunting and giving away his meat. When it arrives in the kitchen it is part of the property of the household itself, and the

3. Descola's (1989) tallies of meat caught by the Yanomami and the Achuar are considerably higher than among the Arakmbut.

woman is the key decision-making person with regard to the prac-
ticalities of sharing the spoils of the hunt. Without the women, meat
would be neither edible nor distributed, and so to some extent they
share in the prestige for hunting.

2. Prestige in Garden Work

Clearing gardens is considered by the Arakmbut to be the hardest
activity. It is carried out by the men, and offers of help from neighbours and close relatives is appreciated and considered generous.
The routine garden work of planting, weeding, and harvesting is
organised by women, occasionally with help from the men. This
work provides women with an opportunity to be generous in their
own right. Women who have lived longest in the community have
the advantage of sharing cuttings and seeds with their younger sisters, daughters, and daughters-in-law. These are distributed informally and without so much discussion as meat distribution.
Nevertheless an accomplished woman who manages her production
well receives significant prestige, and the rest of the community
recognise the gardens as hers by referring to them by her name.

3. Generosity in Gold Work

A man who wishes to be respected should also be successful at gold
work and, with a strong clan or strong wambet alliances, he will be
able to mine larger areas, produce more, and demonstrate his generosity through a fiesta. In San José, looking for gold deposits and
hunting often take place at once: a hunter will take out a testing rod
to see whether he can find any dried up gold-bearing streams while
seeking prey.

If he comes across a dried river bed with gold deposits, he must
share it with relatives outside of the work group, whom he will invite
to mine in the same area; if not, he will be accused of hoarding the
placer for himself. Sometimes a man will hire a group of gold mining workers from the highlands in order to exploit larger areas, but
unless he shares some of the beach with others, conflicts will quickly
arise. In 1990, a man and his sons were criticised by the rest of San
José because they were not prepared to share a gold beach. This was
the trigger for a series of incidents including a refusal of marriage,
which resulted in part of the household moving to Puerto Luz. Disagreements in other communities over the division of gold-bearing
beaches have caused serious ructions, such as a conflict in Boca

Inambari in 1991 which was only resolved after recourse to independent community arbitration by an indigenous student. A person who wishes to be respected has to share the fruits of his success.

The Arakmbut usually distribute their gold profits through fiestas, which are discussed in the next chapter. They can be hosted by one person alone or several people can buy rounds of drinks to keep the party going. Although certain Arakmbut with a higher general income from their gold work can afford luxury items such as watches, radios, and corrugated iron roofs for their houses, this depends on the luck of moment, rather than a fixed monetary division. Furthermore, everyone has to demonstrate generosity in providing drink at a fiesta. This distribution of gold profits in drink ensures that distinctive and permanent inequalities between rich and poor do not arise within the community.

In the pre-mission period, the importance of women in providing drink at a fiesta paralleled their significance in the meat distribution. Women were responsible for making the drink *(wawing)* from the maize they grew in their gardens and distributing it to all the guests at the fiesta. Since the introduction of gold and money, however, women are no longer involved in the drinking fiestas which constitute the majority of parties. Nevertheless, should food be provided, the women in the household will be responsible for ensuring that the food is gathered, prepared, and distributed in enough quantities to feed the community. In this way, although the importance of women in distributing drink at a community level has diminished, their capacity to provide food at certain fiestas is still prestigious.

Some Arakmbut make their gold and money from buying or selling and they too are obliged to demonstrate their generosity. In San José, the owner of the small community store invited the community to his son's birthday party in 1992, despite his difficulties in making a profit. His wife and mother-in-law provided food for everyone and he gave free drinks and cigarettes. This went a considerable way to ward off criticism that he was making profits at the community's expense.

Generosity with Knowledge

As knowledge (e'nopwe) accumulates during life, certain Arakmbut receive prestige for their capacity to learn from observation and memorise information which benefits others. A hunter who knows species' names, characteristics, behaviour, and relationships with other creatures is a significant resource for the community. If a young man wants to build a house, he has to chose from a whole forest of wood; but a knowledgeable person, who has built his own house and observed the fate of others, will be able to demonstrate which branches are resistant to ants, which types repel ants, and which woods last the longest in which parts of the house.

Women have a broad knowledge of wild fruits for gathering, crops in the chacras, the effects of certain weeds, soils, and how to plant or harvest crops. All of this information is shared within the household and the women's work groups. Whereas mothers and grandmothers are the main source of knowledge, other women have particular specialities which are greatly in demand. Old women who are experienced in childbirth accompany and support younger women when they give birth in the forest. Other old women know chindign for growing barbasco, which is a prized crop in the gardens and important as a resource for communal fishing expeditions. These elderly women will offer their services to others in the community and are respected for their knowledge. There are two main contexts in which knowledge gives rise to respect:

1. Generosity in Entertainment

The Arakmbut learn stories, songs, and jokes as they grow older, and those who are proficient performers can provide the rest of the community with information, entertainment, and fundamental knowledge about life and the universe. Within a household, men and women pass on myths *(e'mbachapak)* and songs *(e'machinoa)* to their children in the evenings before going to sleep. Elderly men who are considered very knowledgeable will perform myths and songs to groups larger than the household. An old man who is considered a good storyteller will invite people to listen to a myth after the evening meal, while they lie down in the open air on reed mats. He will guide his audience through stories, passing on the details of tales which he learned from his own elders fifty years ago or more. Sometimes these old men will sing, although some are reluctant to do this nowadays without some alcohol to give them confidence.

The Arakmbut enjoy humour, although they are not quick to laugh. When there is a public meeting, someone who can raise the atmosphere by making a small self-deprecatory quip will cheer people and raise a laugh. The Arakmbut consider that laughter is a way of keeping young and avoiding stress which encourages aging, and so funny stories *(waerik)* are an important part of health, providing relaxation and entertainment. Making an audience roar with laughter is not easy, but some people are so adept that they gain respect for their sense of humour as much as anything else.

As with the singing and myth-telling, informal funny stories are told within the household by men and women, but on public occasions it is elderly unmarried men who poke fun and say things which would be considered inappropriate in most other public contexts. Discussions of sexual matters, personal comments about people, and exceptionally anti-social behaviour are turned into a joke by means of reminiscences. The joker's tales can have an audience in hysterics, as did the following example of humour, which refers to actions which the Arakmbut consider disgusting. Because this story was presented at a fiesta, where personal reservations are temporarily suspended, the Arakmbut were highly entertained.

Story of the Dirty Old Man

A person had brought in a mokas (collared peccary). 'Pun' was the sound as he threw it on the ground. Everyone was happy apart from the old man [a character who lived in the Ishiriwe renowned for being a complainer]. The people said, 'You have brought it in really quickly'. But the ill-tempered man said 'When I was young I could hunt mokas, but now I am old I don't'. [At this moment the teller begins to use words which are usually used about young women.] 'Mokas just don't chase me any more. They keep their distance. When I was young they came after me, but now they don't. When I was young I just loved them!' The old man started to stroke the dead mokas which his son had killed, caressing it as if it were a young girl. He touched its head and then the wound it had in its heart. He's getting lower. ['Lower!' shouts the audience. 'Stroke below the stomach!'] He's getting lower … and then he reaches the mokas' arse and puts in his fingers. 'Huhuhu!' he says. 'Ugh! What a terrible stench! After this, he took out his fingers and went off. Now that surely wouldn't happen to anybody here would it? [The teller uses the term *imatachibetonwawika*, which means 'fingers in the vagina', specifically someone who has their fingers in the crotch of a married woman – clearly referring to someone in the audience.]

Understanding these stories is not easy for a non-Arakmbut because they are idiosyncratic examples of personal creativity, often at someone's expense; but whereas the personalised critical songs (see next chapter) are directly challenging, a fight would rarely break out in the good-natured context of a joke.

Oratory is not respected in the same way as in other Amazonian communities and is really another form of entertainment. Someone who can speak well *(e'apak)* may have influence at a meeting, but the style of speaking is often as important as the content. The Arakmbut who receives the best hearing is not an orator who gives a speech several hours long, but rather, one who gives a brief, casual, sincere presentation containing jokes and quips. A light-hearted comment at the end of a serious statement will quickly bring the community around. To show too much emotion is a disastrous oratorical technique in an Arakmbut meeting, as it demonstrates over-zealousness and a concentration of soul-matter. For this reason, many representatives of the national society who feel that oratory should be emotional and serious are often treated with suspicion unless the information imparted is directly relevant to Arakmbut needs. The Arakmbut are generally suspicious of 'slick talkers' and prefer someone who can combine a sense of humour with a serious concern – and preferably briefly.

2. Generosity in Shamanic Qualities

Within a household or household cluster, all men and women know the rudiments of curing, such as blowing and sucking when a member of the family suffers some physical disorder. Some women know chindign to help barbasco grow or to influence the weather, and others have access to Matsigenka herbal knowledge through marriage ties, while most men know the basis of some simple chindign. However these contacts with the spirit world do not involve the complicated relationships and communication which pertain to the most knowledgeable shamans, the wayorokeri and the wamanoka'eri. These men receive credit and respect for their ability to cure and to help the community.

The wamanoka'eri and wayorokeri practitioners are not expected to charge for their information because their generosity and goodwill is essential for ensuring the health of the community. They try to avoid any accusations of meanness which, in the case of shamanic proficiency, can easily be interpreted as pertaining to sorcery. However, in recent years the declining gold has forced several old men to charge for curing in order to contribute to the households in which they live and to provide them with a basic monetary income so that they can participate in fiestas. The community has accepted this payment because the shamanic knowledge is thereby preserved, although a side-effect is that old curers show reluctance to teach their chants to others for fear that they will lose their monopoly on curing. Those who teach without charge are respected for their generosity.

Qualities and Titles

The qualities reviewed above – generosity in production and knowledge – are respected by the Arakmbut. Looking at them together, a union of the two gives a profile of a respected person who is modest and humble yet strong, knowledgeable, and amusing. While it is impossible to find anyone who has all of these qualities, most Arakmbut men and women have at least one or often more. Personal qualities are thus the prerogative of everyone and are largely distributed throughout the community.

Women and men have a slightly different emphasis in the qualities which receive respect. Women receive respect from men and their peers for bearing children, for hard work, for efficiency, and for the quality of the products of their gardens. Much of this skill comes from knowledge of different plants, some chants to help growth and ways of planting crops. Women are also respected for their knowledge of songs, stories, and myths, which they tell within the household and not at public meetings, although there are periods when Arakmbut women are more vocal than at others.

Men receive respect for hunting and gold work, for their knowledge of chindign, and for their capacity to defend the name of household or clan. However, unlike women, certain men receive labels which recognise their shamanic capacity to cure (wamanoka'eri) or to dream (wayorokeri), or which acknowledge their political abilities (wantupa) and general qualities (wairi). Each of these terms refers to a person's authority (matamona), which is the ability of a person to tell others what to do – to decide or determine activities through propositions.[4]

Wairi and Wanamba

The most general term for a respected Arakmbut man is *wairi* ('gentleman'), of which there can be several in each community. A wairi is successful and spreads the fruits of his success broadly. People take note of a wairi's opinions because he listens well and feels responsi-

4.   Occasionally other terms are used such as *wamachunkeri* to refer to a successful hunter or wambarakeri to a warrior, but these do not have the same emphasis as the four labels wamanoka'eri, wayorokeri, wairi and wantupa, which convey considerable respect and relate to the welfare of the community as a whole.

ble for the welfare of the community. A wairi need not be a good speaker, and often at a meeting stands quietly towards the back of the assembly with his arms folded; yet he could be more important in decision-making than the people who are actually talking.

A person can receive respect as a wairi for his generosity and sense of responsibility, but this will only continue as long as his actions reflect his capacity. Whereas most men are endowed with some of the qualities respected in a wairi, there are a few people called *wanamba* who are considered to be lacking in them. A *wanamba* has little or no social standing, is usually single, puny, and a poor hunter, and on the whole people pay little or no attention to him.

More often than not, a wanamba is an outsider with no neighbouring kin or affines and is in the process of integrating. For these reasons he is at a disadvantage when hunting and gaining community recognition. If he can integrate, his position can improve. However, this is not to say that everyone necessarily agrees as to who are wanamba or wairi. Someone who is closely related to a man considered a wanamba will defend him while recognition as a wairi can vary between households and emerge or disappear over time.

A wairi is the opposite of a wanamba. The wairi is a 'gentleman' whom the community considers competent to act as a mediator within and between communities; the wanamba someone whose lack of hunting or mining skills separates him from the others. Non-Arakmbut people who visit the community are considered to be wanamba if they are sent there to work (such as teachers or anthropologists) but as wairi if they visit as representatives of an organisation.[5]

Ohpu and Wantupa

Whereas the term wairi denotes respect and influence, the terms ohpu and wantupa concern political positions. The ohpu is a now extinct form of leader (discussed briefly in Volume 1, chapter ten) who was recognised as such when a small child and endowed with power from the kurudneri sky spirits at the mbakoykoy festival in order to capture the strength of the jaguar for his future as a warrior. Mamatone from San José witnessed such a ceremony and described it as follows:

'The Arakmbut would collect *tori* (an edible plant), which the ohpu's mother took to produce special breast milk for the child. While taking

---

5.   For this reason, my position in the community was as a wanamba in 1980-1981 when I was a student, whereas, on my return in 1991 as a representative of an organisation, I was a wairi.

tori there was a song *(wapong)* to make the milk effective. The song is dedicated to the ohpu, who claps his hands and says 'hayayaya!'. The ohpu is then brushed with the tail feather of a species of oriole called *mbaimbai* (sun-coloured). This will ensure that the child will become a warrior – *wambarakeri*. The father of the ohpu then sings a song, and the ohpu claps his hands and says 'ehehehehe!' The child is placed on a balsa wood platform and everyone chants around him. The sky will then come down to the ohpu. His father leads the singing and quickly the sky comes down. Afterwards a blue bird comes down with the sky and grants the 'jaguar' strength to the child in the presence of the kurud-neri sky spirits.[6]

The ohpu was recognised as a warrior chief but the word has now been replaced by the title wantupa, which Califano (1982) says is the term for a political leader and 'master of the animals'. However, in San José, as was noted in chapter two, the word wachipai refers to the spirit controller and wantupa only to a political leader. Helberg (pers. comm.) learnt in Shintuya that prior to mission contact, wantupa referred to a military leader who brought together one or more communal houses to fight against an enemy. In 1980 the Arakmbut of San José gave me the names of four influential men who were wantupa, but ten years later I was told that there were no wantupa in the community and that the term was obsolete, like ohpu. One person even went so far as to say that the term wantupa never existed in the past but was a term used to denote the bishop, the chief of the missionaries. Thus whereas the wairi and wanamba are constant parts of the Arakmbut community scene, the ohpu and wantupa are not.

In the past, the wantupa was a warrior, respected for his physical strength and ability to use his powers for the benefit of his clan, household, or community. Whereas the wairi receives prestige from the community, the wantupa has a concentration of strength which can be termed 'power'. As noted earlier, the question of power among the Arakmbut is one of degree where social relations, respect, and prestige become intensified into personal power and a person's responsibility enables him to exercise matamona and to determine or decide for others. However, no wantupa would risk ordering people to do what they do not want to, as a refusal would weaken his power and position. For this reason, a successful wantupa is responsive to community wishes and knows in advance the extent of his power.

6. An analysis of this ceremony and its relationship with other aspects of Arakmbut life is discussed in Volume 1, chapter ten.

President and Officers of the Community

In recent years, young men have taken over the political offices recognised by the Law of Native Communities (President, Secretary, Treasurer, and Spokesmen) because they have some formal education and are considered adept at dealing with non-indigenous outsiders. In jest, they are sometimes referred to as wantupa by older men, but their youth and inexperience make them a new category of leader among the Arakmbut. Few Arakmbut offer themselves for election because holding office is not prestigious and a young official has nothing to distribute.

One of the first ungrounded accusations which faces a community President is that he is misappropriating money. This stems from the need for a young leader to seek donations from households for a community fund rather than basing his prestige on generosity. A young leader can end up considerably poorer after two years in office because the Arakmbut do not understand why he should be subsidised for his activities, which often involve expensive trips to Puerto Maldonado. Those few Arakmbut who do offer themselves for election are motivated by the desire for prestige among their peers and the possibility of making contacts with non-indigenous Peruvians, particularly the municipal officials at the Boca Colorado settlement.[7]

However, the community officials are confusing to outsiders who assume that the President is in charge. The President is not an Arakmbut political authority in the same sense as the wairi, even though, ironically, the Arakmbut talk of the President as responsible for community affairs. Occasionally non-indigenous settlers in Boca Colorado take community officials for a drink in order to entice them with deals and to try to influence the community, without realising that these officials cannot decide anything substantial. The problem for community officials who talk too much to colonists, however, is that they are criticised for making personal deals at the expense of wider indigenous interests. The result of these difficulties means that the President of a community rarely lasts more than one term of office and retires complaining of being misunderstood.

However this is not to say that the young officials of a community are without any position. If they work together and listen respectfully

---

7. Rosengren (1987) makes a detailed study among the Matsigenka concerning the differences between traditional leaders and those of the 'community' according to Peruvian law. His conclusions reflect several of the difficulties in reconciling the two aspects of political life mentioned here.

to their elders, they can make decisions and take initiatives which will influence the community. On the few occasions when older officials are elected, prestige and influence are far more apparent.

A common feature of all the titles reviewed here, including the wamanoka'eri and wayorokeri, is that all the men referred to by these terms mediate boundaries. Wamanoka'eri and wayorokeri are titles given to people who are proficient at contacting the spirit world and utilise their contacts to benefit the health of the household, clan, wambet, and community from the dangers of the invisible world. Their power stems from the invisible world and consists of being able to communicate with the spirits. The wantupa (and the ohpu before him), and to some extent the wairi, refers to Arakmbut who defend the community politically and sometimes even physically from threats from other indigenous communities, both Arakmbut and non-Arakmbut. Their relationship with the community is based on power as well as prestige, and they can communicate with other indigenous peoples in the region without fear of being exposed to danger. With the disappearance of the ohpu, the wantupa became more exposed to outside threats, and with his gradual disappearance in recent years, the young community officials are becoming the last bastion against threats from outside. To some extent this shift in political leadership reflects the different forms of defence used by the Arakmbut. The ohpu used spiritual strength to fight the non-Arakmbut 'Taka'; the wantupa fought against other Arakmbut and represented them during encounters with missionaries while the younger officials oppose the more recent land invasions.

The new community officials also mediate boundaries in an even more accentuated form because, unlike the shamanic and political leaders, they have little or no internal prestige arising from their capacity to distribute the fruits of their skills. The President and other community officers constitute a form of 'Foreign Affairs Ministry'[8] which deals with external relations without taking important decisions. The difference between these traditional and modern notions of leadership is between men whose mediation is based on internal political relationships and officials of the community who are purely boundary leaders (Gray 1986:21). Whereas the internal leaders directly represent the needs and desires of the people within a community by listening carefully at social encounters and demonstrating their generosity, the outside boundary leaders are elected at formal

8.   Thomas Moore suggested this highly appropriate analogy.

meetings and, because of their youth, have fewer resources to prove their generosity.

The terms of prestige for men cover two dimensions: internal/ external and wairi/wanamba. From within the community, persons with prestige have a responsibility wider than that of the household and, through their skills and intelligent participation in social encounters, they are able to articulate the opinions and views of the clan, the wambet, or even the community as a whole. From an outside perspective, men with prestige titles are the focal point of contact with the community; in the spirit world, the wayorokeri and the wamanoka'eri are the intermediaries, whereas in relation to other communities, the wairi and the wantupa are the mediators. Looking at the Arakmbut from the margins of their social life, it is tempting to place a strong emphasis on these titles because they stand out above the rest of the community, but this is largely due to the social position of the holders who face out from the community and consequently meet the gaze of outsiders first.

Certain qualities can be combined and others cannot. A wayorokeri dreamer is always a wamanoka'eri curer, but only a few curers have the capacity to contact the spirits on the level of a dreamer. A shamanic specialist would not want to be a political leader such as a wantupa, in case he appears too self-interested and opens himself to accusations of sorcery by mixing his personal ambitions with his spiritual contacts. The wayorokeri is closer to the spirit world than the wamanoka'eri.

The ohpu, in the past, was the political equivalent of the wayorokeri but with a close and powerful relationship to the spirit world. The wantupa was more common and there could be one or more in any community; rather like the wamanoka'eri, he had less spiritual power.

The terms wairi and wanamba are of a different order than the other terms because they are part of a continuum between respected and denigrated. The terms are relative to the extent that there can be disagreement as to who is respected or not. However, a wairi can be recognised by everyone in a community if the breadth of his generosity and skills are apparent to all. The young community officials are sometimes criticised for giving themselves airs when they are not wairi, and on one occasion I have heard the President of the community referred to as a wanamba, which would never be applied to a holder of a traditional title.

The following diagram shows how titles relate to the internal/ external and wairi/wanamba co-ordinates:

Figure 7.1 Arakmbut titles

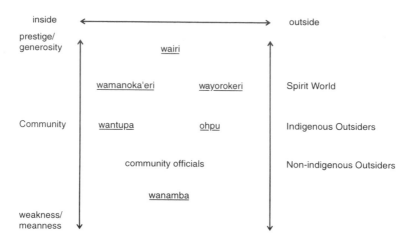

Power, Authority and Access to Resources

The relationship between the Arakmbut and authority of any kind is highly ambivalent. Whereas people with status are respected, unless they demonstrate qualities of humility and generosity they will become unpopular and treated with suspicion. All of the titles reviewed in this chapter imply access to power and resources from the outside. Power is an intensification of the relationship of desire and has to be accompanied by means to disperse its effects generously. Failing to do so causes problems for the person in authority. In the period before conquest, this ambivalence was apparent in the behaviour shown to those who were considered strong potential leaders, as expressed in the song of the Mayari. If this song were to be sung to an outsider with a western orientation, it might sound complimentary:

Song of Mayari (jaguar)

Mayari goes alone because he is secure in himself. He knows he will kill his prey. He goes making his cry. The Mayari has gone to the other river where there are beaches and he shouts aloud because he has no fear. He makes a noise and makes his way to the headwaters. No one can stop him. He has no fear. Petpet has spots and comes through the forest. He comes from a distant place to an Arakmbut community. When he comes from afar there is rain and lightening. He comes to seek out Arakmbut people to kill. He knows where to go. He knows the wandari (territory).

But the song is not complimentary – quite the opposite. When it was sung in the *sinei* (fiesta), the singer would address an assertive and arrogant young man whose power is likened to the confidence of a jaguar (petpet) in order to insult him. The song really means that although the young man is strong and like a jaguar, everyone hates him and the singer conveys through his glance a challenge to fight at dawn. An old man explained the song: 'If I sing this to someone, we will fight. The song is not used often. It is an insult.'

The ambivalence expressed in this Mayari song shows the respect mixed with dislike which people feel for a powerful person who thinks nothing of others. The nokiren of a person becomes more powerful and concentrated with hatred and more dispersed with altruism and concern and so the behaviour of a tyrannical person who terrorises others is seen as dangerous both physically and spiritually, attracting fear and dislike. The same ambivalence can be seen in any situation where people try to bully or boss the Arakmbut, and although their response may be gentle or morose, dislike lurks beneath. A person, whether Arakmbut or not, may attract respect but if he uses power for himself and boasts of his abilities, the Arakmbut will begin to undermine that person.

The ultimate test comes if the leader wants the community to do something and they refuse; when he realises that he has overstepped his position, he can either take on the fight which he will not 'win' in the eyes of the rest of the community or lower his high profile. If there is a problem with a political leader in an Arakmbut community, he will no longer be considered a wairi and should lower his profile for a period. The need to hide power within the community makes it difficult for an outsider to see clearly who really holds authority in an Arakmbut community.

These terms for men of prestige give the initial impression that Arakmbut political life is dominated by certain men who have a monopoly on respect because of their titles. To some extent men have a higher public profile than women because in meetings larger than the household or work group, they are the predominant exponents of myths, speeches, songs, and stories and initiate all the shamanic activities. However, the titles referring to qualities are not used by the Arakmbut within the community, but rather when explaining them to an outsider.

The terms should not therefore be seen as titles which endow position on a person, but rather as titles which state something about where a person is placed within the community. The closer to the boundaries an Arakmbut stands, the more likely that the qualities needed to defend, protect and support the community will receive a label as a means of projecting the person to the outside world as a barrier behind which the rest of the village can continue their lives. For this reason, non-indigenous outsiders consider the President to be head of the community because he is the first person encountered. Similarly women should not be thought of as lacking political influence or prestige because they are without titles. Their apparent internal orientation to the household and its reproduction contrasts with the externally oriented male who deals with the spirit world, other Arakmbut communities or the non-indigenous colonising powers. Yet women's knowledge and awareness are crucial in these relations, although muted. This balanced gender relation is found through much of Arakmbut social life. However, gender is also asymmetrical because of the patrilineal clan relationship (see Volume 1, chapter two) and in certain circumstances conflict can arise leading to clearly unequal relations (see next chapter).

Personal qualities are aspects of all Arakmbut and provide the criteria for looking at the status system of prestige. However, personal qualities in themselves are not the exclusive basis of politics in an Arakmbut community because, were that the case, forms of behaviour would explain all status differences. As we saw in the last chapter, Arakmbut politics is also about access to resources. People desire material goods, knowledge, and a pleasant life. Those persons who have the means to obtain such benefits demonstrate their skill and receive recognition for their talents from the community because they have a constructive relationship with the spirit world, have elderly relatives who teach them this esoteric knowledge, or have non-indigenous sources of cash, goods, and services. In spite of the shortage of gold, game, and land resulting from invasions, the Arakmbut have not reached the point at which they cannot afford to share their benefits. Access to resources is not based on political control but on relationships with outside forces, skill and knowledge, which with few exceptions, is technically available to all.

The political framework of desire and generosity which has been described in these two chapters only comes to life in a context in which skill and knowledge provide access to desirable resources. Prestige and power only arise when a person is able to demonstrate generosity in giving, not in saving. This does not mean that an Arakmbut community is egalitarian or without exploitation. Inequalities can be demonstrated through certain prestige items which are never exchanged: radios, outboard motors, corrugated iron, or, among the young men, fashionable clothes. Exploitation does take place in certain contexts, particularly of people with no immediate relatives nearby (women from other communities and newly married young men living with their in-laws are the most frequent examples). Nevertheless, these are based on the dyadic relations of the political economy rather than on any rudiments of class inequality. Thus there is no internal restriction on access to resources but, on the contrary, any person can demonstrate his or her generosity and consequently his or her success as curer, dreamer, hunter, or warrior providing that he or she has access to external power. The political economy of the Arakmbut consists of qualities which are proven through material efficacy of knowledge or skill by means of contact with the outside world, both visible and invisible.

The political system of the Arakmbut operates with outsiders in a manner which parallels the relationships with the spirit world discussed in earlier chapters of this volume. In both cases qualities or capacities which are available to all people, are particularly developed by certain persons who use their skills to deal with external powers. The socio-political organisation and the spirit world are both highly relative and much of the skill involves breaking out of ethnocentric understandings of life and applying insights for the benefit of the community as a whole. Whereas shamans carry out their work through encounters with spirits in dreams or curing rituals, the encounters in the community are the focus whereby each level of social organisation is expressed socially and politically through personal communication. The most experienced shaman carries out complete two-way communication with spirits in order to defend the community while the wantupa or President has the capacity to carry out full communication with outsiders, creating alliances or fighting enemies.

Both politics and shamanism are attempts by the Arakmbut to harness outside forces for internal benefit. Providing those benefits are shared, the person will be respected and maybe even receive the title wairi, but if they are hoarded, the concentration of power will make him a danger. Power is about the relationship between soul and body and so has to be controlled and shared in order to be beneficial. Simply to accumulate power is selfish, in the same way that to accumulate goods is anti-social. Success in the political economy of the Arakmbut spirit and social worlds consists of preserving as much material goods and power as is possible without causing danger, and of being prepared, through open communication based on the principles of e'pak and e'yok, to distribute any accumulation at the first sign of trouble, or preferably before. The system, as far as it can be seen as a system, is flexible and dynamic and therefore contains the possibility of scope for change. These two chapters have looked at the principles of the political organisation of the Arakmbut. The next chapter looks at the way in which Arakmbut social and political life operates in practice. By looking at the encounters which take place in the community it is possible to bring all the elements surveyed here to life.

Chapter 8

ENCOUNTERS

A visitor entering an Arakmbut community in the late afternoon *(baysik)* will probably, after greeting the cluster of curious villagers assembled on the clifftop, take a walk around the households to meet people and find out how they are. A leisurely stroll will reveal groups of Arakmbut sitting on seats outside kitchens or leaning against steps which lead up to the door of a house, watching the new arrival curiously and punctuating the silence with pithy comments.

The Arakmbut do not talk for the sake of it. Sometimes there are silences and breaks in a conversation. Participants often let one or two talk while the rest sit, listen, and comment with the sceptical 'paah!', a curious 'oo'oh!' or an agreed 'kene!' as the commentary passes from one subject or person to another, rapidly flitting from topic to topic. These encounters are informal and significant for the daily spread of information within the community.

The apparently casual atmosphere is belied by the inscrutable Arakmbut faces which in an instant can break into sceptical laughter at a quip, become serious if the visitor is asked a revealing question, or remain fixed and quizzical. If the outsider demonstrates knowledge and understanding of the community and its problems, both parties begin to banter and the atmosphere becomes warm and friendly as topics come and go.

This banter and atmosphere characterises the hundreds of informal encounters which take place among the Arakmbut on a daily basis, in which they discuss and negotiate events occupying their attention, ranging from incidents in the community to news heard at the nearby settlements or on the radio. The Arakmbut constantly act on and react to the variety of information, such as activities of the spirit world, the threats or support from non-indigenous people in the area, the planning and fruition of production activities, and the ever-changing state of relations within and outside of the community.

An Encounter

The evening of 5 November 1991 was fairly typical in San José. The rain had held off for the day and the men had worked gold or hunted and were washing in the river. The women had already returned to the community after tending their crops and, after washing themselves and their pots and carrying water to the kitchens, were preparing food. The men were wandering around the village or sitting outside houses while the women listened when possible from the nearby kitchens, or passed by from time to time, making comments on the discussion.

Four or five men sat outside a house close to the football pitch. Children played around them and periodically shouted at them when the noise approached a level which might irritate the spirits. I sat with the men and wrote down each snippet of casual conversation which occurred during the encounter. The participants were a hunter and his brother, a gold miner, who constituted the basis of a sibling core, and an old man and his younger friend, neighbours related through the hunter's wife and members of the wambet of a sick child.

Someone handed around cigarettes … The hunter is talking of his day: he talks slowly and the conversation is punctuated by exclamations from the others of surprise, approval, or agreement. The hunter went to the other side of the river and saw tapir footsteps clearly, following them through the forest for several hours, and then they double-tracked like tapirs do and he missed them, but maybe the tapir was avoiding a jaguar; he had seen one there a year ago flashing off into the forest.

[During the conversation on hunting, the hunter's decision to seek a tapir reflects his own expectations and those of his clan, while providing an explanation to his clan and affinal relatives as to why they would get no meat that night. The reference to the jaguar makes his failure to catch the prey arise less from his lack of skill than from the general danger surrounding the area in which he was hunting.]

'The clouds are gathering. There will probably be rain in the night,' says someone. 'Kene', the group agrees. The hunter's brother has been gold working; if the river rises it will make gold work difficult, but it will stop the road. 'The mud will stop their road until the dry season and …'

[The group is familiar with the gold mining activities of each member of the community – where they work, how much they gain, and the workers employed. The hunter's brother has been working gold, but his concern is for the welfare of the community, which was threatened by the building of a road by the municipality through San José's territory in face of Arakmbut opposition (see Volume 3 chapter seven). He thinks that no action should be taken by the Arakmbut as long as the weather continues to disrupt its construction.]

The hunter's wife passes, carrying her youngest baby, who had been crying all day in the chacras. 'I couldn't do anything with her; as soon as one of the children started to look after her she began to cry for her mother.' The old man replies: 'It sounds like the purak' (oriole). He could do a curing session after the meal. 'Have you got sing feathers?' 'Yes', says the hunter. He was going to use them for some arrows, but they will do. As the woman moves off, the others begin to leave. The old man and his younger friend are left on the bench. The younger man says: 'Maybe if the weather holds we could do an ayahuasca session for the child tomorrow?' 'Maybe', says the old man. They go off to eat.

[The hunter's wife expresses the concerns of the household, while the two remaining men refer to different methods of curing. The older man suggesting the curing by a chindign while the younger man proposes ayahuasca. This reflects the age difference between them.]

The whole discussion lasted five to ten minutes yet encapsulated some of the basic concerns of a Arakmbut community: hunting, invasions of colonists, health, and the main social categories. Throughout the conversation, people speak in brief sentences which contain much mutually understood communication; in this manner they discuss issues and clarify responsibilities in the knowledge that information quickly passes around the community. The Arakmbut exchange news while keeping a constant eye on each other, permanently monitoring village life. Although few people receive unqualified respect, few are completely censured either. The community is largely tolerant and will go to extremes to avoid open conflict, but information is stored deep within oral memory, ready to emerge at any moment to explain an event, character trait, or precedent.

Information passes around the community at varying speeds, depending on the general interest. But because every encounter is a continuation of another, each conversation picks up on previous incidents or situations and analyses them anew. Clusters of houses exchange information on a regular basis without even appearing to do so and news spreads, particularly when crises occur. Gossiping is considered a dangerous and troublesome practice and people do their best not to appear to spread rumours; but one person's gossip is another's news.

The conversation is unending. What or who killed the dogs? Who is the father of that pregnant unmarried woman's child? What happened after he hit his uncle? Did you hear toto last night? Better move the canoes – the river is rising. Wamambuey Andrés must have been killed in the Gulf War ... .

From the perspective of the Arakmbut, environmental conditions, the potential for production, and the presence of the spirit world are all related to the social system of the community.[1] The Arakmbut do not see these conditions operating in a mechanical way, providing the background to a static social organisation, but rather conceive of a social system based on the dynamics of desire, in its full ambiguous range of meaning from love to want, which coalesces all of these factors into activities of communication, exemplified in daily encounters. When witnessing an encounter, much of the intricacy described here is known but not expressed. In the same way as with myth, in which the exegesis is unspoken because collective understanding makes its meaning 'immediate', so in any social encounter, much of the communication is unspoken but understood.

The political organisation of the Arakmbut is a dynamic aspect of their social relations, in which desire and generosity are converted into prestige and sometimes power through demonstrating access to and sound use of resources with the help of external forces. The distinction between social and political relations is one of degree. Social relations and the way they are organised are manifestations of principles such as gender, age, residence, descent, or alliance; among the Arakmbut, political relations provide the catalyst for focusing on different principles and bringing them into social prominence according to the situation. Thus for example, the principle of descent can be emphasised as significant social relations because of the political activity giving prominence to patrilineal clan relations.

The Arakmbut have few ritual contexts to define political relationships, and so the political system operates through informal daily encounters; during these encounters, perspectives of the world from social categories and groups are discussed, and social organisation is

1. The use of the term 'system' here does not imply that Arakmbut social life is somehow 'systematic', but that it has certain areas of coherence and consistency which make manipulation and strategy possible. How this relates to the non-indigenous world gives rise to other relationships frequently involving conflicts which are covered in a subsequent volume.

constantly created. Arakmbut society is neither totally ordered nor completely anarchic, but rather consists of a permanent dialogue as to the limits of acceptable behaviour and the context in which certain principles are more appropriate than others.

These encounters could be interpreted as sets of social interactions between individuals which articulate social relations, but this approach slips again into a mechanical metaphor rather than reflecting the dynamic relativity of Arakmbut life, in which opinions are formed and attitudes changed. As people discuss and comment on community affairs they make statements which bring together reflections on their social life and the material and spiritual conditions which affect them. Social action and interpretation are entwined and the difference between what people do, what they say they do, and what they ought to do become topics of negotiation asserted for approval or criticism. Social expectations are constantly under review and reformulated according to people and their interpretation.

With the exception of the community meetings dealing with external questions, all internal matters in San José and other Arakmbut communities are decided and discussed on the basis of these informal encounters and the spread of information. A striking aspect of encounters is the speed with which information flows through the community.

Apart from people moving from one encounter to another, this speed of information flow is dominated by a group of mercurial messengers about whom everyone complains but whom everyone uses – children. Children are the prime vehicles for passing information because they play openly throughout the community, have the easiest opportunities to go into others' kitchens and are always hanging around the evening meetings listening to comments and news. A clear way of attracting parental attention is to provide some news, and it is therefore not unknown for children to embellish a story over and above acceptable dramatic nuances to attract some notice. For this reason, children's statements are treated with more scepticism – unless directly supporting an ongoing theory of the household.

An example of this took place in 1981. A visitor came to the community who could not speak Arakmbut and although I acted as a go-between to some extent, the community found communication difficult and were not well-disposed to the outsider. However, as there was no communication with him, no one could gain any ammunition with which to criticise him. Eventually some children came into the kitchen and said that the foreigner had called them all 'Mashcos'. The visitor did not even know that the people were Arakmbut and such a specialised knowledge of the term 'Mashco' was clearly impossible, but the parents of the children ignored this point and took this as proof that he was not a good person and hoped that he would go soon. He did.

The informal encounters during the day are crucial for the smooth running of an Arakmbut community. The evening meetings are occasions when diplomacy between clans, wambet, and households are frequently needed to prevent conflicts from reaching a community level and causing destructive divisions. The encounters consist of various features which have political consequences. The exchange of information and the formation of opinions arises from spreading news and listening carefully to the response. When a person is sure of the reaction he or she will make the decision.

The effect is a process of permanent consultation. The Arakmbut do not have meetings to decide whether there will be a fishing expedition tomorrow or whether a group of women will go to gather aguajes. What happens is that a someone will casually remark at an evening encounter that the weather looks good for fishing or that the aguajales look good for fruit. The person will listen carefully to the response to ensure that there is no disagreement and then will announce a 'decision' or simply go ahead. The political skill rests in interpreting the responses in order to effect a collective decision based on consensus.

Daily Encounters in an Arakmbut Community

The Arakmbut are not a garrulous people. Long oratorical speeches are treated with suspicion and many of the encounters described here are brief and epigrammatic in the manner of communicating information. Throughout the day, the Arakmbut meet regularly with different groups and through these snippets of conversation build up opinions and positions and make collective decisions. Daily encounters begin and end in the house. The case study below describes a period of marital discord which demonstrates how, through informal encounters, people can spread messages, form opinions, and make decisions. The types of encounter described here are daily occurrences and the example can stand for almost any major event which takes place in the community.

The series of events took place in March 1981. One night a young women had a serious altercation with her husband, who proceded to hit her. The fight was provoked by criticisms of her made by the husband's elderly relative who also lived in the house. The fight could be heard in neighbouring houses after most people had turned in for the night. Immediately those living nearby began to discuss what was happening.

The most intimate Arakmbut encounters take place within the privacy of the house, usually before going to sleep or after waking up in the morning, when a husband and wife discuss family or community affairs, exchange news, and formulate opinions on the basis of information gleaned the previous day. The couple lie in bed with a paraffin lamp, wrapped in their blankets or inside a mosquito net, and quietly chat. Sometimes in the evening the soft murmur of talking couples can be heard from house to house, usually too quiet for the curious to follow. What takes place is confidential.

In spite of their apparent invisibility in the public organisation of the community, Arakmbut women exercise influence from their position of responsibility within the household. However, this can vary according to the relationship between the couple; some respected women discuss their opinions openly with their husbands, while others are ignored. Much of the communication between husband and wife concerns only themselves, although women know that these private talks provide them with an opportunity for participating in decision-making within the house and, through the husband, to affect community opinion.

The conflict in the case study was centred around the discrepancies between different social principles. The marriage was under threat because the husband's elderly uncle lived in the same house and constantly criticised the wife for not being efficient. Because of his respect for an elder member of his clan, the husband beat his wife. The conflict of personality was a conflict of social principles: gender, age, residence, and descent.

During the night she left the community with her children and went downriver to a Harakmbut group living on the Pukiri, where she was sure of a welcome. The husband was left alone with his elderly relative. That morning, down at the port, the women heard what had happened as they collected water and washed pots for breakfast, and each household began to gather information. This was taken back to the kitchens, and before breakfast was finished the whole community knew what had happened.

Periods of washing at dawn or dusk provide opportunities for the Arakmbut to discuss events. The women spend more time washing pots and bringing water than the men, and so more news is exchanged between them at these times. A slightly larger 'hearth group' meets together at meal times in the kitchen, which is a small hut built next to the house. These groups consist of relatives and neighbours who share food, even though they may not necessarily all sleep in the same building. Over breakfast or the evening meal, in the comparative privacy of a kitchen, Arakmbut share information and discuss the latest events; women participate as much as men. After eating, both in the morning and in the evening, friends of children or older relatives drop by to catch up on news, to see what food is available and maybe to scrounge a tid-bit.

The Arakmbut consider it ill-mannered to look at or talk to another person as they are eating. However, everyone talks immediately before and immediately after a meal, passing on information they have heard, commenting, telling jokes, or repeating interesting stories. After the evening meal, the hearth group moves to sit on the benches outside or maybe lie on reed mats to continue chatting or to listen to a myth. Sometimes close neighbours come by and more news is exchanged. These late encounters provide a household with the opportunity to catch up on information which they may have missed during the day.

The wife in the case study left because she could see no solution by remaining in the community. She knew that when she left her husband, he would have to resolve the situation with her clan members and face the humiliation of making his own food. The elderly relative would have to consider his options too if he wanted to remain in the household.

Throughout the day the husband worked gold. He discussed the problem with his in-laws and tried to ensure that there would be no conflict between the clans. The wife's mother and father's sisters discussed the question in their work groups. At night he had to cook his own meal.

In the morning after breakfast, the men sharpen their machetes on whetstones or gather together their gold tools, guns, or axes before work while the women collect their string bags (*wenpu*) which they make or mend at different times during the day. The open slatted walls of the buildings enable people still sitting in the kitchen to follow a conversation from inside and occasionally punctuate the flow with relevant comments.

When men and women separate after breakfast they meet up with close relatives from neighbouring households related by clan or wambet ties (parents, brothers, sisters, or close in-laws) and go to work.

The men go off into the forest to hunt and fish or take a canoe to their gold placers. Gold is a more communal activity than hunting, although even there the men do not talk a lot during the day. Conversations are brief and predominantly concerned with the activity at hand, or else are light and joking. Nevertheless, during the course of the work, topics of current interest arise and there are opportunities to sound out close relatives about certain matters and decisions which were raised at breakfast or the night before, such as a potential marriage, a sickness, a death, or the rumour of a new colonist or death threat. All of this information and opinion is exchanged in quite a casual way.

Women sit at the houses in groups of various sizes and work their string bags (wenpu) after the men have gone, talking to each other about village affairs. Afterwards they make their way in small groups, sharing canoes to the gardens. A woman will go with her daughters and often a neighbour, such as sister or in-law with gardens near to her own, where they will tend the crops with boundless energy, punctuating the tiring routine with moments of conversation and relaxation when they eat wild fruits.

The wenpu and garden work groups are the largest women's discussion group, and, although topics of discussion vary, of particular concern to women are marriage prospects, children's health, the quality of husbands, and garden production. Within the discussions emerge their own problems; they are over-worked, feel unwell, find their responsibilities heavy or consider that they are taken for granted. Rarely will a woman say these things openly, but others interpret theirs from the way they talk and pass the observations on.

A woman's influence is largely related to her experience, her standing in the community, and her relationship with the other women. The work groups are therefore important. A female political arena becomes apparent as women exchange views and reflect on the information passing through the households. The marital tie is significant when defining the position of a woman in a community; influential women are almost always those who have good communications with their husbands. Not only is this because the husband is open to listening to his wife, but because the channel provides knowledge of community affairs which are respected by the other women. This trust between husband and wife is not always apparent, however, and suspicion sometimes arises where the man fears that his authority in the household is being undermined through 'gossip'. In this case a man will accuse his wife of planting a rumour to stir up trouble with another man in the community which could result in an attack against him at the next fiesta. In fact, rather than saying anything about gossip, this opinion reflects more on the confidence and openness in a marital relationship.

Throughout the day, the husband was eager to ensure that there was no problem with his in-laws. As a man with no brothers, he had to work gold with them to ensure his basic income. As the evening drew on the husband walked around the different clusters of Arakmbut and gave his account of what had happened, making his case without criticising his wife too strongly as he wanted her back. The husband's main support came from his clan, while his wife's father's family, with whom he worked gold, did not interfere. They had discussed the matter during the day and had agreed not to fight. Furthermore, the women did not express any solidarity with the wife but acted very much as if she had brought the conflict on herself.

Women return from their gardens before the evening and, after a rest, begin to wash the pots, to bring water, and to light the fire for the evening meal. The men return, wash, and begin to relax and visit each other, informally congregating in clusters at different points throughout the community. It is baysik. Some Arakmbut sit or lounge around a bench or house as others pass by; women participate to a lesser extent than men because they are cooking the evening meal, but there are usually some women present, listening from their kitchens or leaving a child to mind the pots to go by and make a comment.

Rain permitting, there are about four or five clusters of these meetings in San José every night, each of which consists of a group of neighbours related by clan or wambet. However, the participation in the groups is quite flexible; some people will switch groups in the evening, while others will casually saunter up to see if there is any news. Thus each group usually has someone present from another part of the village at some point during the evening's chat to ensure that any information passes throughout the community. If, however, one group's discussion appears of exceptional importance, someone will spread the word (usually a child) and then people from all over the village will move over to listen.

These evening groups are 'fed' by a distribution of cigarettes between men when they are available; someone usually hands around a packet and acts as a sort of unofficial host to the discussion. The provider of cigarettes will not necessarily discuss matters any more than another, but the generosity from someone who has recently produced some gold is appreciated. Alcohol is not a part of these casual meetings.

The preferred settings for the meetings are not necessarily the houses of the people with the most influence, but those whose dwellings are situated at nodal points in the community topography. There are four such nodal points in San José which link the two halves of the village with the river and stream where people wash in the evenings. Two sites are on benches at the respective ends of the main path, linking the two parts of the community at the access points between the village and the paths to the main river Karene. This provides easy access to groups across both parts of the community and enables those coming up from the river to hear enough of what is being said to participate if they wish. The third point is at the corner of the football pitch linking the houses around the football pitch with a cluster of dwellings behind the path to the clear water stream which is favoured by some families for evening washing. The fourth nodal point is on the other side of the community, at the point between the houses and another access path to the clear stream (see map 4).

The husband in the case study used the evening meetings to ensure that he had the support of his own clan, which was influential in the community, without alienating his in-laws, who remained neutral. Whereas he had warded off possible consequences in the community, he still had the problem of bringing his wife back.

Map 4: Map of San José in 1989 (Rummenhöller K, C. Cárdenas & M. Lazarte, 1991.)

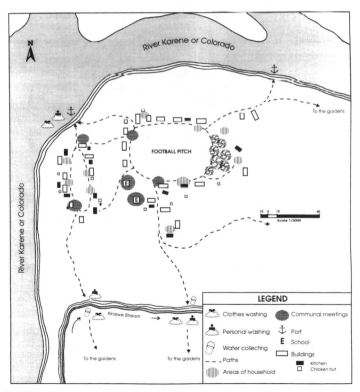

The husband initially refused to go and find his wife and children and bring them back. However, living without a wife and missing his children soon made him feel the strain of bachelor life. During subsequent evening meetings, the in-laws and the husband sought a compromise solution: the husband and an elderly relative would go down river together with the in-laws, not to bring the wife and children back but for a week's fishing expedition. After a week's fishing, the wife and children returned with the husband and they settled down again.

This case study shows how potentially conflictive situations within or between households can be resolved on an informal basis without conflict at a community level. In these cases, the informal encounters can be crucial. The households received the initial news and discussed it among themselves, collecting information and taking a position on the issue. The news passed rapidly around the community from the time that the women were collecting water in the morning, and soon the whole community was aware of what had happened. The man made his case through the evening meetings, initially to ensure the backing of his clan and to check that there was no serious animosity from his in-laws, and then to seek the compromise solution.

The original problem was a marital clash which involved several factors age, residence, descent, and affinity. However, gender, in this case was of particular significance because the relationship was fragile and rather than emphasising complementarity, had, through strains in the marriage, become asymmetrical and, eventually clearly unequal. The woman was suffering because clan and age were being used to diminish her responsibility within the household. She left and the husband used his clan relatives to back him in re-establishing relations with his allies. With a potential rift in his relations of affinity, he had initially emphasised his clan contacts. However, as negotiations smoothed out the conflict, the wambet relations of his children improved and his clan alliance became less emphatic. The elderly man was told to curb his tongue in future, while the willingness of the affines to seek a solution re-established the wife's position in the household. The encounters thus used political means to shift emphasis between different social principles and thereby seek a solution to the problems.

When the woman returned, she did not mention the matter and swiftly returned to life as a diligent wife. She had made her point by demonstrating to her husband the dire effects for him of having to live alone without the rest of the household, open to ridicule. Since this period they have lived together happily. Thus, although the husband's treatment of his wife reached the limits of Arakmbut acceptable behaviour (many Arakmbut do not approve of physical violence), by leaving the community, the wife was able to demonstrate that she was by no means a passive victim.

Because the encounters are spread throughout the community, conflicts can usually be avoided in a public context and the problem can be contained. However, should serious disputes arise, another forum enables the Arakmbut to drop their diplomacy and openly voice their discontent – the fiesta.

The Fiesta

Whereas evening meetings, operating together with the household and work group encounters, can patch over potential rifts in the community, there are many tensions which cannot be resolved, and a small spark can ignite a disagreement into an open conflict. Resolving these disputes is considerably more difficult, and frequently they take on an important profile at the fiesta. The fiesta has a long history in Arakmbut social life and appears in myths as an occasion for young men and women to meet each other and for separate communities or factions to meet peacefully and discuss problems. Whereas there have been changes in the structure of fiestas over the last forty years, several elements remain today, particularly the singing, which is the principal way for the Arakmbut to communicate openly with the spirit world and with other people.

Pre-mission fiestas were called for various reasons, but the main occasions were the male age-grade festivals of e'ohot (nose-piercing) and e'mbaipak (lip-piercing), when the elders of a maloca called together its members and invited neighbouring malocas to attend. An old woman in San José described it as follows:

'We used to *emba'a* or *embachia* in the maloca. This was a round dance which included women. It was not *watawata* (individual) but *watawataewe* (collective). We used to prepare pineapple (*ka*), sugar cane (*apik*), and coca and then invite people. When the *esweri* (outsiders) arrived, the *wanakeri* (people from the host maloca) would greet them outside. *"Ihchagi Ihchagi!"* (I arrive), they would shout. This was the *o'monkudn* (entrance), and the sinei (fiesta) would start. The men would wear their *tombi* (shell rattles), *tanka* (head dress), and *mbakuopidn* (arm bands). They were dressed up at the moment of e'mbaipak when, although they were wanakeri, they appeared like esweri (because they were painted and looked like strangers). These are the wambo (young men), who will become wambokerek (adults). They also wore their *sakmba* (collar). The dances took place with men and women standing alternately in a circle were called *embaipageri*. There was a fire in the centre of the maloca to provide light. "Put more wood on so that we can see more clearly!"'

During the night, the Arakmbut would drink a maize beer (waw-ing) which was provided by the women of the maloca, and everyone would eat and dance. The men, all dressed up in their feathers and paint, would use this as an opportunity to meet the women; during breaks in the dancing, men would sing in groups or solo. Various different types of song are still sung among the Arakmbut which are similar to those recorded by Lyon (1967) among the Wachipaeri: songs about animals and personal drinking songs are the most common now, although in the past there were also challenges to wrestling and boxing duels. The following morning at dawn the old men would rouse the youngsters to fight, repeating the call to arms which was usually given before they left the maloca and which clearly shows the prestige endowed upon a good fighter which continues to this day:

'Wawing (chicha) is ready. Young people, you have to be in high spirits to be in this fiesta. It may surprise you but we have to fight anyone who offends us. So no one should hang behind in a fight. The youths here must fear nothing. This fight is not to the end; it is not like a fight with bows and arrows. It is easy to get close to an enemy. Have no fear. All wambo should prepare who is going to receive the e'mbaipak in this fiesta. Who will get the mbogntokoy (pierced lip)? In this fight you have to defend the *wamankeri* (people from one's own community). Don't get tired in the fight. You will not confront any danger. You have practised too. Use your strength to resist the punches. 'Kukuku', the punches sound horrible from far away. People get afraid. But don't get afraid. This is a lie. When you confront them have no fear. The fight is short. It won't last long, only a short while. You fight in the middle, where there are men. After a few minutes fight, the old men can tell you are good. They will praise you as a good fighter *(wamankeri)*. Let's go to the Karene, Kipodnue. Come on!'

After a night of singing would come the wrestling and boxing matches in which the young men would contest for recognition as brave and fearless. The people would then make their way home to their maloca and wait for a return fiesta.

Fiestas in the past were more formal than today, with ritualistic arrivals and departures, singing, dancing, and fighting; yet all these activities continue to play an important part of the enjoyment. The increased use of alcohol has made the fiesta generally a more ad hoc occasion nowadays but, whereas there have been some changes in style, a fiesta is an important social gathering and significant as a place of encounter. Fiestas usually consist of several households and friends who meet to get drunk, but larger celebrations take place every few months to which at least half or even all of the community are invited. Only at the very largest fiesta is there food for all the community, and this takes place about once or twice a year when a household has gained enough gold money to buy the food.

The invited guests make their way to the host's house, sit outside on a bench, log stool, or mat, and receive beer or pisco. With bought alcohol, women are no longer responsible for making the *wawing* and so they sometimes drink together to the side of the men or, occasionally, drink after the night is well on or even wait until the following morning. Drinking and smoking cigarettes take place together and the men chat or discuss topics similar to those of the evening's meeting, although the topics often linger on more serious subjects such as the invasions of colonists, the future of the children, health, and education.

The Arakmbut drink in a form of a 'potlatch'. Since the discovery of gold on their territory, groups of kin and affines have sought deposits in old streams or on the beaches of the river and gained money through selling the dust, and with gold at about $10 a gram there are opportunities for lucky Arakmbut miners to earn money. However, the results are varied; sometimes Arakmbut are fortunate enough to gain considerable amounts in a short burst; more usually, though, they employ a few workers, and the gold is not enough to cover the costs of machinery and labour. Some profit from gold work is invested in pumps, tubes, and capital goods such as motors for the canoes, but any person who gains money should also distribute profits to other Arakmbut in the community. The fiestas are attempts to distribute any excess gold profit in the form of beer and to allow people the chance to demonstrate their generosity.

Drinking takes place usually at the weekends and since 1990 has consisted of people spending their gold money in the community canteen shop where beer and pisco are available. Those who have been working together drink and chat and then invite their relatives for a drink, after which the fiesta moves into a house and small groups discuss things in detail as they become progressively intoxicated. At larger fiestas, after an hour or so someone puts on a tape recorder of rainforest rock music and the young men and women dance together, which provides them with a chance to talk and meet in much in the same way as in the old *sinei*. However at this stage the fiesta would appear to someone from outside as indistinguishable from the colonists' style of drinking, except that there are far more people being invited to drink. The host takes around the pisco, pouring a glass for each guest or offering beer; as beer is expensive, after a few bottles for everyone, others will be expected to buy from the canteen or else the drink will become exclusively pisco.

As the evening moves on and the alcohol takes effect, people become *e'simbore*. This is translated as 'drunk', but it is closer in meaning to the word 'high', in the sense that a person is transported to another plane. The term comes from the days when men would blow dried tobacco up each other's noses and get quite a kick from it.[2] When the Arakmbut become e'simbore with alcohol, their form of drunkenness makes them look glazed, their bodies become uncoordinated when walking and their speech slurred; however, their singing voice does not suffer at all. At this point the older men begin to sing.

There are several types of song which the Arakmbut men sing during fiestas, and although women have their own songs, they are very reluctant to sing them publicly. Old people say now that they prefer to feel e'simbore before they sing because, as one old man explained, 'you need to raise your spirits to sing'. The greeting songs and duets are only rarely heard now, while those sung at contemporary fiestas are predominantly the animal and personal songs.

Animal songs are described as 'celebrations of the animal', and tell of behavioral traits and aesthetic qualities of the species. Singing is not a means of making contact with the spirit of the creature but of raising people's spirits, making them feel happy and appreciate the animals. Each man usually learns songs from his father or a close relative in the clan or wambet, and through the idiosyncratic use of personal style becomes associated with that person in the same way that species can become attached to people. Some men can pick up a song quickly and can even memorise them in other styles, as for example in Shintuya in June 1992, when an old man sang several songs in the style of dead elders, receiving commendations from the audience who sighed and appreciated the particular accent and throat control. In Arakmbut singing, getting a clear note out is less important than utilising the throat to open and close the sound. The idea behind the song draws attention to an animal or more rarely, as

2. The Arakmbut often say i'simbore (you are drunk) if you sneeze. This presumably comes from the sneeze which would take place after a person had received a good blow of tobacco into their nostrils.

in the third song, to some feature of forest or river life. Here are some examples:[3]

Keme Song (Tapir)

The *weika* bird accompanies keme. It is its domesticated animal and takes ticks from keme's skin with its beak. When keme is near it does this. The *siro* (an oriole) also takes ticks out with its beak. Keme talks to the birds coquettishly. Keme sings 'sss'. The hunter, hearing the weika and the hiss, can kill keme because he can hear where he is. When keme is shot he runs with happiness. Keme does not feel the wound and dies happy. Keme dies. When keme dies there is lightning and there is thunder. Kemesipo (young keme) follows the old keme on the path. First the old one then the *isipo*. The small keme goes with the parents for a year. When they reproduce keme boys mate with the mother and girls with the father. The *windak* arrow has to be strong to kill keme.

Nekei Song (Blue and yellow macaw)

Nekei is beautiful. But *kaikai* (sing – harpy eagle) is crying 'akaakaaka'. Nekei sits in the *witpi* (pona) tree. When he flies he sings. Other nekei are coming and there is a *koimbedn* (scarlet macaw) too. They look beautiful as they come. They fly to *koragn* (pacay palm) where they eat the fruit. They eat a lot. The birds come from afar. But here is *erekn wasing* (white harpy eagle). Nekei is very afraid. When you kill one of a pair of parrots the other flies away singing. The *wakapak* (tail feather) of the nekei is beautiful. The parrot brings the feathers so that the Arakmbut can dance. The parrots settle on all the trees. There they sing.

Wakey Wakey Song (Wind)

The wind blows through the branches in our land. The branch moves with the wind. Before coming the wind roars as if people are talking. All the trees rustle. The wind makes tall trees move and sway in the forest. When branches rub together in the wind they make a noise. Small trees in the wind are easily blown down. When the wind reaches the

3. All these songs were translated for me by a young student who asked the singer to clarify words he did not know. On the whole they were in language he understood and not in the very complicated language of the chindign noted in chapter four.

kotsi (aguaje), the leaves move and make a 'skusha' like talking people. The kotsi branches make much noise in the wind. When the wind comes, the branches of the trees seem to be talking. The following day sometimes trees are found fallen on the earth, blown by the wind.

These songs demonstrate a mixture of aesthetics in which melody, singing technique, and choice of words conjure up a poignant atmosphere during the fiesta. At the same time, the songs themselves are reservoirs of knowledge about animals and birds which can be very useful when hunting or in other production activities. Several of the references, particularly to the keme, deal with the difficult issue of killing animals, which is of general concern for Arakmbut not only because of the illness it can bring but because of the guilt people feel from killing creatures. At the same time, the songs express friendship and good spirits. When a man sings a song at a fiesta he is relaxed and conversation will be positive, covering subjects of mutual interest and expressing solidarity.

As the evening moves on, people become very e'simbore and begin to sing personal songs which allow the singer to communicate those things which would normally be unacceptable to say directly without creating much antagonism. Instead of speech, the song places the criticism on a different plane, which enables the recipient to whom it is directed to choose how to react. Sometimes people pay no attention, but occasionally the song can be seen as a challenge and an invitation for a fight. The songs are usually fairly short with the words, which are improvised or composed just before the fiesta, repeated often.

Personal Song One

We are brothers. We are brothers and you hate me. I feel Yaromba. We are both Yaromba. It is because I have a woman that you hate me. I leave you nothing (drink). Go! Go! Why do you tell me to go?

Personal Song Two

You people are going to say 'go home!' So I will go. We are brothers. but you do not consider me as a brother, even though I am. So I will go. I am alone and so I have no friendship. Your fiesta is a farewell party because I have no friendship.

Personal Song Three

At this fiesta of Amikos we are drinking, brother. We are brothers. We want to drink a lot, not a little. I want to get drunk. When we are drunk we can say anything. We can call each other brothers even though we are not brothers. We might offend each other so must keep calm. You are an adult. You can control your drunkenness. Don't speak offensive words. We brothers-in-law must insist that we want to carry on drinking. Let's go to Jaime's (local colonist who sells alcohol) and sleep there.

Personal Song Four

You brother have criticised me. You should not make pure lies at the people, brother. You brother have criticised me.

Personal Song Five

There was a wanamba, a rubbish person [he imitates the person to laughter]. He has a long back and short arms and legs. [Looking at a woman nearby, presumably related to the person he is insulting.] Some women are serious and when they come by they don't laugh.

Personal Song Six

He sings 'I rob sugar cane from my own chacra' in the hope that the real thief will listen and not do it any more.

All of these songs, according to the singer's careful strategies, say things which a sober man would not dare say. The first two songs question the loyalty of brothers from the same clan, while the third refers to the question of calling an in-law 'brother', which reflects the manipulation of the relationship terminology noted in the previous chapter. The others are directly critical, such as insulting someone with the term wanamba or subtly switching first and third person to accuse someone indirectly of stealing from a garden. Arakmbut would consider stating any of these things openly highly offensive and ill-mannered.[4]

After these songs have been sung, the recipient decides if he wants let the insult drop because the singer is drunk, or to use the song as a pretext to resolve the difference of opinion by fighting. Although fighting is treated by the Arakmbut largely as a sport, it can sometimes get out of hand. Fights usually take place on the morning after the fiesta and follow several unspoken rules: a man

---

4. Women do not sing in fiestas but in the house. This is becoming increasingly rare, and young women claim that they do not know songs.

should not hit another in the face, only the chest, and no one should use sticks or stones – although they have been used when people are really angry.

Behaviour at a fiesta should be relaxed and happy; tempers should be kept under control and discussions open and friendly. However, as conversations become tense and alcohol has its way, arguments can become heated, and during this time the songs provide a means of controlling pent-up anger and frustration. On the other hand, while drinking, people also move in the other direction and emotionally embrace alliances and friendships which would not be deemed appropriate while sober. The Arakmbut are not normally demonstrative people, but when they have drunk they frequently express deep-rooted feelings.

The household, work groups, informal evening encounters, and fiestas are the main contexts for encounters in which socio-political issues are discussed and negotiated through the exchange of information and the formation of opinions. Each of these encounters contains information which is relevant only to that forum and information which is serious enough to move onto the next level of encounter. For example, discussion within the house may concern relations internal to the immediate household and unless they become 'public knowledge', the information need not pass to the work groups or the evening meetings. In the case of the couple who temporarily separated, the household, work groups, and evening meetings were sufficient to tap any strong altercation at a community level and the discussion of that topic never became conflictive at a fiesta. The husband's clan gave their support, the in-laws refused to interfere, and in this way the potential for extending the conflict was quashed.

However, this is not always the case. A particularly intense example occurred in early 1981 when a household prepared a fiesta of food and drink for the whole community to celebrate the birthday of a daughter. The atmosphere was pleasant and people were telling stories and singing but in one corner some people were in earnest conversation and suddenly a fight broke out. Two young men from different clans were courting the same woman and one had insulted the clan name of the other. Allies of the clan tried to stop the fighting, but they in their turn were attacked and the fighting spread to such an extent that in a short time the whole community, men and women, was involved in the brawl. Although the fight broke up after an hour, the feelings on both side were so intense that no mediating clan or affinal relatives appeared, and

Psyche was no longer alive to ease the bitterness. The conflict at the fiesta was never fully resolved, and one of the parties involved eventually moved away from San José.

The daily life of the Arakmbut lurches from periods of tranquillity to upheaval which range from sickness, marital problems, and marriage negotiations to invasions of indigenous territory. All of them involve threats to community life. At the different levels of encounter described here, the Arakmbut discuss and try to solve their problems. The fiesta is the largest informal setting in which to deal with internal matters. However, there are two other contexts in which external events are brought into the socio-political organisation of the Arakmbut: formal meetings and the inter-community 'kermesse'.

Community Meetings

Occasionally San José has a community meeting called by the President or Vice-President. The meeting is usually held in the school and focuses on community decisions about policy relating to external affairs such as the school, the local municipality, colonists, researchers studying in the community, or gold work. Although decisions can be taken at these meetings by show of hand, often these votes are symbolic because the informal encounters have already sized up feelings and anyone making a proposal has usually ensured he has consensus support. After speeches by those presenting the problem and speeches in reply from the elders, a murmur arises and the assent is given. Women are present at the meetings but they either participate in silence or make comments during the speeches. When visitors come to the community, particularly members of FENAMAD, the officers will call a meeting in the school so that the representatives can make a speech giving information on the latest political questions in the Madre de Dios. These meetings do not usually involve a vote, but several older members of the community will be expected to present the perspective of the community as a whole. Those who do this have to ensure that they regularly participate in the informal encounters and test opinion so that on occasions when spokespeople are called, they are ready with a statement which reflects the views of those present. In this way, Arakmbut democracy is direct and consensus-based and avoids as far as possible a vote which would lead to a split in the community. A formal meeting rarely takes on an issue unresolved at the previous levels because it should be an expression of community solidarity in the face of invaders, the government, or visitors.

The Kermesse – An Inter-Community Fiesta

In recent years, the school teachers have started the custom of an annual 'kermesse' to which Puerto Luz and local colonists on friendly terms with the community are invited. The day consists of an afternoon football tournament and an evening fiesta with live music from a band from Puerto Maldonado. The presence of visitors is a sign that relations are reasonably good and, on the whole, all parties try to avoid conflict and violence, with varying success. At these parties, there are opportunities for different members from Puerto Luz and San José to discuss matters of mutual concern and compare opinions on questions relating to the invasions of mining colonists.

By comparing aspects of Arakmbut social organisation with the encounters described in this chapter, it is possible to establish several correlations. At the level of the household, men, women, and children discuss personal questions within the context of gender and age relationships. This occurs in bed or at the time of preparation and consumption of meals.

The work groups take the discussions into gender groups which bring together siblings and/or immediate affines and occur during the periods of production activities during the day. Here neighbouring clan and wambet relations are discussed on the basis of the encounter groups. The informal evening meetings try to bring together closer relatives of both sexes on the basis of house clusters and extend the discussion more widely in the community.

Fiestas are the moments of distribution which bring together people from different house clusters, with men and women seated separately. They sometimes consist of a broader clan and wambet group embracing the whole community, and in this context the manipulation of the relationship terminology, coupled with the singing, enables people to express more shifting and uncertain sets of social and political relationships. Fiestas are occasions when people can become irritable, particularly when discussing unsolved conflicts, which can often lead to a fight after which the loser withdraws or else feels obliged to leave the community.

In this way, informal encounters articulate the potential within the social structure and provide the Arakmbut with the means to take note and make use of the particular principles which are dominant at any one time. Encounters are also bound up in resource acquisition because they take place at moments of production (work groups), consumption (household meetings) and exchange (evening encounters and fiestas).

This chapter argues that the relativity of the different social groupings and categories mentioned in the previous chapters are expressed in terms of encounters which the Arakmbut use constantly
throughout their lives. In any situation, a person will communicate
and discuss with people in the category or group which seems most
appropriate, depending on whether clan, household, gender, age,
wambet, or community take precedence. The encounters highlight
the effects of any particular principle over another and experience
the social consequences. The effect is a constant dynamic shift
between social principles which takes place during the production,
consumption, and distribution activities of the community.

This is a constant manifestation of Arakmbut life in action. It also
provides a context for looking at change in a long-term view. A
dynamic socio-political world is unlikely to lead to a static or even stable existence. The effect of constant change has lead to broad shifts in
the community of San José during the twelve-year period under
review. The next chapter outlines the main features of this change.

SOCIAL CHANGE
AMONG THE ARAKMBUT

A rakmbut spiritual and political relations are centred around the organisation of production, consumption, and exchange. The dynamic behind production stems from the notion of desire which draws people together and motivates them to transform resources into goods. The spirit world controls and regulates production activities through dream contact, but the dangers inherent in overproduction mean that shamanic techniques are needed to ensure the health of the community.

Arakmbut exchange is centred around the notions of selflessness, generosity, and responsibility, which provide the grounds for political organisation. This is most effective when power is dispersed within a bounded framework of accepted behaviour and ideas. A political leader is someone who uses his generosity within the bounds of spiritual acceptability. If he is too mean, he will be accused of sorcery; if he is too generous, the spirit world may attack him for excessive exploitation of resources.

The importance of exchange is clearly noted in the context of encounters among the Arakmbut. From dawn until dusk they not only produce and consume but exchange information, formulate ideas and opinions, and make decisions. Through these encounters the very flexibility and dynamism of the social organisation becomes apparent as a person makes use of his or her gender, age, clan, or wambet when relating to other Arakmbut.

The previous chapters show that, rather than being static, Arakmbut life is constantly moving. Rather than seeing the world as an ordered body which is under threat from outside forces, the impression is of a dynamism stemming from the animating invisible world. Without shamanic intervention with the help of beneficial spirits, the world would be completely disordered. Life and order is negotiated between people with shamanic skills and the spirits through dreams, visions, and curing rituals. Thus shamanic experience creates order by readjusting a largely recalcitrant world through spirit contacts.

The interpretations arising from these experiences in the invisible world have political implications, particularly in times of crisis such as during a sickness or after a death, reflecting the relationships between different groups and categories in Arakmbut communities. The spiritual influence on political life is manifest daily through the state of each person's soul as it reacts to, reflects on, and interprets social encounters with other people. The effects are dynamic processes which relate spiritual, social, and personal life and affect material production, reproduction, distribution, and consumption within the community.

Simultaneously, the principles of desire and generosity which are the basis of socio-political organisation among the Arakmbut are aspects of the social attributes of shamanism. Curers and dreamers have to be generous with their skills to ensure the well-being of the community and to avoid accusations of sorcery. Political leaders have less contact with the spirit world but are strong, active, innovative and responsible for a group of people larger than the household. The shamanic specialists are older, more knowledgeable regarding spirit matters, but are above the internal politics of the community. The two areas complement each other and, in certain household clusters, a political leader often works in harmony with an older shamanic specialist within his clan or wambet. Depending on the history of the community, political leadership and shamanic practices undergo shifts and changes of emphasis.

The political leaders and shamanic practitioners are thus part of a constantly changing world. This chapter illustrates this argument by looking at the changes which have taken place in San José over a period of twelve years between 1980 and 1992. Between the beginning of my first visit to the Arakmbut in 1980 and the end of my last extended period there in 1992 a marked shift took place in the social organisation of the community which seemed surprising in view of the entrenched appearance of the clan system and the dominant political leaders in 1980. The changes, furthermore, covered several distinct aspects of Arakmbut social organisation in a manner which initially looked fairly arbitrary and even insignificant but which, at a closer glance, revealed a whole series of correlations.

Change in San José del Karene

This case study looks at San José as it was in 1980, provides an account of the main events which took place subsequently, and contrasts this with the view in 1992. The shift in San José from the social organisation of 1980 to a distinct version of 1992 did not take place overnight, but was a long-term change made up of several factors, the most important of which were marriage negotiations, choice of post-marital residence, and desire by both men and women to establish independent households within a limited set of obligations to affines or clan members. The changes took place as a result of specific events and the effects of those events on the social formation.

The community of San José was first formed after the flight from Shintuya in 1969. The Arakmbut returned to the homeland of their people and settled at the mouth of the Pukiri. Instead of rebuilding a communal house, they eventually decided to live in houses surrounding a central patio area used for fiestas and football. The original site was on a lower river bank which suffered from flooding and the community moved twice before reaching the present site at the top of the sandstone cliffs of the river Karene in 1974.

The Situation in 1980

Although the community was recognised as one village in 1980, it was divided geographically into two parts. Ten households, under the collective maloca name Kotsimberi, clustered together on an area 100 metres downstream from the ten households of the Wakutangeri. The community was divided into five clans, but at this period the few Masenawa 'shared their kinship' (as the Arakmbut put it) with the Yaromba. This meant that they were considered one clan and treated each other as kin. The following clans made up the community: Yaromba (with Masenawa), Idnsikambo, Wandigpana, and Singperi.

San José consisted at that time of several clan clusters based on a series of households containing members of sibling cores. The Idnsikambo and Yaromba were the main clan cores in San José; the Idnsikambo were pre-eminent in the Wakutangeri half of the community and the Yaromba in the Kotsimberi half. Although the Wandigpana was the largest clan in the Wakutangeri half of the community, the families did not constitute a sibling core and were consequently less influential.

The Arakmbut at that time explained community politics exclusively in terms of clans which fought over resources and competed over their respective interpretations of an illness or death, as described in chapter five. San José gave the overall impression of a community which had a political system run on clan principles.

Table 9.1: Clan demographics, San José, 1980

Wakutangeri:	Number	Percentage
Idnsikambo	22	30
Yaromba	16	22
Wandigpana	23	31
Singperi	5	7
Others	7	10
Total	73	100
Kotsimberi:	**Number**	**Percentage**
Idnsikambo	2	4
Yaromba	23	50
Wandigpana	4	9
Singperi	9	20
Masenawa	7	15
Others	1	2
Total	46	100

The gold work was organised according to the two separate halves of the community. When the Arakmbut work gold, they usually build semi-permanent gold camps where they stay for several months at a time in basic houses with earth floors and low roofs. In 1980, both halves of the community had gold camps, the Kotismberi at Santa Rosa and the Wakutangeri at Chapahal (both downstream from the village), and occasionally they would leave the village to work and live there for a period (as happened after Psyche's death), returning to San José during the weekend to collect crops from the chacras for the following week. At times when they had to work in their gardens they would stop washing gold and return to San José.

In 1980, four political leaders were recognised by the community as wantupa. They were all either Yaromba or Idnsikambo and all aged over twenty-five. They had completed their secondary education and in one case had been in the armed forces. They were elected officers of the community according to the Law of Native Communities and ran the meetings of the whole community which took place every few months.

Furthermore, there were older, more influential people, who had a political interest in and responsibility for members of their extended family and clan. Psyche, the shaman who died, was a wayorokeri known as a wairi rather than wantupa. His position was that of a person who brought the community together and provided spiritual protection for the Arakmbut rather than a politician who dealt with human outsiders. Although the wairi was treated with more prestige, the wantupa were not necessarily inferior.

In 1980 women were not assertive. They attended public meetings but usually observed in silence. Within the household, women held an important position by controlling the cooking and co-ordinating gardening and gathering. Men usually respected this and rarely make a public decision without some discussion with their wives or sisters. However, during this period there were several examples of men beating their wives (as mentioned in the case study in the previous chapter).

In 1980, age was important in terms of the age grades among men and the physical growth of women. Whereas women emphasised residence in their internal status relationships, men emphasised age over residence (Volume 1, chapter three). An older person was higher in the status system than a younger person, who rarely interfered in community affairs and would not presume to know more than their elders.

A rough definition of the community in 1980 would have consisted of a list of five clans realigned into four patrilineal clan groups, allied in two household blocks sharing gold production activities. At that time, fiestas took place every few weeks involving most, if not all, the community, and sometimes this involved fighting to defend clan interests or to resolve personal disputes. Nevertheless, in retrospect, the community considers that the Arakmbut were united in the face of common enemies in 1980 and could respond quickly to violations of land rights, throwing some colonists off their lands as soon as they arrived.

Changes in San José between 1980 and 1992

In subsequent years, the two clan blocks broke up. A series of events took place which led to a substantial change in community organisation. This can only be explained by looking at each clan cluster and sibling group to see how this occurred.

1. The Wakutangeri Block

In 1980 the influential Idnsikambo block consisted of five households living close to each other: three brothers (one a widower) and two sisters married to influential single men from Yaromba and Wandigpana clans. By 1985 these brothers-in-law had children who were either in Puerto Maldonado for their secondary education or were preparing to get married. As their children grew up, the older affines of the Wakutangeri block became more independent and began to seek possible marital arrangements for them.

Figure 9.1: Wakutangeri clan block

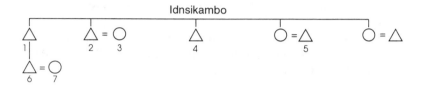

In 1980, the eldest son [6] of the Idnsikambo widowed brother [1] married and brought his wife [7] to live close to his father. After a few years in San José, they moved to the Pukiri river in 1984, until his grandchildren reached school age and returned to the community. During this period, the father no longer needed the support of his sisters-in-law, but become increasingly connected to his children's households. Nevertheless, his youngest Idnsikambo brother [4] and his family remained in close personal contact and also moved for a period to the Pukiri. He eventually returned to San José in 1987, but settled in a house away from the others at a spot which he had always liked by a clear stream.

The wife [3] of the middle Idnsikambo brother [2] lived virilocally, but her relatives stayed on the other side of the community. She became increasingly dissatisfied with being distanced from her clan relations and persuaded her husband to move to the other side of the community where there was more physical space for her growing children. They moved to be close to the wife's relatives in 1988. The husband was becoming increasingly interested in learning shamanic skills from an elderly classificatory father-in-law, who was willing to teach and work with him.

Thus, by 1988, the three Idnsikambo brothers had moved apart from each other. They continued to remain in regular contact and met daily to discuss news. However, their community orientation became primarily to their growing households rather than to their clan or affinal connections.

Over time, the Wandigpana affine [5] no longer felt an obligation to remain in the same part of the village and moved upstream in 1990. This was not seen as a hostile act, but as a part of the process of children growing up and the household gradually orienting its activities to the affines of the children's generation.

The three Idnsikambo brothers and their wives and affines all sought a change during the period from 1980-1992. The brothers explained that they wanted a life which would enable them to be more independent without feeling the responsibility of the community constantly on their shoulders, leaving the political decisions to younger people. This constituted the shift noted above from wantupa to wairi.

The key moments in this change were several types of event: marriage negotiations; the establishment of new households; and the moving of a household out of the clan cluster.

2. The Kotsimberi Block

Figure 9.2: Kotsimberi clan block

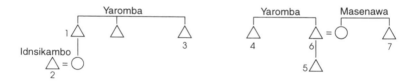

This consisted of two sets of Yaromba siblings, one comprising three brothers, their wives, and their in-laws, and the other of Psyche [4], his brother [6], and the large household of a Masenawa brother-in-law [7]. Psyche's death in 1980 weakened the block substantially, and it was further debilitated when the son-in-law [2] of the eldest three Yaromba brothers [1] died in 1983.

During this period, tensions between the Masenawa and the Wakutangeri from the other side of the village arose because of extended and unresolved marriage negotiations. These lasted several years and although a marriage took place with one of the Wakutangeri, relations were difficult. Eventually, after intra-community conflicts, the Masenawa household, their children and some Singperi relatives left San José in 1986 to live in Barranco Chico. In 1982, 1984, and 1986, several households left San José as a result of conflicts or a desire to move to another community to be closer to relatives.

However, the Masenawa and Singperi households had given their original maloca name to the Kotsimberi half of the community. The result was that in 1986 the whole of San José became Wakutangeri.

To a large extent this diffused some of the rivalry between the two parts of the community, which were no longer considered Kotsimberi and Wakutangeri but became completely Wakutangeri. The Yaromba cluster on the Kotsimberi side was further weakened when the children of the youngest Yaromba brother [3] married and, after differences of opinion within San José, the couple moved to Puerto Luz in 1992. During the same year, Psyche's brother's son [5] married a young women from the Wakutangeri half of the village.

The Situation in 1992

During the twelve years under review, both blocks became more dispersed, lessening the political strength of their clan ties and reinforcing intra-household and alternative affinal connections. The effect was to connect the two parts of the community by means of six marriages which forged alliances between the halves. San José now consisted of a fluid arrangement of friendships and loose alliances between wambet, resulting in a community which was both physically and socially dispersed, coupled with a complicated informal political system.

By 1992 the clans were less important in internal political struggles, and the community consisted of twelve extended alliance clusters linking households that work gold together and celebrate their finds with fiestas. During the twelve years, the power of the clans had dispersed throughout the community and the agonistic and relatively hierarchical relations of competition between clans was replaced with the alliance category wambet. On the ground, these small groups give the impression of a community made up of alliances of household clusters rather than larger groups bound by clan solidarity.

The clan still existed as an important principle of social identity, however. When sending messages to relatives in other communities, people always mention their own clan members first, and men in San José still ally with their patrilineal relatives. Notwithstanding this, the whole community had made a shift in emphasis from clan to wambet in terms of defining the links between households and the main daily relationships.

In 1992 San José looked more dispersed. Although the community was still divided into two parts, with most houses organised in the 'maloca' style facing inwards towards a patio or a cleared space, other houses had been built further away by a clear stream. In addition, four houses had been built an hour's walk upriver where several households had re-established their gardens and raised domesticated animals such as ducks, chickens, and pigs. When asked why they had moved, they insisted that there had not been a conflict with the other Arakmbut in San José but that they wanted to live further away from the main community because it was more pleasant upstream.[1]

By 1992, gold working groups were smaller and household clusters had their gold camps situated in different parts of the community's territory on the banks of the main rivers and streams. In twelve years, the overall spatial organisation of San José changed from a concentrated settlement in two parts (Kotsimberi and Wakutangeri) to a single residential name (Wakutangeri) consisting of more dispersed houses spreading out from the main village settlement. The gold camps proliferated along the beaches, often together with small gardens and new hunting paths. San José's territory thus changed from one large settlement into a population dispersed concentrically out from the centre.

During this period, the Arakmbut suffered increasingly from the effects of the gold rush. One of the consequences was the presence of highland workers in the community. Initially these were young men who had escaped from the ill-treatment they suffered from the local patrons and fled to San José for protection. By 1985, several households were employing highland workers and by 1992 there were about twenty-five men employed by the Arakmbut. One of the effects of this influx of outsiders has been that some young Arakmbut have been attracted to them and several short-lived liaisons have resulted.

At the same time, the political influence of the Yaromba and Idnsikambo wantupa, as described in the case studies, began to shift into the more revered prestige of the wairi. The community officials in 1992 were all in their late teens or early twenties and were considered too young to be either wantupa or wairi. The term wantupa indicates a more hierarchical concept of the political organisation of an Arakmbut village because he is a person with political qualities of influence and authority. The notion of hierarchy in an Arakmbut context refers to a differential recognition of prestige based on generosity from gold work, capacity to make decisions which the community approves (consensus anticipation), and a sense of responsibility.

---

1. This separation of households is something which has happened in all the other Arakmbut communities over the last ten years. Although it is always said that this was done by choice, I am unable to say with confidence whether the same explanations are used as in San José.

The dispersed settlement of the community meant that those who lived in the households outside of the main village had difficulty co-ordinating with the community for meetings. By 1992, raising Arakmbut interest in community affairs was considerably more difficult than it had been hitherto, and there were only two assemblies held over the year. Furthermore, at that time, the Arakmbut took several months to complain against a planned road which threatened to carve their territory into two parts (see Volume 3, chapter seven). Several Arakmbut commented that they were not able to organise quickly to respond to threats because everyone 'looks after themselves'.

Fiestas were not as large in 1992 as they had been. Only one or two community parties took place over the whole year, the usual practice being to drink in smaller groups of several households. However, the more dispersed fiestas led to a consequent decrease in violence over the period until 1992.

Female participation in public events had increased, to the extent that when decisions were made in meetings, the older women shouted out their comments and made their feelings felt along with the men. Women spoke more outside of the household and in mixed company, rather than just in the company of other women. There were no cases of wife-beating between 1991 and 1992, which could be connected to the lessening of clan chauvinism and the dispersion of the men through its wambet ties, which give more recognition to the solidarity of women.

Some women even mentioned that they liked to have intercourse with several different men from different clans with distinct characteristics, in order to blend features and conceive a strong and flexible child who would be more resilient than those produced by one clan alone. This information is a direct questioning by the women of the 'purity' ideology of the clan, and advocates a different perspective. The Arakmbut have not changed their fundamental idea that children are formed from the semen of the father, that the mother produces no substance which contributes to her offspring apart from the shape of her womb. However, the blending of father's semen does reflect the emphasis on the main clan-bridging social category – the ego-centred wambet. Thus the shift of attention onto the wambet in the social organisation has parallelled the more egalitarian relationship between men and women and a weakening of the clan's monopoly on reproduction.[2]

2. This connects to Dumont's (1972) thesis of the relationship in India between hierarchy and purity as the value of distinction. However, among the Arakmbut

In 1992, the youth in the community held different views to those of their predecessors, and although most older youths still respected their elders and did not openly criticise them, several youths banded together to ensure several changes. One was the removal of the school-teachers, which was undertaken without consultation with the elders, some of whom strongly opposed the action. As the majority of the community was non-committal, the initiative of the youths succeeded.

The reason for the increased facility of young Arakmbut to take certain decisions relating to the non-indigenous world (of which the school is considered a part) is the increase in educational opportunities. Nevertheless, after forty years of mission contact, some of the older Arakmbut men are also educated, and so education is not the only reason. Another factor is the larger number of young official representatives in the community who, although they have limited status, can use their contacts with the outside national society to achieve certain aims and to provide themselves with a political niche from which to assert their influence. In order to remove the teachers, the young people asserted their position in the community by making an alliance across the clan divisions with others of a similar age to oppose the teachers and their supporters among the older members of the community. At one point in this conflict, the older Arakmbut were dismayed to hear a young man talk about the 'revolution of the youth'. Cross-clan alliance according to age was unheard of twelve years previously and illustrates the increased emphasis on household alliances through the wambet in conjunction with weakening clan allegiances.

The main events which took place in San José between 1980 and 1992 led to a community which was clearly Arakmbut, but which was markedly different socially. The events here are not the only occurrences during this period contributing to the changes in the community, but they were the main catalytic events which speeded up the cumulative and gradual movement of dispersal.

Political and social relations among the Arakmbut are dynamic in two senses: on a daily basis there is a relativity of relationships by which alliances shift and realign according to the contextual circumstances of the moment. There are also certain events which act as catalysts and which can rapidly change the profile of the community – such as the separation of a household from the community. Com-

---

clans, exogamy is a crucial factor because one must marry into a different source of purity in order to reproduce one's line. As we have seen the women enable this to happen.

paring the situation in San José in 1980 and 1992 on a long-term basis, the shifts can be summarised on the following table:

Table 9.2: Organisational emphasis in San José between 1980 and 1992

1981	1991
Clan	Wambet
Descent	Alliance
Concentrated settlement	Dispersed settlement
More hierarchical	More egalitarian
More conflict/violence	Less conflict/violence
Community unite and resist	Community more resigned
Presence of wantupa	Absence of wantupa
Women stay out of public politics	Women in public politics
Youth obedient to elders	Youth oppose elders

Although this may appear somewhat impressionistic, this table was discussed with several Arakmbut in 1992 who all concurred with the general direction in which the community had changed. In 1980, the clan was predominant and the only factor which indicated its epiphenomenal position in relation to other parts of the social organisation was its relationship with the terminology. Whereas according to clan exogamy a person can marry into any other clan, the terminological prohibition on marrying the daughter of a MZ *(asign)* means that there were cases when the clan exogamy rule was extended to certain members of another clan.[3] This indicated that the clan was not entirely preeminent in spite of its emphasis. Nevertheless, as the clan became weaker during the years subsequent to 1980, its epiphenomenal characteristics became clearly apparent while the wambet, which in 1980 was difficult to define with accuracy, was much more dominant.

When the clan is in the ascendant, as in 1980, the relationship between brothers is extremely important and their solidarity in work projects and hunting, as well as their collective force in community decisions, was significant in the village as a whole. However when the wambet became more important, affinal relationships gain in significance, not only in terms of alliances with mother's relatives but also with a spouse's kin, constituting the wambet of the child. The

---

3. I have also noted that in practice this prohibition is only for the children and close relatives of an actual MZ. Further afield, the clan exogamy holds and one can marry the child of a distant asign.

main shift is thus from clan ties based on consanguinity to wambet ties based on affinity, both of which are always present and in tension with one another. To some extent it is possible to note that the emphases on clan and wambet ties relate to each other in inverse proportion so that when clans are dominant, wambet are less apparent and when the wambet is dominant, the clan is less apparent.

Placing these features together shows that in 1980, San José was more concentrated spatially, there were more community fiestas, defense was more immediate, and meetings took place more regularly. On the other hand, fighting took place more regularly and clan rivalries were more apparent to the outside observer. As the community became more dispersed, fiestas were smaller, meetings less frequent, and fighting less apparent as clan rivalries subsided.

Along with the shift from concentration to dispersion, several correlations of a shift from a more hierarchical to a more egalitarian social organisation became apparent in San José. The last chapter looked at various shamanic and political titles, some of which have changed considerably since 1980. Whereas the concepts of wairi and wanamba changed little over the twelve years, the term wantupa has practically disappeared from the community. Wantupa indicates a more hierarchical conceptualisation of the political organisation of an Arakmbut village because he is a person with political qualities of influence and sometimes authority. Furthermore those named wantupa in 1980 were all prominent members of dominant clans.[4]

4. Kracke (1978) discusses two styles of leadership among the Kragwahiv. A consensus style based on relative equality is contrasted with a more hierarchical style which is more authoritarian. It is possible to compare the more hierarchical political leader of the Arakmbut with the more egalitarian shamanic leader in a way which parallels the general distinction which Kracke makes. Other authors have also noted the co-existence of hierarchical and egalitarian principles in the same system (Chaumeil 1993). The Arakmbut hierarchical case is far more muted than that of the Kragwahiv. This is because the Arakmbut shaman, with his more egalitarian leadership, has a moral authority which embraces the whole community, restricting the influence of the political leader to solidarity with his clan-based following.

    Although this has the effect of lessening the power of a political leader it does not negate his power altogether, as Clastres (1977) would have argued. For the Arakmbut, power is an aspect of the soul-body relationship which is recognised by others as prestige and consequently influence. A person with power controls the relationship between desire and generosity in order to gain respect and prestige while providing as much authority and influence as possible without attracting accusations of sorcery. Power is not opposed to reciprocity but on the contrary is inextricably linked to production and distribution mechanisms among the Arakmbut, particularly meat from hunting and beer from gold mining (c.f. Sahlins 1974:185-275).

The gender shift demonstrates how the relationship between men and women among the Arakmbut is never completely consistent. Over the twelve years, gender relations among the Arakmbut have changed from a comparatively hierarchical relationship to one which is more egalitarian, in which women have more visible presence in the socio-political system. Community relations with the outside world are still dominated by Arakmbut men, but with less emphasis on the clan system, the lack of a mediating wayorokeri after Psyche's death and greater dispersion of households, community, and male groups demonstrate less solidarity. The absence of a wayorokeri, coupled with the increasing importance of affinal relations, could account for the growth in importance of women as intermediaries in solving community problems.

During this period, therefore, women have demonstrated more freedom within the community to express their opinions publicly. However, this does not mean that there has been a complete change in the social organisation of the Arakmbut. Rather, the effect has been a shift in emphasis from one aspect of the political system to another. These changes are largely subtle features which only appear significant when listed together.

The changes outlined here have had an effect on the community as a whole. When the clans were more prominent, political life was divided by blocks of patrilineal descent, although ties stretched throughout both halves of the community. At moments of crisis, the divisions could become temporarily sealed as brothers and cousins of the same clan informed each other and the community would unite to meet. However, in 1992, the wambet was sufficiently dispersed that to gather everyone together meant visiting all the households and talking with the residents separately. For example, when colonists came upriver in 1980 the community rallied around immediately, took off for the camp in an armed canoe, and told them to leave. When a similar event took place in 1991, with a German colonist, it took four months before the Arakmbut opposed the colonist's presence on their territory and they did not expel them until nine months had passed (see Volume 3, chapter eight).

The events which took place in San José between 1980 and 1992 are not structural changes as much as differences of emphasis or focus. The changes did not taken place suddenly, but gradually, whereby a multitude of events in daily experience shape and rearrange the community. Conflict and other dramatic crises such as illness or death are the most common catalysts for change. However, the changes which have been noted in twelve years may not necessarily be relevant to any other long-term views of Arakmbut social life and so it is necessary to place the information established hitherto in a broader context.

Change in Arakmbut Organisation

The comparison between the 1980s and 1990s provides some insights into Arakmbut community rearrangements but it tells us little as to whether this is a unique phenomenon occurring only now, or whether there are certain patterns which can be traced to other periods in Arakmbut history or in Arakmbut ideas of what their social formation ought to be. Placing these changes into a broader perspective, it is possible to look at different ideological systems which share several of the features discussed in the contrast between 1980 and 1992.

The Maloca and Dominant Clan Image – Hierarchy

Elderly Arakmbut sometimes talk about their past before contact with the missionaries in the 1950s, when they lived in malocas on the banks of the rivers Wandakwe and Kipodnue. There were many of these communal houses, each of which was reputed to have had only one clan of male relatives, while all of the women came from other communities and lived virilocally after marriage. Each maloca community was, in this way, ideally coterminous with its clan membership. According to this view, the Arakmbut maloca was a residential group housing a number of agnatically related men. (These would correspond to the sibling cores encountered in San José in 1980.) The men in one clan/maloca arranged marriage exchanges with neighbouring malocas and there were few, if any, negotiated alliances outside of the groups of houses on the Wandakwe or Kipodnwe rivers. The people in these areas were therefore members of the same territorial groups (Wandakweri and Kipodneri) and were related either as potential or actual affines, leaving a shifting patchwork of marriage alliances between different residence groups within an overall territorial group.

According to Helberg (forthcoming), three recognised titles were used for all Arakmbut before life in the mission, arranged in a strict hierarchy. The wantupa was the highest military leader; wairi came next and was respected for an act of bravery; while the wanamba was without any position at all. (This hierarchical structure was reflected by the use of the term wantupa to refer to the Dominican bishop at the time of mission contact.) The hierarchical use of the terms is a more extreme version of the 1980 San José version of the Arakmbut socio-political system.[5]

Helberg's data is congruent with the 'ideal' Arakmbut description of the maloca before the period in the mission which I received. Clans and malocas were meant to coincide and a hierarchy of titles existed within the organisation of each house. The clans were strong in their presence and were physically purer (onyu) than they are today (the Yaromba were thought to be shorter and darker than the Idnsikambo).

This 'ideal type' of Arakmbut maloca organisation did not necessarily ever exist, and, on the basis of other perspectives from old men, the model appears to be conceptual rather than historical. However as a composite picture of an ideal past, the model provides an exaggerated version of the 1980 organisation of San José with parallels that emphasise clan purity, the presence of sibling cores, and wantupa leaders.

Age grade ceremonies were basic to Arakmbut ritual, bringing together boys of the same age. Before the arrival of the missions, during the ritual initiation for young men, the youths had their noses and later their lips pierced. These ceremonies were an integral part of life in the malocas and acted as a form of status differentiation for men within the clan and maloca. Women did not have initiation ceremonies and in the 'ideal' view of the maloca, they came from the outside and consequently had a lower status than men.

The Image of Complementarity and Equality

Several old men, when asked to describe life in a maloca, provided information which questioned the model of pre-mission Arakmbut social organisation mentioned above. Their lists of people living in the malocas demonstrate clearly that men from several clans lived

5. There is no mention of the wambet in this idealised description of the malocas. According to one person from Boca Inambari, the term wambet was first made relevant in Shintuya because the Arakmbut moved out of malocas and began to live in individual houses and so it was necessary to find a social category which would join together people who were separated by the demise of the communal house. However, when Helberg was in Shintuya, he reported (1993) that the term wambet is currently used to refer to the clan (see chapter six). By taking maloca description (Helberg forthcoming) and the discussion of the clan and wambet (Helberg 1993) the result is that Helberg's account is perfectly consistent with an Arakmbut context in which the clan is emphasised.

together under one roof as co-operating affines and that conflicts between brothers sent some men from one communal house to another. People who moved into a maloca group would initially establish themselves in small individual houses outside the main building before moving in and joining the rest of the residential group. Furthermore, in the past, hunters would disappear into the forest for extended periods and build smaller temporary malocas. The significance of this information is that there was a dispersed dimension to life in the malocas, apart from the hierarchical version mentioned above and that in addition, affinal relations co-existed with clan agnates within the same building, providing alternative forms of alliance.

Mythology and ritual provide more evidence that the social organisation of the maloca was not the only model for pre-mission Arakmbut. The relationship between male and female in Arakmbut mythology demonstrates clearly a complementarity between the sexes (discussed in Volume 1, chapter two) through ritual exchanges after marriage and in myths of the Sun and Moon. This counterbalances the view of women as outsiders coming from rival malocas and having a lower status. Similarly, when talking to old men about the initiation rites, it seems that the young men had another perspective. These age groups cut across clan ties and formed small batches of young men who shared the same experience and were connected more by their residential ties to the maloca than by their agnatic connections.

These factors demonstrate that mythologically and ritually, gender complementarity and age-grades can be seen as counteracting the clan-based hierarchical system of the malocas and opened the possibility of a more dispersed system, relying more on affinal relations and equality. It is therefore hard to say that gender complementarity or youth solidarity are factors which the Arakmbut have only developed in the last ten years.

In contrast to the ideal model of maloca life, which relates to the 1980 version of Arakmbut social organisation, it is possible to consider the description of 1992 as consisting of these alternative elements. They were present at the time of the malocas and were expressed mythologically and ritually, constituting an alternative set of organisational principles by which affinity is not dangerous and gender complementarity is a cosmological principle. This alternative is embedded within Arakmbut social relations and presents a more 'egalitarian view' of life than the more 'hierarchical' version based on the clan and wantupa title. The effect is of a system which contains different principles within one framework and which manifests distinct features through history. The features are constituted by different emphasises of the framework reviewed in chapter six, articulated through the encounters described in chapter seven and linked to persons through the qualities covered in chapter eight.[6]

The conclusion here questions the view that Amazonian peoples live in an unchanging world. On the contrary, change is a part of everyday life. However, change in Amazonia need not necessarily be open-ended but operates within a framework established by the people concerned. For example, Arakmbut myths show that too much dispersion and marriage with outsiders who are not Arakmbut (usually represented as toto or animals) can be dangerous. At the same time, we have also seen that too much hierarchy is dangerous. A person who is so powerful that his interests are distinguishable from those of the community can become a sorcerer who threatens the rest of the people.

It is not possible to evaluate whether these changes are cyclical, oscillatory, unidirectional, or random. The reason for this is that changes in the community arise at moments of crisis such as sickness, death, and rivalry over women. Production initiatives, accidents, and threats from the outside can all act as catalysts, questioning the situation in the community at any one time and establishing the criteria through which social life has to be re-interpreted. The re-interpretation and practical revitalisation of Arakmbut social life take place through the processes of shamanic and political practices described in previous chapters.

The result is a multifaceted collage of change, juxtaposing material, social, hermeneutic, and spiritual elements. Rather than reduce change to any one of these factors, the approach here has been to see how they relate. The changes which have occurred in San José between 1980 and 1992 have been the result of many factors which punctuate daily life with illness, death, marriage negotiation, and threats from outside colonists. The next three chapters look at these different factors and evaluate the part they have in community change as a whole.

6. The approach here has certain similarities with the work of Leach (1954), in that the Arakmbut have different aspects of socio-political organisation through which they shift, one of which is more hierarchical than the other. However, there are several differences: the importance of access to resources through knowledge and skill are crucial for the Arakmbut and were ignored by Leach, although taken up by Friedman (1975). The second difference is the importance of process and human activity in the Arakmbut case. The third difference is the importance of history and the presence of colonisation. To a large extent this approach takes its orientation from my work on Nagaland (Gray 1976) and my attempt to see whether that work has any relevance in the Amazon.

Chapter 10

THE COLONIAL CONTEXT OF
SOCIAL CHANGE

The relentless waves of colonisation which have destroyed so many indigenous peoples of the Amazon over the last five hundred years have swept through the territory of the Harakmbut with a vengeance during this century.[1] The devastating effects of contact with the colonial frontier in the Madre de Dios have resulted in massive losses of indigenous life through disease, slavery, and murder since the time of the rubber boom in the 1890s which decimated the Toyeri and Arasaeri. Since then, the upheaval has continued thanks to the boom-and-bust economic cycles of colonisation, which have often left the indigenous peoples of the area at the mercy of powerful forces beyond their control.

Colonisation consists of the invasion of indigenous peoples' territories, attracting them into exploitative economic relationships, political subjugation, and acculturation. The enormous power of the colonisation process creates a temptation for any study of social change, as it offers an account of the internal and external transformations in indigenous communities. However, this explanation effectively makes indigenous peoples appear as silent victims who only respond to change, living in a static, timeless society.

---

1. Ribeiro's work on Brazilian Indians (1970) has been fundamental in the literature, as has Dostal (1972) and Shelton Davis (1977), who have charted the ethnocide and genocide of the indigenous peoples of the Americas. Particularly important have been the IWGIA publications from Copenhagen which, since 1972, have kept up a steady stream of information about the problems facing the peoples of lowland South America.

Clearly colonisation disrupts indigenous peoples' lives enormously, depriving them of their freedoms and resources. The question which this chapter raises is the extent to which responsibilities for the social changes described in the previous chapter can be placed at the feet of the colonial encounter, or whether some of those changes were Arakmbut-induced, although taking place within conditions established through the national society and the international economy. This chapter examines the effects of colonisation on the Arakmbut in several areas: technology, demography, environment, economics, and culture. In each case, the marked influence on community life is tempered by the strategies of the Arakmbut to retain control over their lives.

The Colonial Context

The Arakmbut began working gold in about 1975 through the initiative of young men who had recently completed their secondary education with the help of missionaries, who themselves were renewing ties with the communities which had fled from Shintuya. The community of San José began to wash gold with buckets and sieves at placers on the river banks and, by 1979, San José had bought two motor pumps which enabled each half of the village to do its own gold work. Gradually the miners expanded their work from the beaches to deposits inland left by old rivers.

Old patrons who had been living on the river Karene since the early 1960s were quick to take advantage of the rise in price of gold in the late 1970s. A serious depression within the national economy caused a massive influx of gold miners who made their way down to Madre de Dios, bringing scores of workers from the highlands to mine gold on the rivers. The patrons became mining bosses and, during the 1980s, their relatives moved in to take advantage of the gold and quickly held sway over the Pukiri and Karene rivers downstream from San José. Those who remained in the area have as many as fifty peons working for them in appalling conditions. However the life of a patron also has its drawbacks: two in the Karene were murdered or died in suspicious circumstances in the late 1970s and early 1980s, while armed conflict between colonists setting themselves up in the area takes place regularly.

The peon workers who come to the Madre de Dios are the most numerous of the colonists but they are not the greatest threat to the indigenous people. Traders travel to Cusco and, through the 'enganche' system, offer them a contract to work for ninety days for a patron with free transportation by lorry and river to the Madre de Dios. The workers are usually not paid, work twelve hours a day for six days a week and receive terrible food, mainly plantain soup. Disease is rife and the high number of deaths among workers led to an international scandal during 1991, when several unofficial cemeteries were discovered in Madre de Dios. One of these, belonging to the patron Jaime Sumalave, contained over forty bodies buried over twenty years which, taking into consideration population figures for the area, is twice the death rate in San José. In 1991, several peons escaped from a patron in the Pukiri and provided detailed information on the terrible conditions and instances of child labour.[2]

The main threats to the Arakmbut arose from two sources. First, the old patrons, who had originally been friendly, began to realise that the Arakmbut had rights to resources which they coveted, and relations with the community rapidly deteriorated. Tensions came to a head at the height of the gold rush in 1984-5, when the river Pukiri became a local mining centre. Meanwhile, relatives of the patrons still living in the highlands realised that they could make money quickly and moved down in great numbers from Cusco. By 1986 the Arakmbut were excluded from the Pukiri and their placers on the main Karene river were invaded; although they resisted, they could not stop the ever-increasing invasions (Gray 1986).

During this period, independent miners appeared on the scene who became the second major threat to the Arakmbut. Workers seeking employment and small-scale independent gold miners all rushed to the area during the 1980s and settled in clusters on the Pukiri, both in San José and in Barranco Chico. They formed associations of small miners and established the 'communities' of Boca, Bajo, and Alto Pukiri on indigenous land by applying to the local government at Boca Colorado for financial support. In this way communities of colonists sprang up within the territories of the Arakmbut communities, consisting of poor and mobile workers who shift residence according to the availability of gold and relations with the indigenous communities. With the fluctuation of the gold price, several members of these communities have moved to other parts of the

2. There is a growing literature on the terrible conditions of miners in the Madre de Dios. In 1983 a report by the human rights organisation CODEH-PA drew attention to these abuses, which have been the subject of several articles since (Whittaker 1985; Guillen-Marroquin 1990; Rädda Barnen 1991; Gray 1992). The recent study by Skar (1994) of colonisation from the highlands to the lowlands provides an excellent insight into Andean perspectives of this process.

river, but they still constitute a strong and threatening presence on San José's lands.

From the mid-1980s, the Arakmbut themselves began to employ some highland workers, some of whom had escaped from the slave-like conditions existing in the Pukiri while others were contracted at Boca Colorado. By 1992 there were about twenty-five non-indigenous workers living in camps around the village, some working for indigenous 'patrons' and others working semi-independently because the indigenous patrons had not enough money to pay them.

At the mouth of the river Karene on the river Madre de Dios lies the trading post at Boca Colorado, which grew substantially during the 1980s. By the end of the decade it was recognised as a 'municipality' with a Mayor and Council. Traders are predominantly highland people from Cusco who bring their wares either via Puerto Maldonado to the port of Laberinto on the river Madre de Dios, from where they take a boat to Boca Colorado or via the Cusco-Shintuya road and down the Alto Madre de Dios. The traders sell their wares at the gold camps on the Madre de Dios or else have their own enterprises at specific points on the river, where they have their shops and do some gold work.

The main centre at Boca Colorado was the post of the Banco Minero, which was the only body authorised to buy gold until deregulation in 1991, and the Arakmbut regularly made the two hour trip down to the bank to exchange gold for money and to swap information with the traders about the colonists. Boca Colorado rapidly became the centre of colonial activity in the area and the main opportunity for the Arakmbut to make regular contact with the non-indigenous Peruvian society. In the area of the municipality of the Madre de Dios, which is based at Boca Colorado, there is a group of professionals such as teachers, doctors, and municipal officials such as the state representative local governor ('Teniente Gobernador') and the judge.

The Arakmbut consider that these representatives of the national society treat them with contempt for being indigenous and 'uncivilised'. Occasionally some outsiders have become close to individual members of the community, usually expressed through 'compadrazgo' ties. As was noted in chapter six, this has the effect of dividing loyalties within the community and can hinder unified action on a village level unless the issue is particularly threatening.

At the same time that the over-powering presence of the gold rush increasingly surrounded the Arakmbut, the missions became more active in the community. In 1981, the indigenous schoolteacher realised that he was unable to continue teaching because he was unable to work and carry out the production activities necessary to provide for his large household. Lay missionaries then came to the community to teach. During 1983, two lay missionaries began to reside permanently in the community blending teaching with cate-chisation, a system which is still in operation.

The Dominican priests considered that the escape from the missions in the late 1960s early 1970s had been a major set-back to their programme of 'civilisation'.[3] They had worked gradually throughout the 1970s to restore confidence in their mission through educational services and contacts with community leaders, then, with the lay missionaries' permanent presence, the Dominicans continued their proselytisation policy on a long-term basis. Missionaries have therefore been a consistent influence in San José over the last ten years.

Between 1979 and 1991, there were various visits from anthropologists and members of the Madre de Dios government development corporation (CORDEMAD), who worked on community land titling and raised a political consciousness among the Arakmbut. The influence of these visitors introduced a contrast to the missionary influence among the Arakmbut and provided another perception of the outside world. In 1982 the Federation of the Native Communities of the Amazon (FENAMAD) was established, representing the indigenous communities of the Madre de Dios.

The contrasting influence of the Dominicans and the Native Federation has presented a schismatic rivalry for influence in the community. Whereas the priests provide primary education, the Native Federation provides grants for secondary and tertiary education. The Native Federation is a political body advocating indigenous rights to territory and defence against invasions of colonists, while the mission tries to remain independent from conflicts with colonists. A similar approach has been noted with the Protestant Summer Institute of Linguistics in Puerto Alegre in 1973 (Moore 1979).

Various researchers visiting the Arakmbut in San José (Gray, Aikman, Rummenhöller, Lazarte, and Monnier) have shared the emphasis on indigenous rights to territories and self-determination advocated by the native organisation. However, in comparison with the missionaries, the researchers are present in the communities for short periods. Although the presence of FENAMAD is not as all-embracing as that of the mission, the organisation has succeeded in

3. Several articles have been written concerning this period of missionary history (see Monnier 1982), and Ricardo Alvarez in Torralba (1979).

providing support and advice for the communities of the Madre de Dios, particularly through the technical services of the Eori Centre, an environmental development non-governmental organisation based in Puerto Maldonado.

These are the influences from the non-Arakmbut world which have affected the people of San José over the last ten to fifteen years. Looking at the long-term effects of colonisation, five areas are significant in understanding the features of social change reviewed in the last chapter: technological, demographic, environmental, economic, and cultural.

Technological Change

The social effects of technological change have been marked in San José. When the Arakmbut were first in contact with metal technology in the 1950s, the old men say that a substantial change took place in the style of creating gardens (tamba). Working in the tamba has always been seen as the hardest work *(e'mba'a)* and before missionary contact, cutting a tree could take the best part of a day as opposed to an hour or less now. The intense warfare which took place between the different Harakmbut groups prior to contact with the missions were frequently conflicts to obtain metal tools. (Other reasons were territorial invasion and raiding for women.)

The men in the mission used the time saved with the new metal technology to work for the priests in their gardens, and depending on the priest in charge they would sometimes be paid for this labour. Over the years, working for cash became an increasing aspect of the subsistence economy of the Arakmbut. Salt, sugar, oil, and beer were staples for a household, and so a gradual shift of emphasis took place whereby the market economy became essential for the daily life of the Arakmbut.

With the introduction of gold into the Arakmbut economy, the reliance on money became ever more prominent. Whereas in 1980 salt, sugar, and oil were luxuries which each family bought when available, by 1985 they were essentials and part of the 'subsistence' economy along with meat, yuca, and plantains (Gray 1986). This meant that gaining money in the form of gold (people in the Madre de Dios often buy goods directly in gold) became essential motives for Arakmbut daily labour.

The technology of working gold played a part in this change because it facilitated an increase in production. The simplest way to wash gold is by means of a sieve and bucket, which is very labour-intensive and time-consuming. In San José, the first work was of this type, but production increased with the introduction of two gold pumps which had been bought on extended loan via the mission in 1980. The arrangements for the loan had been organised by the young leaders of the community, who were eager to take advantage of the new technology.

The community organised gold washing around the two pumps on alternative gold placers at Santa Rosa, the mining area situated a few bends down from San José. The effect of San José owning two motor pumps reinforced the community's spatial division into two halves, as the Wakutangeri (dominated by the Idnsikambo) worked with one and the Kotsimberi (mostly Yaromba) worked with the other. The result was that two halves of the community, each one dominated by a clan, clustered around the motor pumps in order to work gold. The men who were considered to be wantupa during this period were influential in the community and were also responsible for the relationship with the mission which had provided the pumps.

The competition between these wantupa increased when they wanted to buy pumps for the use of their own household groups, with the aim of increasing their profits. During this period there were conflicts in the community when certain households began to gain more than others as a result of using their own pumps; this increased when the young men first used highland workers in their placers. However, the importance of generosity as a basis for prestige eventually evened out the economic discrepancies in the community and others in the community gradually took up the new initiatives.

The new initiatives in San José were taken on by enterprising young men, usually (but not exclusively) those recognised as leaders, and that new technology was tried and tested before being taken up by the others. The young leadership took economic risks with the gold technology, which added to their prestige when they shared it, but which contributed to the conflict in the community when they did not. This approach can be seen as the young political leaders acting as a barrier to the forces of colonisation – on the one hand taking advantage of the new technology, but also showing, by example, the problems which can arise.

Twelve years later, the benefits of the gold had reached San José in terms of the availability of mining technology, and each household work group found that it could afford a motor pump. The community had become organised into twelve work groups which related to extended families (the closest active members of a wambet), each of which had by now been able to buy its own small motor pump and was mining either on its own or with a small number of workers from the highlands on a particular beach or inland deposit.

The work groups thus organised themselves around access to motor pumps, which raised the question whether the availability of the appropriate technology for gold mining determined the nature of the social work groups using them. The change of emphasis from clan to wambet, which we noted in the previous chapter, can be explained as resulting from the rise in gold profits enabling households to buy motor pumps thereby increasing the number of working groups from two, based on clan dominance, to the twelve smaller household and alliance groups based on more bilateral wambet ties. Similarly, with each small working group operating with a pump, there was limited scope for young men to demonstrate their initiative and responsibility in gold work.

The increase in profits from the gold making motor pumps accessible to each household has taken place not only in San José but also in Puerto Luz and Boca Inambari, where a similar increase in mining groups had taken place over the last twelve years. However, the changes in San José and Puerto Luz have taken different forms. In Puerto Luz the gold mining model has been based largely on co-operation in the gardens, where the men do the clearing and the women hold the tubes for the water pumps when washing the gold. In San José women rarely participate in the gold washing process, and only a few occasionally help their husbands if they consider that times are hard. Usually the women remain in the community with the children and work in the gardens. In San José the model is primarily one of hunting where the men go out on expeditions to find the gold deposit and then in small groups co-operate to collect the gold. This difference shows that the technology in itself can be present in the context of change but it does not enable us to predict the way in which the conceptualisation of the changes will be expressed through social behaviour.

The increased availability of motor pumps has definitely affected the work groups in San José and other Arakmbut communities and can account for the shift in leadership style. However, this does not mean that the technology itself determined the change. The increased production from the two pumps in 1980 does not provide any evidence to indicate the basis on which the work groups would be organised in subsequent years. Instead of working on a basis of clan or wambet units, it would have been just as possible for the Arakmbut to work in the form of a village co-operative, pooling a proportion of their takings to buy an electric light system or build a new school, or keeping a number of pumps limited to community needs.

The dispersion of the community was a process whereby the Arakmbut decided to use their money to support smaller household work units. This decision was not determined by the technology itself, but consisted of utilising the opportunity offered by the possibility of buying pumps. Technological availability and social change are thus connected but not necessarily linked causally.

Demographic Change

The twelve years of gold rush have had several consequences for San José. In 1980 there were about a hundred workers and patrons on San José's land; by 1985 this had increased to three hundred and by 1990 had risen to five hundred while the community population remained at 150. The repercussions of having so many people on their land turned the Arakmbut from a majority on their own territory in the late 1960s to a minority twenty years later. The occupation by colonists means that the lands have to support almost four times the population of the village.

The number of colonists fluctuates according to the time of year, with considerably more highlanders coming down to the Karene area during the dry season. At this time the gold-bearing beaches are exposed and hold the deposits left by the silty waters of the floods from the previous rainy season.

The reaction of the Arakmbut to the increase in colonisation was not to move away. On several occasions during the twelve years under review, the community of San José resisted the encroachment of colonisation in order to assert their claim over their gold resources. This resistance met with varying success. In the initial period of the gold rush, when the two political blocks of the community were in agreement, the Arakmbut were effective in expelling invaders. For example, in 1981, the Montecarlo company entered San José's territory and, after a month's negotiations by the young leaders, were persuaded to leave. As the colonists were relatively new and there was no non-indigenous support for them, the Arakmbut had the upper hand.

By 1985, the gold rush was at its height. The main patron in the area was Jaime Sumalave and the conflict with San José was far more drawn out and intense (Gray 1986). Sumalave had invaded the mining area known as Santa Rosa and in retaliation the community had expelled his workers from the area. The leadership was effective, but in order to back up their actions, they had to confront armed guards and a Justice of the Peace brought by Sumalave from Puerto Maldonado. Furthermore, the leaders of the community had to go to Puerto Maldonado to denounce the actions of Sumalave to the authorities.

The murder of a young Arakmbut man in 1986, death threats to the leadership of San José, and a mass invasion by eight members of the family of the patron 'Pinto' Bejar with all their workers, made the Pukiri a no-go area. The power of San José's leadership was weakening, and for a period, the community chose younger men as President, which diverted attention from the previous wantupas' growing impotence in the face of violent confrontation.

By 1992, Bajo Pukiri and Boca Pukiri contained about a hundred colonists in all and they were receiving support from the municipality, in spite of being illegal settlements. The new leadership tried to arouse the community, but many felt that defence was hopeless and became resigned to their fate. The Arakmbut still had fight left in them, however, and in 1992, they managed to expel a heavily armed German colonist from their lands and attack Boca Colorado to claim the resources for their school. Nevertheless, the mobilisation took considerable effort, lasting six months, and was not as immediate and effective as that of twelve years previously. The youth of the leaders and the lack of wantupa in 1992 reflects the increasing pressure against San José and the impossible odds against which they were trying to defend their community.

A related consequence of the decreasing power of the leadership in the community has led to another focus of conflict which has increasingly occurred with the school. In education the increasing presence of the lay missionaries in the community is all-pervasive, while the national curriculum does not take local factors into consideration and ignores rainforest peoples altogether. The school is an 'outside' institution that exists within the community, with Spanish-speaking teachers provided by the national society and the missionaries. The Arakmbut see education as a means sent from outside to provide information for those who need to learn the ways of the non-indigenous society and tap into its power.

The relationship between teachers and the Arakmbut is difficult. Parents who have been through the educational system are on the whole the most co-operative, as are those who have high expectations for their children. The main problems, however, have been with the young adults, particularly the leaders, who regularly find themselves in conflict with the teachers over community matters.

This is because teachers in the Amazon are considered responsible by the authorities for certain activities in the community, such as the distribution of food or medicines from outside. This comes into direct conflict with the young leaders, who consider that their position is to represent the community to the external authorities. This came to a head in 1992, when two experienced teachers were forced to move elsewhere because of differences with the young leadership. The effect has been that as the young leadership has found dealing with the external colonists more difficult, they have focused their activities on the representatives of the outside world living within the community.

The weakening of the leadership in the face of the increasing numbers and power of the colonists is another factor showing how outside influence has affected the Arakmbut's capacity to defend themselves. The community's political leadership continues to act as a barrier between San José and the colonising frontier, but over the period under review, self-defence has become ever more difficult.

Environmental Change

Ascertaining the extent of the depletion of resources as a result of colonisation is difficult, but certain patterns can be gained by observing hunting methods, places of work, and the impressions of the community. The amount of hunted meat and fish has decreased between 1980 and 1992 by about a third.[4] Furthermore, hunters take much more time and travel longer distances before finding any prey than twelve years ago. Although the people still go to salt licks (sorok) to kill their animals, those hunting closer to the community have few opportunities for a successful hunt. Instead, hunters have to go to the furthest part of the territory to seek prey at the more distant salt licks.

During the first years of gold production in San José, the working groups mined at places which were within an hour of the community and could return at nights. Between 1980 and 1981, the camps of

---

4. Estimating the decrease in meat between 1980 and 1992 is difficult because the household where I ate had a hunter who made a great point of preserving the old values and spent much time in the forest. He was an excellent hunter and the amount of meat consumed was not appreciably less in quantity than twelve years previously. This was not the case with other households, in which the men who spent more time working gold and were not prepared to take so much time for hunting.

Santa Rosa and Chapahal were more distant, and during the period of Psyche's death the community lived apart from the village settlement. During the middle of the 1980s, when the Pukiri was available for gold, the Arakmbut went in large family groups and worked in areas a few hundred yards inland from the beaches. The deposits in the Pukiri were used by the people of San José until 1987, when the family of the patron Mateo Bejar began to assert their desire to control the Pukiri from within the boundaries of San José to just before its confluence with the Karene. They were prepared to divide the zone with the other patrons of the area and edge the Arakmbut from their territory. After threats and the death of one of the community in 1986, the Arakmbut retreated from the Pukiri, but meanwhile other colonists had invaded both Santa Rosa and Chapahal. The beaches and environs of the Karene and Pukiri were gradually falling to the hands of the colonists, to the extent that by 1992 the Arakmbut only had access to one third of their gold-producing beaches.

Throughout the years 1987 to 1990 the community had to look further afield for their gold deposits and by 1991 several men were working at the 'cumbre', which was on the watershed between the Karene and Pukiri rivers, about two hours walk inland from the community. Others worked at camps in the headwaters of the Mbaraiwe river, which lies about two hours walk downstream from San José. Over the years the Arakmbut have extended their gold working areas ever further away from the village of San José and the encroaching colonists, but all gold camps are temporary.

The families which moved upstream in 1990 moved permanently. They worked gold and hunted in the upper part of San José's territory and so by moving away they have reduced the distance between their houses and the gold camps while providing them with access to new beaches more distant from the colonists, who are mainly downriver. Furthermore, the new houses are closer to the salt licks for hunting, which ensures the men of the households a more regular supply of meat than for the people living in San José village.

The residential patterns of San José have been affected by the increased presence of colonists who took over the gold deposit areas downstream from San José and, through their mining activities, have frightened away animals which the Arakmbut hunt. The environmental pressure caused by the great influx of colonists in the 1980s forced difficult conditions on the community, encouraging the men to move ever further afield to obtain their basic resources of gold or meat and making some households decide to move into areas where life was less troublesome.

Another element which relates to the movement of the Arakmbut comes from the introduction of pigs in the mid-1980s which they purchased at Boca Colorado. Unlike chickens and ducks, which the Arakmbut look after with a minimal amount of interference in daily life, the pigs were a nuisance. Running loose through the community, churning up mud and depositing excrement, the pigs caused increasing irritation and concern for hygiene. The presence of the pigs was one of the reasons given by the households which moved upstream, and the same explanation is given by Arakmbut for a parallel dispersion of households in Boca del Inambari and Puerto Luz at the same period, when, coincidentally, pigs were also introduced. The domestication of pigs has thus been a factor in the physical dispersion of the Arakmbut communities, although access to hunting grounds and gold deposits are probably more significant reasons for moving.

From the perspective of the gold rush, the dispersion of the activities of the community between 1980 and 1992 was a direct response to the influences of colonists from outside. Whether they were encroaching on Arakmbut resources and forcing them to seek subsistence activities further afield or whether they were responsible for introducing new initiatives in herding (pigs) which called for more individual space, the effect of the colonising frontier has been considerable. The decrease in resources is a direct result of the increasing presence of the colonising frontier on San José's territory. However, the Arakmbut themselves do not explicitly refer to this connection; they see the availability of resources dwindling and the increasing presence of colonists as parallel events which occur without any apparent explanation and just have to be accepted.

The expansion of the power of the colonists has also resulted in a parallel decrease in the strength of community mobilisation. However, colonisation does not explain everything. For example, it does not necessarily explain why some households remained in San José, some moved a short way from the centre of the village, and others moved one hour's walk upstream. Similarly, the changing of the leadership in the face of colonisation does not account for why younger leaders should be chosen, as opposed to other adult men. As with the technological and demographic factors, the expansion of colonisation and the resulting decrease in resources provided conditions which influenced shifts in work and residence patterns for the Arakmbut, but the way in which the members of the community decided to alter their lifestyle was not determined by these factors.

Economic Change

The colonising frontier has also brought other influences into the orbit of the native community which, to a varying extent, have affected Arakmbut social and political life: the colonists, the missions, and those supporting indigenous rights. These influences brought innovationswhich have had an effect on the socio-cultural life of the community. A major change which has occurred after increasing contact with the colonists at Boca Colorado has been the use of gold and money within San José. The effect of gold and money has been to place fixed values on certain commodities. To some extent the payment for services or goods has introduced some aspects of individualism into the community and some Arakmbut have more outside workers and make larger profits than others. Those Arakmbut with more resources occasionally sell capital materials such as extra tubes for pumping water to the others. One man, who prefers working wood than working gold, has made money from constructing beds for most of the community households, while others hire out their motor saws to cut wood for houses. A new house style has consequently arisen, with walls made from planks of wood rather than the stripped trunks of the pona tree.

Related to the increase of money in the community has been the appearance of small stores selling drink and groceries for gold or money. This has institutionalised the exchange of commodities at fixed rates within the community, yet in San José the effect has been largely positive in that it has stopped traders from visiting the community to sell goods and has given the members of Puerto Luz, the community living upstream, a reason to return regularly to San José to buy goods and petrol and to drink with their friends and relatives.

In San José, the introduction of gold and money has not fundamentally affected the social relations which already exist in the community. The goods and services which money buys come from the outside, and the barrier between the two worlds still largely preserves untouched the internal distribution of food and beer. Even the people who sell beer from their shops have to distribute some of the profits to the drinkers or to the community as a whole. The conclusion here is that the reaction of a particular people or community to the introduction of money is determined by socio-cultural and historical conditions (Parry & Bloch 1989: 28). Indeed, the use of money is not standard in all Arakmbut communities.

However, whereas money has not led to the break-up of community life as a whole, it has compounded the detrimental effect on the position of women. Prior to the period in the mission, women were responsible for making beer from maize (wawing) but while at Shintuya, the priests prohibited the manufacture of beer. When the Arakmbut reconstructed their community life, they began to use gold and money to buy bottled beer. This meant that women were not reinstated as responsible for the production and distribution of the most prestigious commodity in the community.

The effect has been to shift the focus of the principle of generosity through beer distribution in San José. The period in the 1980s when the leadership of the community provided large parties was coterminous with a lessening of the public presence of women. However, with the decreasing resources and the dispersal of the community, the means to demonstrate generosity has been reduced. This is particularly apparent in the availability of gold or money for beer. As beer is the main means of distributing wealth, the reduced resources have meant a smaller number of fiestas and opportunities to redistribute a surplus. This has occurred at the time when the leaders of the community command less influence than in 1980, and a time when women have reasserted their position to some extent in public life.

Cultural Change

The cultural changes in San José during the period between 1980 and 1992 have been far less apparent. A breadth and variety of interpretation has always existed within an Arakmbut community, as was demonstrated in the case studies of the death of Psyche and the cure of the young Idnsikambo man described earlier. For this reason, a multiplicity of ideas and opinions easily co-existed within San José.

The Arakmbut have a culturally refined view of the visible and invisible worlds which need not change its content substantially in relation to social changes. Cultural changes appear through the way in which information is expressed; for example, spirits in 1992 appeared less tied to clans but more to a hunter and his work associates as the wambet became more dominant in the community. Sorcery accusations within the community were more numerous during the more violent periods of the early 1980s than in the more peaceful times of the 1990s, when alliances came to the fore. However the content of sorcery and spirit ideas did not change substantially over the twelve-year period. Sorcery is still considered to come from neighbouring communities and other indigenous peoples in the area, while the association of a hunter with the ndakyorokeri in contact with certain species remains unchanged.

Cultural influences from the national society affect people in San José in different ways. From the time of missionary contact the Arakmbut have changed visible aspects of their culture. The demise of the maloca, with its ceremonies, body paintings, feathered costumes, and dances, occurred within only a few years of arriving in Shintuya and the adoption of individual houses. The gradual popularity of house styles similar to those of colonists, with their ubiquitous corrugated iron roofs, has led to the replacement of older styles which used materials exclusively from the rainforest.

From time to time an itinerant trader with a video machine comes to San José to show films ranging from 'Rambo' and 'Commando' to 'Aliens' or 'Tarzan'. The changes in musical taste brought about by the use of tape-recorders and radios have involved other cultural innovations. Dances in San José are held with Peruvian rainforest music played on cassettes. The radio is now more frequently listened to for international and national news, a variety of music, and commentary.

The Arakmbut have reacted to the encroachment of an alien culture by a two-way process which obscures the visible elements of their own culture and places external influences into discretely separate contexts of communal entertainment. The Arakmbut thus internalise their own culture without necessarily incorporating destructive external elements and consequently form a barrier between themselves and the national society. For this reason, the lay missionaries and priests have not been able to destroy the most deeply held aspects of Arakmbut religion. One Dominican missionary considers that, in spite of forty years' proselyting, the Christianity encountered among the Arakmbut is skin deep and their own religion is resilient and thriving (Padre Mixtel Fernández pers. comm.). By revealing little of their own culture and religion to outsiders, the Arakmbut preserve their view of the universe by erecting a 'barrier' between their world and the outside. The protective barrier is present in medicine, where the Arakmbut divide sicknesses and medicine from the Christian God with the more dangerous attacks from their invisible spirits.

The Arakmbut speak their own language in all contexts in community life – whether at meetings, at work, or in the household. This helps them defend themselves from some of the ethnocidal consequences arising from state education. As long as the Arakmbut control this relationship between internal and external education, it is possible to protect the indigenous transference of knowledge while taking advantage of the opportunity to learn how to manage in the national society (Aikman 1994). Indigenous values and culture are thus kept separate from what goes on in the school, and the community provides little support for the teachers, who are assumed to bring and impart knowledge from outside of their own good will.

The Arakmbut consequently defend their culture by internalising it and separating it from outside influences. Whereas this has lead to the disappearance of many ceremonies and communal activities, it has effectively preserved their innermost spiritual practices. The Arakmbut who are most responsible for this internalisation are the shamanic practitioners who decide whom they will inform about the spirit world.

This should not give the impression that the Arakmbut are not under considerable threat from the influence of external cultures. In several communities, elders complain of an increasingly dissolute youth who have opted out of school and take no interest in their culture. Their interest is in following trends from the local towns, rejecting their cultural identity. Whereas they are not influential now, the future is uncertain. The increasing desire of young Arakmbut to marry outsiders also constitutes an ethnocidal threat.

The presence of non-indigenous people working in the community as peons for a small wage has brought the outside world of the highlands in direct contact with the Arakmbut. The Arakmbut are on the whole reluctant to reveal their own culture to outsiders, and there has been a consequent reduction in the evening sessions and opportunities for story-telling or singing between 1980 and 1992. The Arakmbut have not stopped telling stories and singing, but are more inclined to do these things in the privacy of the home rather than in open sessions. The limiting of story- and myth-telling, songs, and curing to household activities is another example of the reduction in scale of social encounters, as the smaller wambet alliances groups transmit cultural information more than the larger groups which used to meet in the evenings in 1980 and 1981, when the clans were more dominant.

The breaking down of the means of cultural transmission among the Arakmbut over the last ten years parallels the shift from the clan to the wambet and the dispersion of gold mining production into smaller household and alliance units. The telling of stories indoors continues a process of 'internalising' Arakmbut cosmology in order to protect them from the destructive consequences of outsiders refusing to treat their invisible world with respect.

The only times when the barrier has shown signs of weakening has been with inter-marriage between Arakmbut men and women from the highlands. Unlike the Matsigenka or other indigenous women who have settled with Arakmbut men, highland women do not learn the Harakmbut language, and consequently their children and the household become Spanish-language oriented. The implication of this in the long term is that the strong monolingual defence of Arakmbut culture from within may begin to break down, threatening their world-view.

However, there is another interaction between the Arakmbut and the outside world which might make the barrier less necessary. While highlanders have moved into households in San José, several Arakmbut students from the community have reached the heart of the outside world by participating in university courses in Lima, where they are in close contact with international and national organisations of the indigenous movement. The respect for these Arakmbut students in Arakmbut communities has introduced a different perspective on the indigenous struggle where, rather than constructing a defensive barrier against the outside world, the strategy for survival consists of the revaluation of culture, confidence in traditions, and the assertion of fundamental rights.

In conclusion, it is possible to see three ways in which the Arakmbut have reacted to external influences from outside:

1. External Elements Substituted for Internal

Where elements of pre-missionary Arakmbut socio-cultural life have disappeared, outside influences have provided alternatives. Examples range from metal tools replacing stone ones after contact with the missionaries to Arakmbut ritual. With the demise of the maloca, singing and dancing at fiestas, which formed an important ceremonial part of festive life, have been replaced by rainforest rock music and beer. Similarly, the age-grade ceremonies have disappeared, but the terms are still used and less formalised methods are used to indicate maturity such as education level and military conscription.

2. Internalisation and Barrier Formation

As the Arakmbut realised in the mission that their cosmology and religion were ridiculed, they internalised them. The effect was to create a barrier between inside and outside. The distinction is particularly noticeable in education and schooling as well as health.

The Arakmbut not only internalise some of their ways of life through secrecy, but also by keeping the passing of information within the household. Recently, story-telling within the house and preserving the Arakmbut language have been the means of retaining their integrity. The people have been able to conceal important elements of their life from those who do not respect it. However, to those genuinely interested, Arakmbut elders will talk openly. Money is used inside the community, but rarely, if ever, for internal goods and services, so it does not affect the 'barrier'.

The overall effect is the construction of a barrier between the Arakmbut and non-indigenous domains which is strictly controlled by the community. This does not mean that it is impassable, only that the Arakmbut are the gate-keepers. In fact the 'barrier' should be seen more as a flexible process of protection, rather than a fixed never-changing chasm between inside and outside. On the whole, it is the shamanic leaders who are responsible for this internalisation of Arakmbut culture because they are responsible for telling the stories and projecting the information to a community audience.

3. Breaking the Barrier

The barrier is weakened by the ethnocidal effects of non-indigenous men and women marrying into the community, although until now they have not remained long enough to have had a detrimental effect. However, the barriers can also disappear when people have the confidence that they can defend themselves culturally and socially in the face of an over-powering external world. The Arakmbut students' confidence in their culture in the face of outsiders is reinforced by the knowledge that they have more education than those who try to denigrate them, such as the patrons or non-indigenous workers.

Furthermore, the students in Lima have had the effect of reinforcing cultural values through a cultural strengthening project. Fortified by this project, the people of Boca Inambari are considering starting up the old ceremonies once more under the influence of a university student from the community (Sueyo 1995).

The social changes which have taken place in San José, such as the shift from clan to wambet and the dispersion of the community settlement, can be connected to a multitude of factors which are triggered by the conditions of colonisation: technological, demographic, environmental, economic, and cultural. Whereas there have been enormous socio-economic threats arising from the colonising frontier, the Arakmbut have, on the whole, been able to defend their culture from unwanted outside influences between 1980 and 1992. Part of the reason for this has been that most of the ethnocidal effects of colonisation took place at the beginning of the period at Shintuya mission.

This is not to say that the colonising frontier has not affected the Arakmbut. The encroachment of individualism and the presence of non-indigenous colonists within the communities' territories have established a permanent threat to the capacity of the Arakmbut to survive as a people in the future. The plundering of indigenous resources, the discrimination from outsiders which weakens their confidence in their culture, and the threats against their lives are a constant reminder of their need to defend themselves. The details of this confrontation with the colonising frontier is the point of departure for Volume 3.

This chapter has demonstrated that colonisation affects fundamental aspects of production and social organisation for the Arakmbut, but the way in which the community realigns itself in defence against outside threats is not determined by the frontier itself. The changes which have taken place over the last ten years have been influenced dramatically by the colonisation, but have been decided not by outsiders but by the Arakmbut. The Arakmbut social formation still retains its framework within which all occurs, enabling the people to be self-determining and to retain their sense of identity as Arakmbut. However, factors of colonisation have been instrumental in the changes that have taken place and have provided the conditions within which the Arakmbut have altered their social organisation, a subject which is reviewed in the following chapter.

Throughout this chapter the importance of Arakmbut political organisation has been apparent in the prominence of the young leaders in trying to defend their community from the ravages of colonisation while incorporating those aspects of life which they see as positive. However, the young leaders are only apparent because they are thrust into the public political space. The older men, those with shamanic experience, and the women are all involved in community change. The colonisation frontier on its own has not conquered the Arakmbut and has not changed their world beyond recognition. Indeed, as long as the their socio-cultural system does not change out of recognition, they will survive; but the boundaries are fragile and by no means impervious.

Chapter 11

INTERNAL FACTORS
IN SOCIO-POLITICAL CHANGE

A rakmbut social life does not merely change in response to outside influences, but operates in terms of its own internal dynamics which affect both community life and resistance to the process of colonisation. The changes which took place in San José between 1980 and 1992 may have been triggered by developments such as improved gold mining techniques or the encroachment of colonists on Arakmbut territory, but these factors cannot account for the shifts in emphasis between different social principles such as from clan to wambet or from a relative hierarchy to a more egalitarian system.

This chapter looks into the way in which Arakmbut social life is in constant flux and yet changes within certain consistent limits. The flexible and relativistic social organisation described in chapter six does not in itself provide any clues as to how different elements of social organisation relate, yet the changes between 1980 and 1992 show that there are clear correlations. Chapter eight outlined how several clusters of social features underwent parallel changes during this period: an emphasis on clan, gender inequality, respect for age, and 'hierarchy' was replaced by a greater emphasis on affinity, the wambet kindred, age solidarity, and a more 'egalitarian' ethos.

The Arakmbut conceptualise the impulse of change as arising from growth *(e'kerek),* which is a fundamental process affecting everyone in their personal lives and the community as a whole.[1]

---

1. Although it might be possible to look at this change from childhood to maturity and old age as part of a 'domestic cycle', this would be inaccurate. The domestic cycle of the Arakmbut is primarily about the life of members of a household

Change takes place as a result of time passing (*e'pogika* – 'it always passes'), and as people grow older they not only alter physically, but their relationships and responsibilities undergo substantial changes. Gradually throughout life each Arakmbut's social field constantly expands. At different moments of growth, however, each person is confronted with certain choices or decisions (*matamona*) which can cumulatively affect the potential for change within the community. For example, the choice of marriage partner, post-marital residence, and the organisation of daily activities all involve options which can influence the complexion of the community as a whole.

These choices cover a multitude of different aspects of life, but of particular significance are questions relating to the joining together and separation of households. Several words cover this notion. The first is 'marriage' (*e'toepak*), which is taken from *e'toe*, 'to grasp', with the verbalising particle pak. The other verb is *e'mbet*, which means 'stuck together', from which comes the word wambet. In contrast, the term for 'to divide up' or to 'distribute' is *e'mbayok*. The principles of desire and giving are thus drawn into these important concepts which are based on processes of conjunction and separation which cover material goods as well as social principles.

Until now, the description of Arakmbut community life has been based primarily on notions of flexibility, relativity, generosity, and conflict resolution, thereby giving the impression that the multi-lay ered social organisation runs smoothly. However, encounters can aggravate as well as resolve problems, which can recur on a regular basis to such an extent that there are certain 'fault lines' which run through Arakmbut community life upon which moments of social tension are regular occurrences.[2]

---

from birth to the establishment of an independent unit after marriage, but throughout this period, the main changes within the household cannot be seen separately from the relationships with other households within the community. As households grow and decline at different rates, the effect of each change on the community at large is difficult to ascertain. To talk of a 'domestic cycle' gives the impression of a repetitive form of change which recurs through each generation, forming a neatly balanced life. For the Arakmbut this is not the case; the world is, on the contrary, unbalanced.

2.   These distinctions could be termed 'contradictions' in the sense that they pull the Arakmbut in different directions, but they are not necessarily contradictions in a strict dialectical sense, in which an antithesis resolves with the thesis at another level of analysis. The term contradiction, however, has several meanings. On the one hand, it is a sort of negative, which implies a type of 'irrational' event. On the other hand, in the Engels sense the term contradiction implies the 'negation of a negation', which is something positive. The sense of contradiction is used

At certain moments in Arakmbut life, conflicts can have repercussions throughout the community unless they are identified and brought under control. These are particularly apparent at times of crisis such as illness, death, or problems over marriage arrangements, when the intensity of social relationships makes interpretation particularly sensitive. Whereas change takes place all of the time, at these 'crisis moments', such as in the case studies reviewed earlier, whole features of political life come into focus, expressing the intricate complexities of Arakmbut social organisation.

The Arakmbut see this tension in terms of negative relationships between people – *ioknda* (anger) and *mepuk* (fear – literally 'liver-split') and, in serious cases, ochinosik (hatred – 'concentrated black centre'). The generalised term for this is *pakwe* (dislike), which is the corollary of the verb e'pak which was glossed earlier as 'desire'. The word has a broad set of connotations covering not just lack of desire, but also embarrassment and awkwardness. These negative relations occur at moments of tension within Arakmbut social life.

If there are problems between Arakmbut, factors such as affinity, age or residence are drawn into the relationship. Husband and wife, old and young, competitive brothers or affines can all be the locus of conflict and the critical events arising from these uncertain relationships serve as subject matter for social encounters, punctuating the rhythm of daily life in the community. The effect is an uneasy balance which is constantly in danger of becoming out of control. Should people go beyond these possibilities, serious problems arise and one party may decide to leave the community.

The changes in social organisation which occurred in San José between 1980 and 1992 were primarily based on decisions made by members of the community or through reactions to particular events which were beyond their control. The focus of decision-making in Arakmbut communities surrounds potential or actual marriage arrangements. The main principles of Arakmbut life – gender, age, residence, descent, and affinity – are all affected by decisions about marriage. Choice of spouse, negotiations over residence, the appro-

---

here more in this sense. However, the 'negation of a negation' implies that somehow there is always a positive step forward or a resolution. But resolution is not inevitable and a tension often prevents a permanent resolution. In this sense, social change for the Arakmbut is never fully resolved but only a temporary solution to problems. The distinctions here are constantly playing against each other within Arakmbut social life and provide the cause of many tense relations, for which reason the term 'tension' is more appropriate as it does not imply an assumed resolution.

priate behaviour of the couple, relations between parents and children, and the implications for clan and wambet relationships all involve decisions. These decisions inter-connect and their cumulative consequences can affect the community as a whole.

In addition to delicate decisions, crisis moments can give rise to an intensity of social relationships which, as with the case studies reviewed in chapters one and five, bring whole features of political life into focus and express the intricate complexities of Arakmbut social organisation. Some periods are more conducive to the more hierarchical structure observed in 1980, others to the more dispersed egalitarian system described in 1992. This can be illustrated by looking at different periods of life and showing how relationships spread throughout the community during adulthood and where certain social fault-lines can become prominent.

Marriage Prospects – Competition for Spouses

With the exception of Puerto Luz, all the Arakmbut communities suffer from a demographic pattern where there are discernably fewer women than men. In 1980, of the marriageable young people in San José, two thirds were men, while in 1992 an increase of young women who had grown up in the intervening years decreased the imbalance to 60 percent men and 40 percent women (see demographic pyramid). Unfortunately, the increase in potential wives has been offset by highland workers in the community, three of whom have lived with young Arakmbut women, abandoning them with children who are not recognised as Arakmbut because of the patrilineal clan system.

Men consider that there is a shortage of women in San José and competition for wives is a long-term struggle. Even in those communities where the ratio of men to women is more balanced, suitors from other communities also act as limiting factors to the availability of future wives. Of all the tensions within Arakmbut communities, those surrounding marriage arrangements are the greatest because of all activities in the life cycle of the Arakmbut, finding an appropriate spouse is the most difficult.

The weakest point in relationships between young men lies with those of similar ages who share the same potential marriage partners, thereby establishing a competitive element in their relationship which covers everything from their hunting ability to knowledge about the invisible world. Rivalries between siblings are usually

Figure 11.1 A population pyramid for San José, 1986-1988

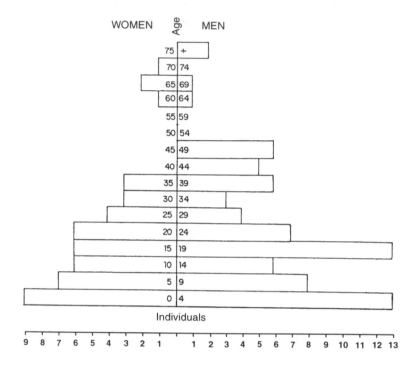

Source: Rummenhöller, Cardenas - Lazarte, 1991.

contained within the house, but they become more open between young men of different households trying to compete for the attentions of a young woman. In December 1993, two young men who were mother's sister's (MZ) children to each other fought fiercely at a fiesta over an apparently trivial issue when one mocked the other for wearing old-fashioned clothes and not keeping up with the contemporary Peruvian styles. However, beneath this aggression was a rivalry over their capacity to attract women, because fashionable clothes are expensive and reflect successful gold production. The close relatives of both young men quickly entered the fray and separated them, however, before the conflict spread to other households.

Problems internal to the household arise primarily between men who are rivals with their brothers for women and with fathers who are reluctant to encourage their sons to assert their adulthood at too young an age, for their own physical safety (see myth of Chipomeme,

Volume 1, chapter six). Throughout this period, young men and women refer to each other primarily by kin terms and, as far as possible, suppress reference to potential affinity. This effectively blurs the distinction between clans and avoids publicly drawing attention to eligible partners for marriage.

The tensions surrounding potential marriage partners are thus either kept within the household or quickly smothered by close relatives of the rivals. Young men competing for women should try to prevent the problem from affecting more than the immediate people concerned, but as soon as the parents of two couples and their wambet begin to discuss a possible union in earnest, the possibility of an expansion of the tension increases considerably.

Negotiations for marriage are fraught with diplomatic pitfalls into which insensitive members of a household can speedily stumble. The imbalance of men and women means that as marriage negotiations become more open, the possibilities of conflict between households increase. Thus internal household conflicts become less apparent as tensions arise between potential affines during marriage negotiations.

Women are extremely important in marriage negotiations. Although the decision is made by the wambet of both parties, the evaluation is a constant activity. Discussions over the relative merits or defects of a suitor take place in the household and women's working groups, consisting of an evaluation of his hunting ability, success at gold work, the length of his education and the relationship between the parents through clan and residential group as well as whether there are any signs of sexual malpractice in his antecedents. A prospective young wife will give her preferences for certain men and gradually an acceptable suitor emerges and discussions take place between wambet. The key persons in marriage negotiations are the mothers of the couple, whose encyclopedic knowledge of genealogical connections are fundamental sources of information and interpretation throughout the discussions.

Parents of young men who are eager to help their sons find an appropriate spouse use various methods to achieve their aims. Some fathers help their sons hunt the chindoi meat which is offered as a proposal of marriage. If a woman refuses to accept the chindoi meat, serious repercussions can follow, including fighting at the next fiesta, and in one case during 1992, a father and rejected son moved out of the community.

Between 1980 and 1992 two strategies were used in San José to try and secure wives for sons by expanding or constricting the use of the relationship terminology, which has given rise to tensions between households with daughters available for marriages and those without. In 1980, for example, sister exchange was considered a reasonable form of marriage, although the practice was rare because of lack of women. The implication of sister exchange was that it would enable a man to forfeit his bride service and increase the possibility of brothers living together forming clan blocks. However ten years later, sister exchange was being criticised by households without women eligible for marriage because men with sons and daughters would 'wrap up' marriage negotiations and ensure wives for their sons by providing daughters in exchange *(wayawaya)*. In this way a husband is no longer desirable because of his hunting record and competence as an Arakmbut adult, but because of the capacity of his family to provide a wife.

On the other hand, households with more men than women have, during the twelve year period, extended the options for potential wives by expanding the relationship terminology. For example, in 1980 I was told by the Arakmbut that a young man should not marry the daughter of someone in the category of an asign (MZD), but those people in the community who missed out from the sister exchanges, by 1992, considered that such a marriage could take place as long it was not with anyone who was the genealogical daughter of a mother's sister. Furthermore, these households spoke clearly of the importance of marrying women 'at a distance'. This effectively increases the range of exogamy and casts a more negative light on the marriages arranged within the community.

A tension could consequently be discerned within San José in 1992 between those households with several male offspring and few women and those with sons and daughters in equal measure according to the strategies they use to obtain wives. The tension was between desire to receive and the need to give, and could only be resolved by negotiation (Dean 1995). However, the difficulty of finding marriage partners had repercussions on the use of the terminology.

In 1980 the two blocks in San José consisted primarily of married men with young children. The affinal relationships were primarily based on ties through sisters' husbands. The contiguous relationship of members of the same clan was complicated by the imbalance in the numbers of men and women . Agnatic competition between men of the same clan or who have the same relationship to potential wives led to conflict, while negotiations around marriage were also fraught with difficulty as a result of the creation of affinal relationships.

A list of the households which left San José between 1980 and 1992 revealed that all were involved in pre-marital negotiations or post-marital obligations. One household from the Wakutangeri half of the community left for Shintuya in 1982 because the two young men in the household were unable to find wives, leading to conflict with others. The families who moved to Barranco Chico in 1986 did so because the post-marital arrangements were not satisfactory to the wife's parents. The 1992 move of a household to Puerto Luz was concurrent with the rejection of one son who wished to marry in San José while his brother had been successful upriver.

Each of these decisions was influenced by a multitude of other factors, such as personal animosities and conflicts over factors such as meat distribution or access to gold deposits. However, when talking to the Arakmbut, the marital question is the focal point for discussing conflicts. The limited number of women available for marriage has placed considerable stress on households because parents want to ensure that their sons are married and can continue the clan line, support them in old age, and live comfortably.

It is interesting to note that clan solidarity comes to the fore when clusters of households are not actively seeking spouses because the children have just married or partnerships have already been arranged. However, as their children grow up, the clan solidarity becomes weakened because of competition between the young men of the new generation, while those men with more daughters are able to take their pick of the in-laws to work bride service. With only a few exceptions they expect uxorilocal marriage arrangements, which draws the young men out of the clan blocks. This emphasises marital alliance and strong affinity over clan solidarity and can be seen as one of the factors which changed San José from being organised on the basis of clan blocks in 1980 to being more oriented to dispersed alliances in 1992.

Residence and Social Organisation

Once a marriage has taken place, the conflicts between potential affines and between brothers appear to subside as they establish relationships based on friendship or co-operation. However, the fault lines continue to exist and tensions between brothers or affines arise particularly over the delicate matter of post-marital residence. Immediately after marriage, the couple live uxorilocally or virilocally for a period while they have children and care for them as they grow up. This can involve actually living in the same house or sharing a kitchen with a parent, sibling, or in-law, or else living in a neighbouring building. Raising off-spring and providing an independent production base can take as long as fifteen years.

A woman usually desires uxorilocal residence because it enables her to keep a close tie to her mother and to rely on the support of her father's clan. Until marriage, an Arakmbut man shares a room with his brothers and sisters or sleeps in a partitioned section within his father's house; but after marriage he is expected to move in with his spouse's family and work with his father-in-law. All the meat that he catches goes to his mother-in-law, who distributes it from the household. The period of uxorilocality within the in-laws' house lasts for two to four years, after which time the couple move to a house of their own nearby. Eventually elderly parents with married sons or daughters will move in with their children. The effect of the uxorilocal system is to separate male siblings and distribute them among families with daughters, thereby preventing clan solidarity from permanently taking over the community.

From a male perspective, however, virilocal residence is more convenient, and given the choice a man will usually build a house near his agnatic relatives so as not to have to deal with his parents-in-laws' demands on a daily basis. Furthermore, a husband living near his own relatives is less obliged to give the products of his labour to his in-laws' household and can use these goods to build up a distribution network according to his own priorities.

It might be thought that with these advantages, all men would seek virilocal residence, but this is not the case. In spite of the immediate benefits of living with others of his clan, a man who lives uxorilocally has several long-term benefits. He receives respect from the rest of the community for being prepared to fulfil his marital obligations and knows that, provided he remains patient with his in-laws, his affines will remain loyal and in the next generation will provide the wambet support necessary to obtain a wife for his offspring. Furthermore, a man who marries a woman from outside of the community gains in clan solidarity, but loses the affinal ties which are crucial for support in future marriage negotiations.

In spite of the advantages for a woman and the acceptance of uxorilocality as the appropriate form of post-marital residence, out of sixteen marriages made in San José over the twelve year period under discussion, seven were virilocal. Whereas uxorilocality is not explained, cases of virilocality are usually justified with one of the following three explanations:

1. The uxorilocal rule is not necessary if the woman comes from another community and the husband has carried out a brief

bride-service to fulfil his obligations. Even this is not necessary if the woman is non-Arakmbut.
2. A couple can live virilocally if the husband's father or mother are widowed or too old to look after themselves. A young man with a mother but no father will try to live near his family in order to help out and ensure that his younger siblings are provided for.
3. Virilocality is also possible if a household has two daughters in close succession and one son-in-law already lives uxorilocally. The second son-in-law is not necessarily obliged to live in his wife's household, but he has to support his father-in-law with work, drink, and meat.

This shows that virilocality is not always connected to the formation of clan blocks but is negotiated according to the conditions of each household. However, when virilocality is combined with the formation of sibling clusters the system takes on features of the 1980 community organisation, in which a group of brothers in the same clan live as neighbouring households. The two residence patterns based on virilocality and uxorilocality present different but complementary aspects to the political system.

Clan Blocks and Virilocality

Male agnates reside virilocally after marriage for one of the reasons cited in the previous section (in one case in San José this was to be near a widowed brother bringing up small children on his own). The brothers either have daughters with young men doing bride service or sisters with husbands who provide important cross-clan affinal allies. The clan cluster of brothers choose to live together and to share a relationship of solidarity which extends to other clan members in the community. The political economy of the arrangement consists of the following elements:

a) The brothers in the same clan are referred to by the name of their father (converted by the priests to a surname after baptism) and their cluster of households makes up a residential grouping in the community.
b) The brothers have affinal relatives living nearby, married either to sisters or daughters, who provide meat, contribute to fiestas, and give political support.

c) All other members of the brothers' clans support them or, if they are affines of the rival block, abstain in periods of conflict.

In this way a clan cluster emerges by co-residence, which means an emphasis on virilocal post-marital residence, in which brothers and sisters live as neighbours. According to their skills as hunters or curers or their proficiency at dealing with the outside world, brothers can gain a high reputation and prestige through their generosity and become influential in the community. This was the basis for the two power blocks in San José – the Kotsimberi, dominated by Yaromba brothers, and the Wakutangeri, dominated by Idnsikambo. However, as each household grew up and became responsible for their own children, the clan solidarity broke down and alliance relationships gradually became more prominent in the community.

Uxorilocality and the Wambet

In contrast, uxorilocally-based marriage emphasises the affinal relationship rather than the clan tie as the pivotal connection between households. This usually leads to a more disparate set of dyadic alliances linking together chains of connections, but not necessarily utilising the group solidarity so apparent among clan siblings. In this case, the incoming husband's political loyalty is to his in-laws, who may themselves be a group of brothers but are just as likely to be older men with grown-up children living independently from their own immediate household. The woman remains in the maternal household and benefits from the support of her mother and sisters in their gardening cultivation. The existing gardens provide a basis for a sustainable production and enable her to produce a surplus and variety of crops more speedily than for a woman who has to start her gardens from nothing.

The political repercussions of this arrangement are two-fold:

a) If the son-in-law or brother-in-law is affine to a sibling group, then he will support his immediate affines, but will try to avoid entering into political questions. These people rapidly become expert at telling witty stories or entertaining, thereby avoiding the complications of community politics.

b) If the son-in-law is affine to a single independent household he can gradually build up his influence and prestige through hard work and generosity, keeping a low profile on larger political questions. If the affines collaborate well together they can begin to establish wambet-style clusters of allies.

Whereas the virilocal option with agnate clusters leads to a concentration of clan power, the uxorilocal option involves the dispersion of a man's clan. In some cases, uxorilocality with the women who are part of clan clusters will reinforce the political alliances based on block formations. However, uxorilocality with households outside of the clan clusters lead to smaller scale alliances and groups based on the wambet of the offspring. The tension between uxorilocality and virilocality is thus a key element in the political framework of the Arakmbut. If a community becomes dominant in one form as opposed to the other, in-built tensions act to destabilise the system.

The destabilisation for the virilocal clan clusters is that in order for children to have marriage partners, the cluster has to disperse. However, for the uxorilocal residence, the dispersion leads to a weak community in which it becomes increasingly difficult to regulate its affairs. Whereas the imbalance of men and women works against the clustering of clans over a long-period, community weakness works against the excessive dispersion of households into dyadic alliances.

After the break-up of the clan blocks and the separation of the uxorilocal extended households after marriage, the Arakmbut seek places to establish their independent households. From this point, the children grow through puberty and the cycle begins again. When a community consists of smaller clusters of households in alliance, the capacity to offer large fiestas and express generosity becomes more difficult as the production units are more dispersed and involuted.

With more independent households, members of the community fervently watch each others' production, people want to give meat, but they also want enough for their family; a man wants to be generous and buy beer, but he also needs a new motor pump for his gold work. With no clan blocks in support, being generous is more difficult and has limited political rewards in terms of prestige, as alliances are limited to small groups of households throughout the community. The result is an apparent lack of unity and a desire on the part of the elders to sacrifice themselves for the community.

This gives rise to a frustration among the generation growing up. The tension across the generations was exposed in 1990 during the conflict between young students back from Maldonado, who were impetuously trying to resolve the problems between San José and the non-indigenous people in and around the community, and the more cautious elders, who argued that the youth had no respect and refused to learn Arakmbut ways. The youth, for their part, considered that the older men should take a more decisive role vis-à-vis the threats coming from outside. Furthermore, they said that they wanted to learn Arakmbut knowledge but that the old men did not want to pass it on for fear that their position as knowledgeable people could be usurped. The young thus complained of the selfishness of the old and vice versa.

Tensions between youth and elders increase at times when the community as a whole is more dispersed and does not react to external threats in a unified manner. The delays in making decisions frustrate the young, who try to take decision-making into their own hands by asserting themselves at meetings. Some of the young men are eventually elected onto the community council and slowly begin to enter into the political system with all the disadvantages of official leadership (c.f. chapter eight). The new generation gradually forms alliances on the basis of their clan affiliation or other connections which over several years can lead to the establishment of new power blocks. This is particularly prominent among large groups of siblings who have their marriages negotiated and are not in competition for spouses.

The alliances of young men constitute the beginning of a shift from dispersion to solidarity. Although at this stage the men who are grouping together are young, they form the same sort of alliances as did their parents' generation twenty years previously. An example which illustrates this is the formation of the Idnsikambo clan cluster in the 1970s, which formed the Wakutangeri block. Two of these young men lived in the mission of El Pilar for several years where they learned the new gold working techniques and also how to use ayahuasca. When they returned to the community, they settled with their agnates and in-laws and, with these ideas from outside, utilised the internal structure of the community to implement them.

The alliances consist largely of groups of young brothers who have found their future wives and are no longer rivals in the marriage stakes. Since 1994, I have heard that a similar process is beginning to take place. There are two sets of brothers in San José which have a tense relationship between each other. One is Idnsikambo and the other Wandigpana, and they are the children of members of the old Wakutangeri block. They live in opposite parts of the community and as far as possible avoid conflict. Both have taken initiatives which could affect the community – some siblings have tried to establish shops in the community, while other brothers are taking an interest in the concepts of indigenous rights in order to unite the community to defend its interests.

The possibility is that these two groups are the embryonic formation of new power blocks in the community. Whether they will emerge as new concentrated elements of the community, it is difficult to say, because beneath the possible changes lie many contingencies which make prediction impossible.

An Arakmbut community shifts between periods when there is a status differential between sibling cores who dominate community politics and single men who live with their in-laws to carry out their bride service, and more egalitarian periods, when the blocks break up and older household heads live in a more independent manner, with their growing families eager to influence community life. There is therefore a possibility for every Arakmbut to gain influence in the village at some point in his or her life. Those who do not have brothers to support them politically soon build up relationships with their affines, and by the time adults have grown up children, their influence is comparatively equally dispersed throughout the community.

Throughout this process of change, there are different elements of social life which exhibit tensions within and between kin and affines. When tensions exist between brothers at certain points in their lives, they seek support from their mother's kin through the wambet connection, or from affines through the spouse and the increasingly important wambet of the children. Similarly women who find affinal ties a strain look for opportunities to make contact with other people in their clan and wambet. In this way, kin, mother's relatives, and affines provide alternative sets of relationships for both men and women to organise their lives with as they grow older. The breadth and ambiguity of the wambet is significant because the category, at different times of life, includes kin, mother's relatives, and affines, and acts as a flexible means of drawing together a diverse set of relations within one framework of allies.

Placing all these factors together, several patterns arise out of the choices open to the Arakmbut, particularly concerning marital relationships, which can account for many aspects of the changes which took place in San José between 1980 and 1992:

Figure 11.2: Community change among the Arakmbut Youth to early adulthood

Youth to early adulthood Tensions arise from imbalance of male and female in marriage negotiations	
Men live at home with parents sibling rivalry suppression of affinity friendships through wambet	**Women** live at home with parents sibling solidarity suppression of affinity friendships through wambet
Early adulthood- Post-marital Tensions arise from relative advantages from different residence	
Man lives virilocally Clan alliance advantageous Political support widespread Clan blocks Affines supporting	Woman lives virilocally Production disadvantageous Little political support Clan elsewhere Wambet and affinal contacts
Gender relation more unequal	
or	or
Man lives uxorilocally Works off a 'debt' to his in-laws Politically weaker Supporter of affine & wambet	Woman lives uxorilocally Production advantage Politically stronger Clan and wambet contacts
Gender relation more equal - woman slight advantage	
Mature adulthood Tensions between old and young because of weakness arising from dispersion	
Man moves from virilocal residence Clan clusters disperse Establish independent household Improves contacts with affines to form child's wambet, balancing this with clan relations. For uxorilocal residence affinal ties already strong	Woman independent and influential Affinal contacts expand Garden production full strength Contact with clan, affines, and wambet
Gender relation more balanced Sons live virilocally, moving to take over	
Old Age Couple dependent on married children and moves in with one of them	

The choices which face each person as he or she grows older depend on personal desire, options available, and acceptable behaviour. The following features of social organisation interconnect:

1. Sibling solidarity, virilocality, gender inequality; community concentrated in clan blocks and affinal connections, more united vis-à-vis the outside; problems arise with the pressure for uxorilocal residence and the difficulties men have in finding a spouse, which reinforce this.
2. Sibling tie weaker, maternal/affinal contacts stronger, uxorilocality and gender equality, more use of the wambet kindred and affinity ties; community dispersed in relatively independent households, less united vis-à-vis the outside; young men more assertive in complaining against their parents.

These possibilities are constant sets of options open to all the Arakmbut and negotiations, particularly over marriage, involve exploring either set of options. At any one time each household could consist of a mixture of these possibilities. However, the effect of one change can be felt throughout the neighbouring households until, over a long period, the cumulative effect makes its mark on the community as a whole.

Socio-political events reveal tensions in the system which cause problems and lead to complementary activity diffusing and diverting the situation wherever possible. For example, when clan blocks are in control, the wantupa of the community are blamed for anything which goes wrong and, as unequal power relations take shape, people complain. This provides those in the clan blocks with further impetus to establish their independent households and avoid conflict. On the other hand, when the community is too dispersed, people similarly complain that it is too weak to defend itself. Two related dangers therefore stand to threaten an Arakmbut community: as exploitation and hierarchy become more marked, selfishness and jealously may split the community, then individualism without responsibility may take control, which in its turn encourages younger people to join together to assert themselves politically. In this process, the two extremes of the social formation merge: too much power in the hands of too few will lead to exploitation, and too much dispersion in the guise of individualism will lead to alienation.[3]

---

3. This raises another issue which relates to conflict within Arakmbut social life. In spite of characterisations of Amazonian communities being warlike, such as the Yanomami (Chagnon 1968), it is impossible that the Arakmbut are 'by nature' either aggressive or peaceful. The findings here cohere with those of Overing (1989) and Howell and Willis (1989): that sociality is the fundamental aspect of human life and that aggression or violence are aspects of moral values in reaction to events. The Arakmbut cannot be defined as 'peaceful' or 'warlike', but as

In the previous chapter, a connection was drawn between the colonisation of San José's territory and the position of the leadership (both wantupa and, more recently, the young community leaders) as barriers between colonists and the community. The changes reviewed in this chapter are based on the internal dynamics of community life, and consequently the political activities are not so bound up with leadership qualities (as discussed in chapter seven) but with the everyday activities of all members of the community in their households, clans, and wambet.

The resources affected by colonisation are meat from hunting and gold, which were built into the prestige 'system' of the Arakmbut. However the dynamics of change within the community is highlighted with another problem, the availability of a spouse. According to sources stretching back forty years (Holzmann 1951-56), there has always been some demographic imbalance resulting in more male than female Harakmbut. Competition for wives is therefore built into the system because of the status differences between contrasting marriage relationships. The current imbalance has been made more acute by Arakmbut women living with highland colonists and in three cases actually leaving the community.

The conclusion from this account of community change is that the Arakmbut experience a periodic shift from times when clans are more dominant to times when the clans disperse and the wambet come to the fore. Marriage arrangements are key factors in this change. However, a question remains as to why a whole community should change as a result of a few marriages. For example, clan clusters of sibling core-groups could easily co-exist with uxorilocally based household clusters and furthermore, marriages take place with sufficient frequency to allow the smooth co-existence of the two systems.

Several reasons could explain why this has not yet occurred. In the first place, the population of Arakmbut malocas has been in the past about fifty to a hundred people (about a third or half the size of the current population of San José). The reason could therefore simply be that there are not enough people for the system to operate in a balanced manner. The two clan clusters in 1980, for example, embraced about 60 percent of the marriages in the community, and included the main political leaders. As the two blocks dispersed in subsequent years, no other sibling cluster of young adults existed.

---

people with both elements present in their social life. Sometimes their history is more conflictive than others, but the competitive and co-operative aspects of their social life co-exist.

Only in 1992 did the first rudiments of a reformed political organisation began to take shape.

Another factor is that a sibling cluster development among the Arakmbut spans a time dimension of between ten and fifteen years. Several sibling clusters can live virilocally in the same vicinity for over a decade between marriage and establishing a more independent household. They effectively dominate the social organisation of the community for about five to ten years but eventually disperse. Yet as the clusters break up, other clusters do not necessarily automatically assert themselves, even though they exist. For example, if an external threat places the future of the community in jeopardy, older members of the community might reassert themselves as wantupa in order to defend the interests of the people as a whole. This would weaken the influence of a sibling core temporarily until the group is strong enough to deal with problems facing the community. This is the very discussion which was taking place in San José in August 1995.

The way of encapsulating the internal shifts in San José is therefore to see the household as embracing connections through clans and wambet. Both features of social organisation co-exist and at certain times one takes precedence over the other. Marriage rules and community organisation are influences which prevent one from becoming too dominant, and the community lives in a state of uneasy imbalance. Between 1980 and 1992 the system shifted markedly from one feature to the other; in the future it is impossible to predict whether this will necessarily be repeated, but similar processes of change will continue to be present.

This chapter has shown that many aspects of change within San José between 1980 and 1992 can be seen within the framework of the larger changes which were taking place as household, clan, and affinal relations waxed and waned. However, this should not give the impression that an Arakmbut community is somehow a neatly functioning self-regulating organisation. Nevertheless, in many respects Arakmbut conflicts are resolved and the community of San José has remained intact for the twelve years under study.

However, when no solutions can be found, households leave the community because the self-regulating aspects of Arakmbut social life break down. People are never expelled from the community, but they choose to go because they realise that they have lost the support of their former allies. In small communities, serious conflicts can cause a complete disintegration, as happened at the small settlement of Boca Karene, close to Boca Colorado, in 1983 because of personal conflicts between sibling groups coupled with serious threats from the colonists at Boca Colorado. Some went to San José, the majority to Puerto Luz. A community as a whole can thus break down when the borderlines of acceptable behaviour are transgressed and non-Arakmbut aspects of socio-political life enter into the system.

The Arakmbut are aware of the dangers of a community being destroyed, which perhaps makes them more concerned to avoid the conflict which causes internal ruptures. Indeed, the changes in San José which have taken place over the last twelve years constitute a major realignment of the residential maloca groups to such an extent that it is difficult to argue that the result has been simply consolidating or divisive. It has been both.

Many of the changes which took place in San José between 1980 and 1992 occurred as a result of a series of contingent events. Even though marriage has influenced the direction of change among the Arakmbut in a particular way between 1980 and 1992, the evidence is not sufficient to make any predictions about the future. The account given here is based on specific events and persons with their own ways of interacting which took the community in a certain direction during twelve years and says nothing about change in general, apart from giving some indications of the points at which the system weakens.

Over the next ten or twelve years, San José will change in other ways as the different households move in different directions. For example, the loss of so many Arakmbut to disease at the time of missionary contact in the 1950s has affected the number of older people in the community; since the 1960s the population has become more balanced in terms of the ratio between men and women; and the Arakmbut population as a whole is growing faster than at any other period since their first contact with white people. These three demographic factors could considerably affect the way in which the community moves over the next twenty years. Looking at social change is largely a question of looking at patterns in historical events rather than establishing any permanent principles of how a community is going to change.

This chapter has looked at the ways in which change has occurred in a community from a social perspective and has discussed the tensions which provoke social movement. If this were a discussion of the dialectic, these tensions would be seen as contradictions, placed in the context of marriage potential and dwindling resources (imbalance of the sexes and the encroachment by colonists onto Arakmbut territory). According to this perspective, in order to retain control of the community, the Arakmbut male sibling groups control access to too many resources and the social conflicts arise from competition over them. Through emphasising affinal ties, the concentration of the power struggle becomes resolved and the community disperses the tension until it rises up again in another form.

The conflict between access to resources and social relations would be sufficient to explain the generation of movement within the framework discussed up until now. To a large extent this explanation is logical and has the advantage of bringing social, environmental, and political elements into the same explanatory framework. However, the elements which generate the change are assumed to arise out of the tensions between persons and groups, yet this does not answer the question as to what generates and regulates change. For the Arakmbut, the answer lies in the world of the spirits, which is the subject of the next chapter.

Chapter 12

THE INVISIBLE WORLD AND ITS CHANGELESS QUALITIES

Accounts of change rarely include a discussion of the impact of the spirit world because it is invisible and is usually conceptualised as peripheral to the visible world which changes through time. However, from the perspective of the practical philosophy of the Arakmbut, spirits are an ever-present reality which can only be seen in moments of heightened consciousness in dreams and visions (wayorok). Grasping the nature of the invisible world is difficult because it combines concepts which, to an observer, are often separated.

The Arakmbut explained the invisible world to me by comparing a dead animal with a live one. Life (e'e) is the generating force within all living beings. The more intensely the soul-matter occupies a body, the more it takes on the form of a soul (nokiren). Souls are the prerogative of large animals and humans, which is why it is not possible to use the term universally for all living things. The invisible world is the animating cause of life in the visible world, which fits with the general sense of animism used by Tylor that 'spirits are personified causes'.[1]

Change is a process which, like the spirit world, is essentially invisible from the perspective of the material world of form, and is bound up with intangible qualities which only shamanic activities can penetrate. For the Arakmbut, change is not a unitary concept. When they use the word in a general sense they say 'kambiaka' – which combines the Spanish verb 'cambiar' (change) with the

---

1. Alan Campbell (1989:61), gives a detailed and inspiring discussion of the relationship between causality and the spirit world of the Wayapi.

Arakmbut *e'ka* (to do, make). Even then this refers as much to exchanging something as to change which is intrinsic to something. However, by looking at several contexts, it becomes possible to look at a spread of meanings in which a broader notion of change emerges. In each case it is connected to the relationship between the visible and invisible worlds.

Growth and Death

For the Arakmbut, growth and death are based on relationships between the visible and invisible world. E'kerek means 'to grow' and is the continuous passage through life of all living things – plants, animals, birds, fish, and human beings. It is not guaranteed, however, and only takes place with sustenance – soil and rain for plants; fruits and other creatures for fauna; or for human beings activities of production and reproduction. Chapter two looked in detail at how these activities involved a relationship between humans, the species of the environment, and the spirit world which relate to secure the controlled growth of each Arakmbut by means of the sustenance of food and spiritual support against death, sickness, and weakness. Growth is a phenomenon which is only encountered in the visible world.

E'mbuey means death. Death occurs in those contexts when the soul separates from the body. This occurs at moments of orgasm, fainting, fits, and the termination of life. The change of existence at death is the moment when the connection between the soul and body, which constitutes life, is broken and the nokiren moves to the invisible level of experience. Death thus frames life between conception and death.

From the perspective of Arakmbut daily life, the relationship between growth and the constant threat of death from disease and sickness constitutes the main form of personal and social movement. This book has reviewed this movement from several perspectives: production methods, curing techniques, and dreaming are all ways in which human beings use contacts with the invisible spirit world to ensure that growth takes place within certain limits and does not become dangerous. The spirit world provides the basis for understanding the points at which the boundaries of the acceptable are transgressed and threats and dangers are let loose on the community.

Arakmbut consider that the spirit world generates and animates movement with growth and death, and consequently spiritual experience can provide some illumination of change. These concepts are difficult to grasp because the phenomena under discussion are fundamentally experiential and not conceptual.[2] However, two connected areas can shed some light on how the relationship between the invisible and visible worlds relates to change: time and causality.

For the Arakmbut, time is not conceptualised as a general movement from the past to the future in which all existence floats, but as movement which passes by human beings by (o'pogika), leaving them to grow older and change. The metaphor is thus not of people drifting in the river of time, but watching from the banks as it goes on its way. The passage of time is measured by how things change. Thus, day/night, new moon/full moon, wet season/dry season, and what the Arakmbut call the 'calendar of flowers' provide a periodic or cyclic view of change by which time passes certain sequences.[3]

To move with time would be a form of 'timelessness' in which nothing appears to change and from which future and past would be visible. This is how I have tried to conceptualise what the Arakmbut mean when they say that in the spirit world one can see the future as clearly as the past. The spirit world is a place of potentiality beyond time and space. Time, as it passes, facilitates growth, decay, and change, in the same way that spirits, when they pass within or by human beings, animate and generate change. This is not to say that the spirit world is time, but that free spirits are beyond the constrictions of time and space until they are caught up in a body and name from which they receive their form.

The visible world thus provides the timelessness of the spirit realm with time-space co-ordinates. Meanwhile, the invisible world provides physical existence with animation and life which is channelled into directions through growth and death which permeate all existence. These directions are in space – *kuta* (up, along) or *toyo*

---

2. The methodology of explaining a world which is experienced by a heightened form of consciousness is difficult. Analysing concepts and causal statements can provide a limited glimpse, but the Arakmbut have repeatedly told me that it is impossible to understand these things unless I accept them as real. This approach is somewhat experimental: I am perhaps trying to penetrate the impenetrable.

3. Gell (1991), contrasts 'Series A' time, which is based on the distinction past-present-future and reflects the notion of time passing, with 'Series B', which looks at ways whereby time is measured by temporal points. The Arakmbut would relate to this, as B for them would be seen as the visible markers for showing that A has occurred. The Arakmbut see time as something which passes by as one 'faces the future arse-forwards'. This is a Quechua expression for a similar notion (Sarah Skar pers. comm.). The effect is a strongly spatial sense of time.

(down) – and in time – *anenda* (before, in the past, just now) and *wambwanda* (right now, soon after). Rivers flow from kuta to toyo, while time passes from anenda to wambwanda. Temporal change is thus fundamentally related to spatial positioning, and its dynamism stems from a world outside of these criteria.

The invisible world also provides the Arakmbut with a generative structural causality, according to which behaviour is a visible sign of an invisible animating cause which can only be seen in its effect. Arakmbut ideas of what causes other things include several different concepts. When talking about connections between phenomena or making statements with causal features, the Arakmbut say '*o'epo*' (for this reason). The word *mon'ka* is also used to express a necessary relationship and was translated into Spanish as 'causal'. It means literally 'it must be done so'. Out of these examples, the notion of causality is a combination of two contiguous elements which are related to each other and an imperative force (*mon-* is an imperative form).

Causality for the Arakmbut can be seen both as a generative energy which, in making an effect, causes a situation to change, as well as a succession of two states which, juxtaposed through association, appear to be connected. The successionist perspective is primarily the way of looking at the visible aspects of change between two juxtaposed visible states, which are temporal, whereas the relationship between the visible and invisible world involves, on the one hand, the imposition of form onto spirit and, on the other hand, the animation of form by spirit. In the Arakmbut causal system, soul-matter is the only aspect of causality which provides any connotation of generative change.[4]

The causal complex of the Arakmbut consists of different permutations across the visible/invisible divisions where successionist causality (o'epo) is dominant in the visible world and generative causality (monka) relates to the invisible world. The different possibilities cover four areas.

Visible causes with visible effects are based in the material conditions of the world and concern all features of daily life which can be juxtaposed. For example, statements such as 'It is raining so I will stay in' or 'The man made a spear' express connections between contiguous items.

---

4. The successionist approach to causality, which is based on the Arakmbut visible world, relates closely to Hume's approach to causality, while the generative view connects more with the perspective of Aristotle.

Visible causes with invisible effects refer to how the invisible world receives its form from the visible world. For example, the body gives the nokiren a personal shape and form which it retains even after death – usually that of a human being in adulthood. An example of this aspect of causality is 'The toto was in the form of a long, thin, pale creature like a white man.'

Invisible causes with visible effects refer to the dynamic generative animating power of the nokiren – this is human activity where the soul acts as intermediary between the invisible world of spirits and dreams and the visible world of the body. Human activities involving the soul would be one example here, as in the statement 'The hunter killed the tapir' or 'The old man was angry'.

Invisible causes resulting in invisible effects refer to the interaction between different spirits and souls which occurs during illness or in dreams and visions. This can only be understood in states of heightened awareness, and can be encapsulated in statements such as 'The toto attacked the soul of the sick man.'

During Arakmbut daily life all these aspects of causality are connected. To some extent, this separation into four contexts is artificial because all of these features are present in any form of causality. However, the generative and contiguous aspects of causality do appear in the way the Arakmbut use causal statements. No priority need be put on any one of this group of causal connections, because, as with Aristotle's theory of causality, they are four aspects of one movement and interaction between phenomena, which in the Arakmbut case are shared between the visible and invisible worlds.

Thus, rather than change over time being solely a property of physical attributes and social interaction, any activity is a combination of different factors, and the invisible world is as critical an element as the visible. By viewing Arakmbut spirit cosmology from the perspective of time and causal principles, it is possible to see how the spirit world provides the only way in which life can be generated and consequently the only means of understanding, from an Arakmbut perspective, how things change.

Time and causality are examples of how the animating movement of the invisible world relates with the visible world of form to enable the directional processes of birth, growth, and death to take place in a controlled manner. Arakmbut cosmology sees an invisible world beyond time which animates material phenomena by moving from a level of experience beyond time and space to one which is fundamentally directional, spatially and temporally. This directionality links the experience of time, the nature of causality and the process of growth from birth to death in a way which connects change and places its dynamism in the spirit world.

The Spirit World and Community Change

Change in the invisible world takes a form which does not operate in a linear manner such as growth. Soul-matter can change from concentrated to dispersed and back according to the situation of each person or spirit. The invisible world is only known through its effects, and so the Arakmbut do not talk of the process whereby spirits change from one form to another, only that in any particular context they are acting in either a concentrated or a dispersed manner. Spirit transformational change is not necessarily temporal. The same features arise when Arakmbut say that a spirit can take the form of a person or an animal and change instantaneously. Spirits do not grow and die except in as much as they are tied to a growing body through life, and transform into free-spirits after death.

The soul of a person (nokiren) has many parallels with the spirit world, but lives within the framework of a body to which it is tied by the name. The soul is formed by the passing of semen *(wandawe)* from father to mother during intercourse by means of the orgasm (e'mbuey), which also means the moment when the nokiren or part of it leaves the body. The nokiren is nurtured first in the womb by the mother and then after birth, with growth of the body through eating meat. Protecting the body with black huito paint (o) or immersing a child in cold water at dawn causes it to breath deeply and become stronger. As the body grows, so does the soul, reaching full growth point with adulthood.

Concentrated and dispersed aspects of soul-matter have different manifestations inside or outside of persons. The nokiren has an external form which appears in dreams and visions. This reflects the person as a totality, condensing all the attributes into one image. This image of a person's nokiren becomes as fixed as that of a fully grown adult and remains in this form after death. The other aspect of the soul, the wamawere, can travel 'like the wind'. For example, when torch-lights were seen passing through the community in February 1992, several Arakmbut commented that it was my wamawere coming in advance to warn the community that I would be arriving the following day (which I did). Wamawere also refers to dispersed free spirits, associated with dead people or species, which can cause harm, but to a lesser extent than toto.

Soul-matter changes within a person according to the circumstances in which he or she lives, where form and spirit co-exist in an uneasy balance. Each person, at any one moment, manifests the state of the soul. Sickness occurs when this unsteady balance breaks down and one of two things happen: either the nokiren is enticed out of the body by a spirit or else a spirit enters a person's body and attacks the soul. A person becomes sick at the moment when the normal limits of concentration and dispersion of the nokiren within the body are exceeded, which can cause the ultimate dispersion of the nokiren from the body – death.

For an Arakmbut, thinking or feeling something strongly is a constantly altering state reflecting the situation of a person's nokiren at any one time in reaction to visible events and invisible spirit contacts which provide the person with the drive to act on the world. The relationship between thought and feeling is a matter of degree rather than kind, and the nokiren changes in a manner which is not always predictable. However, any change in the nokiren arises from some encounter between the Arakmbut and other people or spirits, which provide the reasons why a person thinks or feels certain things. Human 'sociality' is a manifestation of the state of the nokiren.

The spirit world relates to human beings through the nokiren. It also provides the generative animation which constitutes change. The effect of this is that the Arakmbut can change their world through the animating power of their soul while, at the same time, the state of the soul reflects the state of the person and his or her social relationships. The nokiren is a permanent aspect of the invisible world present in all activities of the Arakmbut, reflecting each person's relationship with the rest of the community and beyond.

The spirits which roam in freedom are separate from the nokiren of humans except for the occasions in which they are able to communicate through dreams and visions. For example, the relationship between a hunter and the dispersed beneficial ndakyorokeri provides him with information and skills which are extremely important for knowing how many animals to kill and the limits beyond which it is dangerous to hunt. The capacity of a man to hunt is a prerequisite for marriage and the presentation of chindoi meat is the most delicate part of the negotiations. The significance of meat for the growth of the household is also crucial for a man and woman's prestige, as his hunting and her distribution are the factors enabling them to show their generosity. All of this depends on support from the ndakyorokeri.

In a situation in which gaining a marriage partner involves competition between men and, in some cases, households, positive skills are a demonstration of contacts with beneficial spirits, whereas ill-feeling occurs when relationships with the invisible world are poor. Spirits can therefore provide the key element in the negotiation of a marriage through knowledge and advice.

The case studies of death and sickness in chapters one and five demonstrated how members of the community were regularly in touch with spirits in order to diagnose the reason for the misfortunes, either through wayorokeri dreaming or wamanoka'eri talking to the chongpai during ayahuasca sessions. The different clans in the community fight over different reasons for an illness and different theoretical constructs of the cosmological principles behind the trauma facing the households concerned. During these periods of illness, invisible spirits not only directly harm a person, but also provide advice as to ways of restoring life or community stability.

Within the community, people with influence and prestige are also open to certain risks. For example, if a political leader fails to show responsibility or generosity he will encounter problems. This is amply illustrated by the young president of San José, who in December 1991 requested that the community pay for him to travel to Puerto Maldonado, two days away, in order to lodge a complaint on behalf of the community against some invading colonists. The response of the community was that the President was clearly going to take the money for himself and no one collaborated. I was told that as a leader, it was the President's job to support the community, not the other way round. Meanwhile, the President became depressed and disappeared from the community for several days. This scenario has been repeated so often that it has almost become a regular feature of community life and demonstrates the debilitating effect of political life on the state of a leader's nokiren.

Another example of a political leader arose in 1981, after the death of Psyche. Here a successful gold miner had built up support and influence from his generosity. However, he began to consider negotiating permission for a local colonist to work near a community placer. This led to ruminations and concern among the rest of the community, who complained that the leader would open them up to more colonists and that he was going to gain personally at the expense of everyone else. The alliance with the colonist was made and at the next drinking party the leader was accused of sorcery in the context of Psyche's death. Tensions in the community were running high, and the deal ultimately came to nothing. These examples show how too little and too much concentration of power in a leader can be harmful to the community as a whole. These phenomena are expressed by the Arakmbut as too concentrated or dispersed aspects of the soul.

Any man whose political ambitions make him favour his own interests rather than those of the community is considered mean and selfish (senopo). Depending on his power, he appears weak and depressed (nowenda) or else, if bitter, a concentration of nokiren (hatred – ochinosik) can lead to accusations of sorcery. By acts of altruism and generosity, a powerful person distributes his success to others in the community and disperses his emotions. This is expressed by the Arakmbut in the similarity between the words e'yok (to give), e'mbayok (to distribute), and the particle – ok which means to separate.

Although words in themselves do not necessarily relate to peoples' behaviour, these examples provide some orientation as to how the state of the soul is intricately bound up with political activity. Thus spirits directly intervene in Arakmbut affairs and consequently play a part in changes affecting the community. At all the major events in Arakmbut life, such as birth, death, illness, marriage, and at other less predictable moments, spirit influence is keenly felt, animating or depressing those involved and generating the heightened intensity of social encounters which take place at these 'crisis' periods. The following table summarises the different states of the nokiren and how they parallel the spirit world, placing both of these into the context of certain social activities when the invisible world enters directly into Arakmbut community life. This table is not intended to convey a tightly structured, harmonious universe. Rather, the axes are points on a continuum, linking the concepts of concentrated and dispersed in different contexts connecting the personal state of the nokiren, the forms of spirits, social activities, and political positions discussed in chapter eight.

Figure 12.1: Concentration and dispersion of nokiren and spirits

	Concentration		Dispersion	
	Excess	Normal	Normal	Excess
state of nokiren	ochinosik/senopo hatred/meanness	wanopo affections	e'nopwe thought	nowe depression
spirit	toto harmful	chongpai beneficial	ndakyorokeri beneficial	wamawere harmful
social activities	chindign sorcery	e'pak desire	e'yok generosity	kawe inactivity
social	more hierarchy	clan	wambet	more equality

The invisible world affects community change directly through the activity of the nokiren within each person. During daily life, the encounters which punctuate the socio-political arena of community life consist of meetings between different people. Each nokiren reflects the social and personal effects of these encounters at any moment and provides the stimulus to continue or avoid particular relationships. As all human activity has a spiritual dimension through the operation of the nokiren, encounters are imbued with the invisible world in both thought and emotion.

In addition to the nokiren, spirits can intervene directly in human affairs. In productive or reproductive activities, whether hunting, cooking, or sexual relations, spirits are involved and behaviour has to be controlled in order to avoid harmful consequences. This regulates the social relationships which take place within the community and defines the boundaries of the acceptable. Sickness and death are always attributable in some respect to the activity of the spirit world in response to accidental or careless transgression.

At certain periods of crisis, particularly after a death or after particularly intense internal conflict, the community acts in particular ways in order to control the dangers facing its members and to reduce the chances of harm spreading further. This change of settlement affects the relationships between the nokiren of the community and frequently takes place as a result of messages from the invisible world.

During crises, the Arakmbut separate from the village centre in order to avoid the dangers of hostile spirits (as in the case of a death) or to escape the possibility that the intense hatred affecting a particular section might turn into sorcery. Arakmbut communities thus go through periods when, temporarily or permanently, people move away to avoid the concentration of soul-matter either in the nokiren of living enemies or for fear of toto. By physically spreading themselves out, the Arakmbut effectively counterbalance the concentration of the soul-matter.

In contrast, during periods when the community is spread out and weaker thanks to lack of co-ordination, the reverse process can be seen, and the youth seek out some new initiative to try to draw the community together in meetings or larger work groups in order to bring some more life into its political activities; the main examples over the last twenty years were the introduction of ayahuasca and gold mining. This is not to say that the concentration and dispersion of settlement is of the same order as that of soul-matter. However the animating generative consequences of the invisible world have to be controlled by the living, and often the only way to do this is by closer co-operation within the community or by separation.

Those who stand on the frontier between the visible and invisible worlds are the people with shamanic expertise: the wamanoka'eri and the wayorokeri. Whereas everyone to some extent can interpret the spirit world, the shamanic specialists try to regulate the world so that there is neither excess nor absence of soul-matter. This is the basis of spiritual health. The wamanoka'eri curer does this with the sick and the wayorokeri dreamer with the community as a whole. These specialists try to ensure harmony within the community because this prevents either weakness and lethargy or hatred and sorcery. For this reason a shaman should be 'above politics'. A shaman who is too involved politically is assumed to be using his spirit contacts to better his own interests and this opens him to charges of sorcery.

The death of Psyche can now be seen in the light of the death of a shaman who managed to keep the community together. The conflicts which took place in 1980 were exacerbated by his death. The process whereby the clan blocks broke up began almost immediately after his death and continued throughout the 1980s. Without Psyche's presence mediating between the rivalries, the community suffered from animosity and hatred which there was no one to calm. The position of the wayorokeri as regulator of the spirit forces external and internal to human beings is vital to the strength and survival of the community.

Thus the changes which took place between 1980 and 1992 were, to a large extent, influenced by the spirit world. This occurred as result of its animating causality, the actions of the nokiren of each Arakmbut person, and the lack of a wayorokeri to hold the community together. Whereas Arakmbut with shamanic skills strove to mediate with these forces, without Psyche's presence their effect was limited. Although no one in the community has the power and foresight of Psyche, several of the older men are currently trying to gain more shamanic expertise. There might not be a wayorokeri in the community, but the spiritual strength has by no means disappeared forever.

The tensions and disintegration of the clans during the 1980s took place in the context of accusations of sorcery and highly charged conflict in the community. The result was a dispersion – some moved to areas close by while others moved to other communities altogether. The evidence here demonstrates that colonisation and internal dynamics are not the only factors affecting social change, but the spirit world is extremely important. This relates not only to the 1980s but stretches further back in Arakmbut history.

Change in the Past

Throughout the forty-year history of the Arakmbut since mission contact on the Ishiriwe river, their social life has been changing, but in the late 1940s and early 1950s, events took place which particularly altered community life. In 1950, there were initially seven Wandakweri malocas which divided and reformulated into four new groupings as a consequence of the first deaths from disease arising from contact with whites. For several years the deaths continued and were explained as the result of female sorcery.[5] The crisis in the malocas became even more tense after the yellow fever outbreak in 1956. The unprecedented deaths were attributed to the nokiren of dead Harakmbut who had been killed during the rubber boom and which were taking their revenge. Thus, between 1950 and 1956 there was a period of dispersion from the malocas on the Wandakwe to the Ishiriwe and the Eori (Madre de Dios). Some malocas lost contact with each other.

In 1956, however, lured by the offer of metal goods and medicines for their illnesses, the Arakmbut moved to the mission of Shintuya, where the maloca groups were concentrated in one settlement. This process of concentration lasted from 1956 until 1960, when about three hundred Harakmbut and Matsigenka lived in the mission. At this time, the Arakmbut worked for the missionaries. The youngest were sent away to schools while the young adults were targeted to learn new agricultural methods and cattle-raising. This provided the younger generation with an opportunity to utilise their initiative for the community as a whole and to resist the older Arakmbut.

During the 1960s, problems increased in Shintuya and conflicts arose between the different Arakmbut malocas, which were not used to living so close to each other. Furthermore, the Arakmbut fought with the Wachipaeri, particularly regarding access to the benefits which the missionaries could provide. The result was an increase in accusations of sorcery and the killing of women considered to be sorcerers. The Arakmbut moved their settlements from the centre of the

---

5. There are examples of Arakmbut killing young women as sorcerers during this period. However, this may not have been a permanent state of affairs but rather a panic measure in the face of the horrendous amount of death and blindness which was threatening life in the malocas.

mission and lived downriver in separate settlements for a while. However, this did not solve the problem. The people of San José explain how the sorcery was so rampant that even the dogs were dying. In 1969, the Wakutangeri and Kotsimberi from San José left the mission and founded their community on Harakmbut territory. The increase in sorcery accusations and lack of access to goods in the mission caused problems between the other indigenous peoples and the priests, and eventually other Arakmbut sought seek an independent life downstream from Shintuya.[6]

Between 1969 and 1975, 75 percent of the Arakmbut maloca groups moved away from Shintuya to found their own independent communities on the Karene, Pukiri, and Inambari rivers. This dispersion came after their concentration had reached crisis proportions. The escape of the maloca groups relieved the tension and restored them in their own native communities. The concentration of the Arakmbut in San José happened at the same time that gold mining was becoming significant in the Karene area. In the early 1970s, several young men moved from school at El Pilar to form the Idnsikambo block, which was so prominent in 1980.

These movements of concentration and dispersion over the last forty years affected all the Arakmbut. In each case the break up of communities arose from social tensions and fear of sorcery, specifically during the period of contact with whites, when disease and death were rampant. However, the periods of concentration occurred when the Arakmbut wanted to take advantage of external benefits, initially metal tools and medicines and lately gold and ayahuasca.

The changes which took place between 1980 and 1992 were not sufficiently drastic or traumatic to warrant the disintegration of the community, but they demonstrate that the processes of concentration and dispersion of settlements are a constant feature of Arakmbut life. For example, between 1969 and 1980 there was a gradual concentration of Arakmbut who joined the original fifty or more people who left Shintuya in 1969 for San José. However, between 1980 and 1992, five households, comprising over twenty people, moved from San José to Puerto Luz, Barranco Chico, and Shintuya as a result of conflicts within the community. In this case, the cause of the conflicts

6. The concentration in Shintuya and the dispersion of the Arakmbut is parallelled by events in the origin myth (see Volume 1, chapter twelve). In the myth, the Arakmbut flee from a crisis into the branches of the tree, Wanamey, and then disperse downriver after the fire-flood subsides. The effect of the myth, as with the move to Shintuya, was a unification of the Arakmbut in self-defence, and a dispersion once the crisis had subsided.

did not only include interpretations of death or sickness, in which charges of sorcery were involved, but also finding marriage partners, where conflict is more usually expressed through fighting and argument. The population of San José is now the same size as it was in 1980, in spite of the birth rate outstripping the death rate.

This account demonstrates that the change from a comparatively more 'concentrated period' in 1980 to a more 'dispersed period' in 1990 is part of a periodic fluctuation which occurs from time to time in Arakmbut life, taking different forms and varying in intensity. What took place between 1980 and 1992 was considerably less extreme than the movement of concentration to Shintuya in the late 1950s, and the subsequent dispersion and was probably more similar to the fluctuations which took place within and between malocas prior to 1950.

Several old men in San José recall that in the 1950s, when the Arakmbut lived on the Wandakwe river in the headwaters of the Ishiriwe prior to the arrival of the missionaries, people would move from one maloca to another as a result of conflicts. One man left the Kukambatoeri maloca and moved to the Wakutangeri group after conflicts described in this personal song:

> Before, I was miserable, I was alone. Arakmbut hit me. My brother-in-law was not grown up when I had these difficulties. I was alone in the other maloca. My brother followed me when I left. Now the Yaromba here are my brothers. Only recently they grew up. I admire youth because they understand. I am now pleased and have sufficient family to defend myself against Amiko. I don't even have to say anything to my Yaromba relatives and they will defend me.

The growth and decline of maloca membership was therefore a feature of socio-cultural life before contact with the priests, and is reflected in similar processes which take place in the communities today. It is possible to see the spiritual dimensions of change taking several forms according to the intensity of the tensions and the extent to which they are life-threatening. Community concentration and dispersion ranges from the main epoch-making events in Arakmbut history, when communities break up and reform again over the years, to the short periods when people leave the community after a death or for shorter periods due to some conflict. The twelve year period with which we are concerned here lies somewhere between the two. Although the community has not broken up, the changes which have taken place are not simply variations in the daily routine.

In conclusion, we see that the connection between concentration and dispersion in the spirit world reflects the same process in the social organisation of Arakmbut communities. The connecting factor is the nokiren and the direct influence of spirits on human production and reproduction. People with shamanic skills try to control what is essentially an unbalanced universe, in the same way that those with political skills strive to balance the notions of desire and generosity. Desire draws people together and is a force for social concentration but without generosity, the relationship is affected by senopo (meanness) and hatred (ochinosik), which attract harmful spirits. On the other hand, too much generosity leads to a strain on resources and a risk of the breakdown of the household and a weakening of the community as a whole.

In this way, desire and generosity control the socio-political organisation as visible aspects of the invisible principles of concentration and dispersion which generate change in Arakmbut life. Political and shamanic skills thus become parallel vehicles for the social and spirit world, attempting to regulate the constant imbalance in the world which threatens to move into destruction through conflict or weakness.

The picture of social change has become considerably larger than a shift between one social unit and another. Embedded in social life are the dynamics of political action and spiritual process which together express the form change is taking through a cultural framework. Three factors are thus combined: outside factors, such as the colonising frontier, which trigger changes; tensions between clan and kindred, gender, age, and virilocal or uxorilocal residence, which express socially accepted boundaries of accepted behaviour through informal encounters; and the generating and animating attributes of the invisible world through the nokiren and the spirits.

Each of these three contexts relates to a different aspect of the shamanic and political features of Arakmbut life. The political leaders, in particular the young men, are the in the front line as mediators with the colonising frontier, while the shamanic specialists are prime negotiators and regulators in spiritual matters. The internal changes of the community are based on daily encounters and through these, the Arakmbut deal with periodic problems which regluarly arise.

As crises emerge within the community, tensions grow or weaken, manifesting different aspects of spirit relations, either in terms of direct contact with the invisible world or through the state of the nokiren of the participants. If the tensions grow too much, the community will split from within; if it becomes too weak the community will be prey to forces from outside.

The task of the Arakmbut is thus to try to regulate a cosmos which is in permanent imbalance. The most extreme crisis is in the myth of Wanamey, when the earth was destroyed by a fire-flood; the historical equivalent was the sickness brought by the first contact with the non-indigenous world. However, the fluctuations are usually on a more modest scale, as described for the period between 1980 and 1992.

In this chapter we have seen how the spirit world animates the human visible world in the same way that the nokiren animates the human body and comes close to the notion of process manifest in the dynamics of the social formation. The invisible spirit world is beyond space and time and consists of the potentiality in the universe which, through the spatial and temporal co-ordinates of the visible world, constructs a unidirectional causality; spirit is movement only known through its effects. The relationship between a nokiren and the spirit world is the link between inside desire and outside power – some of which is dangerous and some beneficial according to who is trying to control it. Shamanic skills use the positive power to re-establish order as a form of generosity to help the community, while a sorcerer utilises the imbalance of the world in the form of negative powers to harm.

Arakmbut change can take advantage of benefits from outside of the community, but this is fraught with danger. White people, for example, can provide goods and services of value, such as metal tools or education, and can, in certain circumstances even be a source for marriage partners, but they are also predators on Arakmbut resources and threaten their survival. Spirits provide the opportunity for the Arakmbut to improve production, but also threaten them with sickness and death. The Arakmbut can unify as a community to defend themselves by resisting the outside threats or trying to control them, while taking advantage of their benefits.

Resistance is difficult because the state of the soul reflects its effectiveness. The stronger the resistance becomes, the more likely internal tensions will appear in the community, while the weaker it is, the more likely the Arakmbut will suffer from external threats. Arakmbut social life is a constant battle between these positions, as exemplified by the state of peoples' nokiren, which constantly juxtaposes resignation and resistance in response to outside threats (Gray 1986).

By avoiding any reductionism in this analysis between the levels fluctuating change (external triggers, inner tensions, and invisible powers), it is possible to see the invisible world as the process at the centre of this description of change, thereby sharing the Arakmbut understanding and respect for the spirit world.

One question which arises is the extent to which the change described in San José between 1980 and 1992 is unidirectional or whether it is periodic, in that the social and spiritual movements pass through similar sequences. The answer to this is that both phenomena occur. On the one hand, the events which took place are framed in space-time and not repeatable; on the other, the shift from clan to wambet or from hierarchy to equality are emphases within the social formation which could and have moved through sequences from periods of concentration to dispersion and back to concentration again.

This does not mean to say that Arakmbut social life will necessarily always change in this way. It is perfectly possible that this shifting system has been present in the past but became particularly active during the 'history of contact with the state' which has been inherently unstable and has involved several major relocations over the last forty years. For this reason, no one can predict whether the sequence will repeat itself again or whether eventually a totally new shift will occur, moving the Arakmbut social formation in another direction.

CONCLUSION

Far from being static, timeless, or isolated, the Arakmbut of San José live, and appear to have always lived, in a world dominated by change. The fluctuations of change are part of the normal operations of social life, but occasionally these can become so extreme that the social formation is threatened. The Arakmbut try to regulate their spiritual and political life in order to avoid destruction from internal or external encroachment and to ensure the continuation of their social organisation and cultural practices.

Spiritual regulation consists of communicating with the invisible world in order to correct the imbalances of the universe which affect the Arakmbut. Interpretations of sickness, portentous events, and the repercussions of behaviour are all aspects of their shamanic skills. Political regulation consists of ensuring a balance between desire and giving while steering a course between excessive emotional aggression and debilitating weakness, which are ultimately states of the soul. All Arakmbut have these qualities to some extent, but certain men are recognised as being particularly effective protecting and controlling Arakmbut lives and destinies.

Life is constantly changing, and so the shamanic and political features of community activities are bound up in ensuring that change is harnessed into being beneficial rather than destructive. Several themes illustrate the complexities of change in an Amazonian community. Access to resources is an important factor for understanding the conditions of change. Whereas resources are, on the whole, readily available from the perspective of the community, external influences can be significant. The attraction and influence of innovative technology have made resource acquisition more straightforward for the Arakmbut, yet at the same time the effects of colonisation severely limit the resources which are available.

External features of colonisation and innovation can act as triggers for change. However, these conditions do not necessarily determine how change will take place, because the social framework within which it occurs is based on various criteria such as gender, age, residence, descent, and alliance. These criteria are the loci of the daily encounters through which the Arakmbut make decisions, evaluate, and interpret the world. Arakmbut encounters are commentaries on life and the contexts for decision-making; however, they are also moments when tensions in the social organisation arise. The different interests of siblings, affines, clans, spouses, the young, and their elders are all examples of social areas which can sometimes erupt into conflict. Sickness, death, and threats to the community are occasions when these become most clearly manifest, but the difficulty which all Arakmbut men have in securing a marriage partner has, in recent years, become a major source of conflict. The tensions surrounding these events are focused on the social relations which become emotional 'fault-lines' on which change is generated. In this way, during periods of intra-clan conflict, stronger affinal connections arise, while in periods of inter-clan conflict, internal clan solidarity becomes more prominent.

However, trigger factors and tensions within the community are only two elements accounting for change in an Arakmbut community. The third factor is the generation of change which comes from the spirit world, using human beings as vehicles. The constant presence and influence of the spirit world as it generates change is the most difficult aspect to express. It occurs through the activity of each person's soul operating within the body through encounters with other people. The soul is also the means of communication with the spirits, and in countless activities, ranging from hunting to curing, the Arakmbut enter into dialogue with the invisible word through dreams and visions.

In this way, change among the Arakmbut is about access to environmental resources, available marriage partners, and health. Tensions arise when these are threatened, and the encounters which take place within the community express current social, cultural, spiritual, and political conditions which, in certain circumstances, can cumulatively restructure the social organisation. Since their first contact with the priests in the 1950s, the Arakmbut have shifted periodically between an emphasis on clan relations and hierarchy and a more kindred-oriented emphasis based more on equality and scattered household alliances. This series of shifts has been apparent in the period under discussion in this book from 1980 to 1992, and the question remains as to the extent to which this is the feature of a particular period of fifty years in the history of the Arakmbut or a permanent aspect of their social world.

During this study, variations on the themes encountered in San José have appeared in the other communities. For example, Shintuya (according to Helberg 1993 and forthcoming) concurs more with the clan emphasised aspect of Arakmbut social organisation whereas in San José, Barranco Chico and Boca Inambari, the system fluctuates between the clan and wambet alliance emphases. In Puerto Luz, the wambet is apparently completely cognatic, in which case the organisation is more heavily biased away from the clans. However, in all communities the clans are strong and some form of cognatic-style arrangment exists; The differences are of emphases and the nature of the fluctuating system.

When looking at the other Harakmbut societies in the Madre de Dios, it is possible to see them as more extreme variations of the organisational features encountered here. None of the other Harakmbut peoples emphasise the clan as much as the Arakmbut. The population of peoples such as the Sapiteri has dropped so significantly that there are not sufficient numbers for a clan system; for others, it may never have been emphasised much at all. For example, the Sapiteri and the Wachipaeri both had clan systems which were similar to that of the Arakmbut, sharing patrilineal features. However, regarding the Pukirieri, Arasaeri, Kisambaeri, and Toyeri, information is not clear. The Pukirieri and Arasaeri do not appear to have a clan system, while the Kisambaeri and Toyeri are too small in number to be clear about any social system outside of the mixed communities in which they live (Shintuya and Boca Ishiriwe).

Whereas all the Harakmbut peoples share a relationship terminology based on symmetric prescription and the accompanying marriage arrangements, some emphasise the clans greatly and others not at all. The effect is therefore a spectrum from the Arakmbut, who have a marked clan system, through the Wachipaeri and Sapiteri, whose clans are recognised but not used, and the Arasaeri Toyeri, Kisambaeri and Pukirieri, who no longer have or never had the clan system at all. The Harakmbut as a whole, therefore, reflect the flexible system of the Arakmbut but with different emphases.

However, the similarities and differences become more marked when comparing the two closest indigenous neighbours of the Harakmbut – the Matsigenka to the north and the Ese'eja to the south. The system common to the Matsigenka, who live on the borders of Harakmbut territory and with whom the Wachipaeri frequently intermarry, contains several similar features to the wambet, the dispersed aspect of Arakmbut organisation described above (Lyon 1984; Rosengren 1987). Among the Matsigenka, there are no clans and the wambet exists as a form of kindred in a community which is highly dispersed in the form of residential clusters known as *noneri* (Rosengren 1983, 1987). There is a possibility that the dispersed wambet version of the Arakmbut system could be seen as taking on certain Matsigenka qualities. Indeed, during the period at the mission of Shintuya, both peoples lived in the same community and there were several cases of inter-marriage. However, the aspects of the Matsigenka model which are apparent among the Arakmbut were already present before contact between the two groups.

It is important to realise that these similarities refer to certain attributes of the Matsigenka system and not to the social formation as a whole, which is considerably more complicated and contains other features not present among the Arakmbut (Rosengren op.cit.). For example, according to Rosengren (pers. comm.), gender hierarchy is more emphasised and age conflict less so among the Matsigenka than the Arakmbut. This implies that the connection between hierarchy and equality among the Matsigenka is not necessarily connected to the clan formation in the same way as among the Arakmbut.

The dispersed, relatively egalitarian version of Arakmbut social organisation is, like the maloca version, more an ideal than a reality, and one which is unlikely to take on purely Matsigenka features, i.e. eradicating the clan and the hierarchical expressions of the system. However, looking at the changes which have occurred between 1980 and 1992 to the Arakmbut system, the move or shift has been 'in a Matsigenka direction'.

When looking at the Ese'eja, a different system appears. There the whole people is divided into two patrilineal clans (*batsaja* and *wiiho*), based on a moiety classification whereby each person calls his or her father by one of two terms (Chavarría nd). This distinction relates to 'warrior' and 'shamanic' characteristics, which are reflected in a very general division of labour between the clans (Gareth Burr pers. comm.). The clan system appears to be clearly marked, while there are no reports of any notion of kindred from the Ese'eja.

According to Chavarría, Ese'eja do not seem to have a particularly strong sense of gender inequality, such as is found from time to time among the Arakmbut. Although the research available makes no reference to age conflicts, there is reference to the shamanic ceremony of *eshashapoi*, which Chavarría describes as including a form of male initiation. This presents a similar situation to the Arakmbut who, prior to contact with missionaries, would hold two separate rituals of male initiation during a person's youth (see chapter eleven).

Whereas it is impossible on such scanty data to provide a detailed spectrum of the different indigenous systems operating in the Madre de Dios, it is possible to say that the Ese'eja show certain similarities in terms of the clan-based aspect of the Arakmbut system: patrilineal clans, division of labour between shamans and political leaders, male initiation, and a clustering of clans into two groups. In contrast, the Matsigenka share similarities with the more kindred-based wambet aspect of Arakmbut social organisation, the more dispersed aspects of Arakmbut residence, and the more individualistic activities.

The tentative conclusion we can make, therefore, is that the Arakmbut live in a fluctuating system which combines features encountered in both the Ese'eja and the Matsigenka, combining both clan lineality with a more lateral emphasis on kindred. The wambet is not a completely formed kindred, because it operates as an alliance category, and yet the overall effect is broadly similar. The Arakmbut thus have a system which juxtaposes both elements.

However, this is not the only possible way of combining lineal and lateral aspects of a social formation. According to the work of Kensinger, (1977, 1984), Torralba (1981), and Townsley (1993), the Panoan Cashinahua, Sharanahua, and Yaminahua peoples, who live to the west of the Arakmbut, combine a clan moiety arrangement and a way of naming which alters at each generation and which results in a 'four-section system'. The Panoan peoples mentioned above share with the Arakmbut a distinct mixture of the Matsigenka and the Ese'eja systems.

Instead of juxtaposing both systems in their entirety, as with the Arakmbut, the Cashinahua and Sharanahua blend them together within their system of classification so that both aspects of the system operate simultaneously. On the one hand they have a dual clan system like the Ese'eja, although their generational naming system breaks up clan continuity much as the wambet does for the Arakmbut. However, in contrast to the Arakmbut, the Cashinahua, Yaminahua, and Sharanahua do not share the male initiation ceremony or an emphasis on fauna in their shamanic practices.

Whereas the Panoan peoples share the clan formation of the Ese'eja, they emphasise a female initiation ceremony which appears to be connected to their considerable knowledge of plants. This is shared not with the Arakmbut but with the Matsigenka. The Ese'eja and Arakmbut, on the other hand, connect male initiation with a cosmological emphasis on the animal world. The connections thus appear to be a set of overlapping characteristics which, on a general level, provide the first tentative hypothesis of relations between peoples of the Southwestern Amazon.

This view of the Madre de Dios obviously omits many important features of these non-Arakmbut peoples and it necessarily obscures many of the subtle distinctions. Yet it provides a starting point for looking at broad similarities and distinctions which not only reflect the peoples of the Madre de Dios and beyond, but also broadly relate to their relative geographical positions. Lack of information on peoples such as the Amahuaca (Panoan-speakers who live close to the Ese'eja) or the Kogapakori in the Manu Park, who are related to the Matsigenka but have certain distinctions, may provide more subtle differences which will break down the broad sweeps of this comparison.

Various authors (Århem 1981, 1989; Rivière 1984; Hornborg 1986; and Gow 1991) have looked at the possibility of transformations of social organisation over a broad area in South America, whether in the Guianas, the northwest, or the southwest Amazon. The difference between the kindred and clan-based systems relates very much to the conclusions found by Århem (1989) and also by Ramos and Albert (1977) on the Yanomami, where the Sanuma are clan-based and the Yanoama based on ego-centred kin networks.

In this way, parallel differences can be found throughout Amazonia. In some cases they are spread out across vast areas, such as the Guianas (Rivière 1984), and in others, as with the Arakmbut, differences are encompassed in a temporal and dynamic system. The question remains whether, like the symmetric prescription terminology (or perhaps because of it), different permutations throughout the Amazon region can appear or disappear according to historical conditions.

However, none of these peoples live in a vacuum. The wave of colonisation from outside is the one threat which could surpass the limits of social change for the Arakmbut, thereby haltering the fluctuating movement which has taken place over so many generations. The most serious threat is through decimation, but although the Arakmbut in San José fear this possibility, there are other, more subtle dangers to their social and cultural integrity. Throughout the Amazon there are indigenous peoples who have changed certain aspects of their indigenous identity and become absorbed into the capitalist national state system. For this to happen, a process of change eats away the indigenous social formation from within as well as from without. The Arakmbut system is at its weakest when

Cashinahua, Yaminahua etc. (Panoan)
Clan and moiety
Female initiation
Flora-oriented
Alliance sections

Ese'eja (Tacana)
Clan and strong moiety
Male initiation
Fauna-oriented
Alliance but not kindred

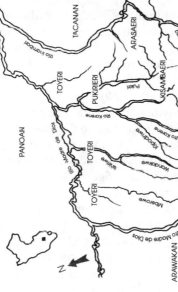

Matsigenka (Arawak)
No clan or moiety
Female initiation
Flora-oriented
Kindred

Arakmbut (Harakmbut)
Clan - locse dual organisation
Male initiation
Fauna-oriented
Alliance and kindred

Figure 13.1: Relationship
between the different peoples
of the Madre de Dios

the generosity principle embedded in internal distribution networks, such as meat distribution and bride service, breaks down. Possibly the Arakmbut, with their resilience and imagination, can invent a new way of incorporating these changes into their social, political, and spiritual systems, but on the other hand, these transformations could be the thin end of the wedge allowing a non-indigenous style of individualism to enter.

In the community of Shintuya, the priests have been working on several projects which members of the community see as detrimental to their internal distribution networks. These changes are concerned with a debt system which arises from a hierarchical financial relationship between the Arakmbut and the priests (Fuentes 1982 and Wahl 1987). For several years, the priests have encouraged logging by men in the community, offering each adult male the opportunity to buy a motor saw by hire-purchase which they pay off with the profits from logging. Sons-in-law have used their debt to the mission as an excuse for refusing to carry out their bride service. They argue that they could not work for their in-laws while paying off their personal debts. The effect has been to make the community more economically individualistic. Although there are some communal activities such as dragging logs to the mission, the breakdown of inter-household obligations has affected the distribution network to the extent that some hunters are obliged to charge for wild meat instead of sharing it because their debts are considerable.

If this increases, Arakmbut obligations will be replaced by a situation in which nuclear families are permanently in debt to the mission and no longer fulfil their obligations to their relatives. Missionisation shows signs of breaking clan and affinal ties linking households together by mutual obligations of distribution, and of encouraging an alien economic individualism to encroach into internal community relationships. A recent change of priests in Shintuya may reverse this trend.

The danger of this form of individualism is that it differs markedly from Arakmbut personal identity. The Arakmbut person is made up not only of a unification of body, soul, and name, but also involves participation in a complicated overlapping network of social groups and categories as well as connections with the spirit world. The effect is an autonomous person whose difference from everyone else is marked because of his or her position in the community, yet at the same time, whose soul is drawn outwards through desire and generosity. Whereas a person participates in a multiplex set of relations, the difference between that person and others is built into his or her self-definition.

The threat from an individualism based on capitalist market-economy definitions is that the Arakmbut become more regimented. With fewer obligations to other members of the community, an Arakmbut becomes an individual, increasingly defined within one production system, rather than a multifaceted person operating on several levels of economic production at once, each with its own sets of obligations and expectations. As the individualism of the market takes over, the nuclear family replaces the clan, community, or other social unit as the central unit of production, consumption, and distribution. The complementarity of gender breaks down as the principal 'wage earner' becomes the husband and the defining principles of status no longer continue to be distribution in return for prestige but their opposite – hoarding leading to political power.

The Arakmbut are surrounded physically not only by colonists, but by a capitalist system which presents the possibility of a destructive overload of their fluctuating social formation. The effect of individualism is to accentuate dispersion until the individual and family constitute the main social units in the society, too weak to effect any meaningful social change and too disintegrated to practice their cultural traditions within a community context. On the other hand, the concentration of power which before was noticeable within the clans would pass to a 'class of employers', from within or without the community, who would exercise more power than the clan ever did and would represent the ultimate form of concentration of soul-matter.

The threat which faces the Arakmbut is thus social and cultural in that it could stretch their system past breaking point. At the point at which it breaks, the Arakmbut would no longer recognise themselves as indigenous but see themselves primarily as members of the proletariat. This is something which has happened to thousands of indigenous people in Peru who have become rainforest agriculturalists – detribalised ribereños. The rise of indigenous representative organisations such as FENAMAD is one attempt to defend the native communities of the Madre de Dios from this destruction. An analysis of this threat and the defence mechanisms which are emerging throughout the indigenous world is the subject of the third volume in this series.

However, there is one form of change which is not often discussed, and which forms the topic of Gow's study of the Piro (Yiné) of the Urubamba (1991). There, after a traumatic history, the people of the area have formed communities which cross-cut particular ethno-linguistic groups and have forged lives based neither on clan nor on kindred but on families bound by concepts of mixed blood and a sense of identity as indigenous people. The implication here is that it is perfectly possible for a people to become increasingly bound into the political economy of the region without losing their sense of identity as indigenous peoples. This is a process which can take place in many communities: there are several in the Madre de Dios which have followed this pattern, such as Boca Ishiriwe. Communities moving in this direction are not acculturated, but find their own indigenous expression.

Indigenous change can therefore take three broad paths in the Peruvian Amazon. The first is to utilise internal strengths to resist colonisation and change within the framework of the social formation (as the Arakmbut do); the second is to develop resistance as an indigenous people, while forming a different type of community (as do the Piro); and the third is to lose indigenous identity altogether and become 'detribalised ribereños'.

The account of the death of Psyche in 1980 crystallised the orientation of this work by illuminating three areas which recurred through the text. The first referred to the invisible shamanic world and its relationship with the visible world. The second connected the political framework of Arakmbut community life to shamanism, relating curing diagnoses to the agonistic features of intra-community rivalries. The third element was the historical importance of his death, which still affects the life of the community today. In 1995, the Arakmbut still discussed the implications of Psyche's death and his importance for them. The ramifications of his death were manifest through the forms of social change which were traced in subsequent chapters.

The death of the shaman has provided a silent commentary which has accompanied the text of this work. His death was the end of an era for the community marked by his prophecy, which was discussed and interpreted by the Arakmbut. San José was affected by the fact that he was no longer with them. For example, on several occasions during his life Psyche carried out acts which defended the community from visible and invisible threats, utilising his contacts with the spirit world, and he was consequently seen as the bulwark of Arakmbut resistance against all enemies.

Psyche was not only an inspiration for the community in their defence against outside threats in times of danger, but he was also a peace-making influence. In the case of the sick man in chapter five, as wayorokeri of San José, Psyche participated directly in the curing, contributing to the recovery, mediating in potential conflicts over the diagnoses between factions within the community, and reassuring the Arakmbut. Since Psyche died, many people have remarked that the community has not had anyone who can really cure them. The wamanoka'eri know the chants, but as a wayorokeri, he really knew the invisible through his river spirit companions.

Furthermore, since his death, there has been no other person who could mediate between the clan rivalries. Indeed, for a period of several years after his death, relations between the clans became more intense and five households left the community (one later returning), contributing to the shift from concentration to dispersion after 1982. His death in 1980 was the catalyst for the events which led to the community changing between 1980 and 1992. The case study of Psyche's death not only prefaces the main areas influencing change, but was the single most important factor precipitating the shift.

The presence of a wayorokeri enables a community to reconcile inter-clan rivalries and to build the strength needed to defend against outsiders. This is not to say that a community cannot defend itself at any other time but that the possibilities for successful resistance are greater. During the period of dispersion in 1985, the community managed to defend itself against the local colonist, Jaime Sumalave, in Puerto Maldonado (Gray 1986). Nevertheless, soon afterwards, community confidence sapped away, and since then it has been more difficult for the Arakmbut to co-ordinate defence strategies. In spite of this, they are still an effective political force against the colonists when the situation arises (see Volume 3, chapters two and eight).

In a sense the wayorokeri enabled a form of limited hierarchy to exist, because he maintained a regulatory balance of power by advising how to connect desire to generosity. Without his presence, the tensions behind the hierarchy were forced into the open and serious conflicts resulted. The community then began the process of dispersion into the more egalitarian aspects of the system. The death of Psyche thus precipitated changes which were in line with the fluctuations which were occurring before contact with the state, although it is impossible to predict the direction in which Arakmbut community life will change at any point. Historically each fluctuation varies in intensity and form, but the overall pattern of alternating concentration and dispersion provides the common factor.

However, the threat of the colonising frontier and harmful spirits has not destroyed the community, and indeed, Psyche thought that his death would mark a turning point in the conflicts with outsiders. The main enemy by 1980 was no longer the Taka or other indigenous peoples but the colonists, and, even though the gold rush had not reached its height during his lifetime, in his death prophecy, he referred to the dangers of colonisation and promised to defend the community from the spirit world. Several Arakmbut report his return to help them at moments of great danger in the guise of a river bird.

Psyche has not been forgotten because his presence was and continues to be essential for the people of San José. He symbolises the strength of Arakmbut shamanic practices and instills a sense of pride in Arakmbut identity. The people of San José see Psyche as a presence protecting them and energising them from beyond the grave in a way which becomes difficult in the community without a wayorokeri. Thus in spite of the weakening and dispersion of the community which took place after his death, his presence ensures the protection of the Arakmbut of San José.

Psyche's death was not only the death of a shaman, it was the death of the last wayorokeri in the community and as such the end of an epoch. The significance of the dying man's prophecy of the need to resist the power of colonisation becomes even more poignant in this light. This is not to say that in the future the adults who are learning shamanic skills will not become the wayorokeri of the next generation, only that nothing is certain.

Since he died, Psyche has not left the community, and even in its moments of weakness the Arakmbut say that he is there. His soul is forever reaching outwards, wandering in the forest through dreams, and at any moment you may see it alighting on a beach by the banks of the Karene, giving hope for the future of the Arakmbut.

ORTHOGRAPHY

The Ministerio de Educación Republica Peruana (1973) has an Arakmbut orthography which was prepared by Robert Tripp of the Summer Institute of Linguistics. This orthography uses an alphabet which conforms to that of Peruvian Spanish. Heinrich Helberg (1984) has adapted this to accommodate the phonetic alphabet. This orthography largely conforms to Peruvian Spanish, but several Arakmbut students have advised me on the spellings they prefer.

Each Arakmbut community has its own accents, words and expressions which means that there is no fixed spelling system for the language as a whole. Some of the words written here may well be rewritten in the future, as young Arakmbut find a system which is appropriate for all the communities.

Some Arakmbut vowels can be un-nasalised or nasalised but I have not made this distinction in the text. I have substituted an 'h' for the Spanish 'j' or 'x' and 'w' for 'hu' except in quotes from Spanish-speaking authors. Where the 1973 orthography has 'ti', I have written 'ch' or 'tch', depending on how strongly the 't' sounds; where it has 'si' I have written 'sh'. The 1973 orthography recognises that 'b' is pronounced 'mb' by the Arakmbut. However, in some cases the 'm' is more apparent than in others. I have therefore written 'mb' where the 'm' is pronounced and 'b' where the 'm' is silent. Similarly the 'd' in the 1973 orthography appears as 'nd' at the beginning or 'dn' at the end of a word. I have written the letters 'n' and 'd' as they sound because in some examples the 'n' is silent. I occasionally heard a 'v' and a 'j' sound which are not in the orthography but are used here.

Vowels

a as in 'apple' (also nasalised)
e as in 'egg' (also nasalised)

i as in 'into'
o as in 'pot' (also nasalised)
u as in 'moon'

Consonants

b as in 'book' but with varying degrees of semi-nasalisation *(mb)*.
ch as in 'church' but also accasionally with a slight *'t'* as in 'pitch'.
d as in 'dog' but with varying degrees of semi-nasalisation as in 'and'.
    At the end of a word, a *'d'* sounds *'dn'*.
g appears with semi-nasalisation (*'ng'* as in tongue) but often at the
    end of a word as *'gn'* as in 'gnu'.
h as in 'hat'
k as in 'kite'
m as in 'mouse' also as semi-nasal to *'b'*
n as in 'nature' but also as semi-nasal to *'d'* and *'g'* or after *'d'* and *'g'*
    at the end of a word.
p as in 'pig'
r as in 'rainbow'
s as in 'sea'
t as in 'top' but sometimes present before *'ch'* or *'sh'* as in 'pitch'
w or *hu* as in 'window'
y as in 'yacht'
'a stop as in the glottal stop before *'I'*

GLOSSARY

akudnui/iari	white-lipped peccary (Tayassu pecari)
ambaru	carp-like fish (boquichicos)
anenda	before
apik	sugar cane
apoining	anaconda/stranger/tipsy
arakmbut	human beings/society
aramburu	armadillo
aroi	plantain
asign	MZ/capybara (Hydrochoerus hydrochaeris)
atodn	fruit
aypo	food
bawi	deer
baysik	dusk
bi'ign	fish
biu	tree
biwi	snake
chimbui	opposite-sex affine of same genealogical level
chindign	curing chant/sorcery
chindignwakeri	sorcerer
chindoi	meat offered to potential spouse
chiokpo	stars
chongpai	ayahuasca, anaconda
chupit	bird
e'anopwe	to understand
e'apak	to speak
e'chipoa	to blow
e'chiri	to feel ill

e'e	to be/life
egn	brother
e'ka	to do, make
e'kerek	to grow
ekhomba	tree
e'machinoa	to sing
e'mba'a	to work
emba'a/embachia	round dance
embachiusu	a fruit
e'mbachpak	to tell a story, myth
e'mbaipak	initiation ceremony
embaipageri	dancers at e'mbaipak
e'mbayok	to distribute
e'mbet	to stick together
e'mbuey	to die
e'mbuiyuk	to suck
e'mepuk	to fear
e'munka	to fight
enchipo	brother in law
e'nopwe	to know
e'ohotokoy	initiation ceremony/nose-piercing
e'pak	to want/desire
e'pe'e	to hear
e'pogika	it is always passing
ereknda	white
e'simbore	to be intoxicated
esweri	outsiders
e'toe	to grasp
e'toepak	to marry
e'yok	to give
hak	house
henpu	string bag
hirengo	bird
ho	peach palm (Guilielma speciosa mart)
hor	monkey (martín)
ihchagi	I come
ihpi	common squirrel monkey (Saimiri sciurecus boliviensis)
ioknda	annoyed
isipo	child
ka	pineapple
kaikai	harpy eagle (Harpia harpyja)

kapiro	heron (Egretta alba)
kapiwi	coati (Nasua nasua)
kayare	paca (Agouti paca)
keme	tapir (Tapirus terrestris)
kemewere	tapir spirit
kerongtogn	tree
kodna	fruit
koimbedn	scarlet macaw (Ara macao)
kokoy/watohpu	Wachipaeri/Arakmbut name for type of eagle
koragn	fruit
kotsi	aguaje (Mauritia flexuosa)
ku'mbarak	cemetery
kumo	barbasco (Lonchocarpus sp.)
kurudn	sky
kurudneri	sky spirits
kuta	up
macherik	nettles
mako	bird
mama	caiman
mamori	sabalo (fish)
mantoro	achiote (Bixa orellana)
mapi	agouti (Dasyprocta aguti)
masamimbi	mud
masonara	watery areas
matamona	decide, order, frighten
matuk	gallinazo black vulture
mawe	stream
mayari	jaguar (Panthera onca)
mbaimbai	sun coloured
mbakokoy	ohpu ceremony/bird from sky
mbakoy	bird
mbakuopidn	arm bands
mbapndik	edible
mbapwendik	inedible
mbaset	fruit
mbedntoktok	species of oriole
mbeyok	give me
mbogntokoy	lip piercing ceremony
mbudn	curassow (Crax carunulata)
mendo	fruit
menke	tree
mepuk	fear
metamera	fruit

miokpo	sun
mokas	collared peccary (Tayassu tajacu)
mokpayomba	bird
monka	must do / causality
muneyo	young woman
ndak	good
ndakmayorokeri/ndakyorokeri	good dream-beings, beneficial spirits
ndakwe	bad
ndoedn	my
ndumba	forest
nekei	blue and yellow macaw (Ara ararauna)
nogn	other
nokiren	soul-matter
nowenda	sorrow
o	huito (black dye)
ochinosik	hatred
o'epo	therefore
ohpai	game animal
ohpu	war leader
okmbu	night monkey (Aotus sp.)
okpi	palisade
ombayok	dry season
o'monkudn	they enter
onyu	'pure', clan
opewadn/opedn	formal term for spouse
paimba	tobacco
painda	bitter
pak	desire
paka	bamboo casing
pawe	dislike
paron	turkey hen
petpet	jaguar
pio	fruit
ponaro	fruit
pugn	moon
purak	species of oriole
prung	bird
sakmba	collar
sawe	tortoise
senopo	mean

shiok	woolly monkey (Lagothrix lagothrica)
sinei	fiesta
sing	harpy eagle
singpa	peach palm tree
sipin	black mantled tamarin (Saguinus nigricollis)
sipo	smaller/younger
siro	type of oriole, metal
sisi	meat
sopi	worms
sorok	soil, salt lick
sowe	black spider monkey (Ateles paniscus chamek)
supi	fruit
suru	trumpeter bird
tainda	power, strength
tamba	chacra
tanka	headdress
tapi chipi	fruit
tapo	mouth of a stream
tare	yuca
tawiresindak	bark of tawire tree
toca	toca monkey
toket	maize
toko	fruit
tombi	shell rattle
tomenkero	fruit
tone	large/older
topobaudnihpi	squirrel
tori	edible plant
torogn	oppossum (Didelphis marsupialis)
toto	dangerous spirit
towanda	fruit
toyo	down
toyori	red howler monkey (Alouatta seniculus)
urunda	beautiful wonderful
wachipai	otiose spirits
waerik	good humour, laughter
waewembedn	red-tailed squirrel
wakapak	tail feathers
wakawa	large pineapple

wakirignayo	where it is misty
wakumbuesindak	bark of the wakumue tree
wakupe	gold
wairi	leader, man of prestige
wamambuey	same-sex sibling
wamachunkeri	hunter
wamanoka'eri	curer
wambachapak	myth, story
wambarakeri	warrior
wambayok	dry season
wambedn	red, fruit
wambet	ego-centred alliance category
wambetoeri	dead spirits of one's relatives
wambign	squirrel
wambo	young man
wambokerek	adult male
wambwanada	now, presently
wamankeri	member of our community
wanakeri	host community
wanamba	rubbish person
wandagnte	on the path
wandaknda	good
wandari	territory
wandawe	semen
wandik	name
wantupa	political leader
wapong	ceremonial song in mbakokoy ceremony
waren	striped heron
wasik	black/grey
wasiwa	fat
waso	body
watawata	individual alone
watawataewe	collective
watoe	spouse
watone	old person
watopakari/topakari	Wachipaeri word for shaman
wawe	river
waweri	river spirits
wawesik	Guayaquil squirrel (Sciurus stramineus)
wawing	maize drink like chicha
wawiyok	wet season
waya	fruit
wayawaya	exact exchange

wayorokeri	dreamer
weika	a bird associated with the tapir
wenpu	string bag
were	dispersed spirits
windak	arrow
witpi	pona tree
wiwimba	bamboo
yaro	a broad leaf used for roofing
yawiru	non-poisonous black snake
yereyere	white heron
yorok	dream
yoromba	fruit

BIBLIOGRPAHY

Aikman, S.H. 1994. *Intercultural Education and Harakmbut Identity: A Case Study of the Community of San Jose in Southeastern Peru*. PhD thesis, University of London.

Alvarez, J. 1946. Creencias y Tradiciones Mashcas. *Misiones Dominicanas del Perú* XXVII 10-15.

d'Ans, A-M et al. 1973. *Problemas de Clasificación de Lenguas No-Andinas en el Sur-Este Peruano*. Centro de Investigación de Lingüística Aplicada. Lima: Unversidad Nacional Mayor de San Marcos.

Appadurai, A. (ed.) 1986. *The Social Life of Things: Commodities in Cultural Perspective*. Cambridge University Press.

Ardener, S. 1975. Introduction. *Perceiving Women*. London: Dent.

Århem, K. 1981. *Makuna Social Organization. A Study in Descent, Alliance and the Formation of Corporate Groups in the North-Western Amazon*. Acta Universitatis Upsaliensis. Uppsala Studies in Cultural Anthropology 4. Stockholm: Liber Tryck.

Århem, K. 1989. 'The Makú, the Makuna and the Guiana System: Transformations of Social Structure in Northern Lowland South America'. *Ethnos* 1-2: 5-22.

Balée W., & D. Posey (eds.) 1989. *Resource Management in Amazonia: Indigenous and Fold Strategies*. Advances in Economic Botany Vol. 7. The New York Botantical Gardens.

Barriales, J. and A. Torralba. 1970. *Los Mashcos*. Lima: Santiago Valverde.

Barth, F. 1965. *Political Leadership Among the Swat Pathans*. LSE Monographs on Social Anthropology No. 19 University of London. The Athlone Press.

Bennet, B., 1991. *Illness and Order: Cultural Transformation among the Machiguenga and Huachipaeri*. Ph.D. thesis. Cornell University.

Best, S., & D. Kellner. 1991. *Postmodern Theory: Critical Interrogations*. Macmillan.

Bloch, M. 1992. *Prey into Hunter: The Politics of Religious Experience*. Cambridge University Press.

Bourdieu, P. 1977. *Outline of a Theory of Practice*. Cambridge Studies in Social Anthropology.

Brown, M. 1984 *Una Paz Incierta: Historia y Cultura de las Comunidades Aguarunas Frente al Impacto de la Caretera Marginal.* Lima: Centro Amazónico de Antropología y Aplicación Práctica, Peru.

Brown, M. 1985. *Tsewa's Gift: Magic and Meaning in an Amazonian Society.* Smithsonian Institution Press.

Brown, M., 1987. 'Ropes of Sand' in B. Tedlock (ed.) *Dreaming: Anthropological and Psychological Interpretations* pp.154-170. School of American Research Advanced Seminar Series. Santa Fe.

CAAAP, 1992. *Propuesta de Politica Educativa Sub-Region de Madre de Dios Linea de Educación Intercultural.* Centro Amazónico de Antropología y Aplicación Práctica. Peru.

Califano, M. 1978a. El Complejo de la Bruja entre los Mashco de la Amazonía sudoccidental (Perú). *Anthropos:* 73, 401-433.

Califano, M. 1978b. *Análisis Comparativo de un Mito Mashco.* Entregas de I.T. Instituto Ticlan, Centro de Investigaciónes Regionales Facultad de Filosofía y Letras. Unversidad de Buenos Aires.

Califano, M. 1982. *Etnografía de los Mashcos de la Amazonía Sud Occidental del Perú.* Buenos Aires: FECIE.

Califano, M & A. Fernandez Distel, 1982: 'The Use of a Hallucinogenic Plant among the Mashco (Southwestern Amazonia, Peru)' *Zeitschrift für Ethnologie* Band 107, Heft 1. pp. 129-143. Berlin.

Campbell, A.T. 1989. *To Square with Genesis: Causal Statements and Shamanic Ideas in Wayapi.* Edinburgh University Press.

Chagnon, N. 1968. *Yanomamo: The Fierce People.* Holt, Rinehart & Winston.

Chaumeil, J-P., 1983: *Voir, Savoir, Pouvoir: Le chamanisme chez les Yagua du Nord-Est Péruvien.* Éditions de L'École des Hautes Étudies en Sciences Sociales.

Chaumeil, J-P. 1993. Des Esprites aux ancêtres. *L'Homme. 126 128. XXXIII. pp.409-427.* Paris.

Chavarría, Mendoza, M.C. nd. *Ejatojabatiji: Buscando las sombras de nosotros mismos (aproximación ethnografica a la cultura Ese'eja).* Mss.

Clastres, P. 1977. *Society Against the State: the Leader as Servant and the Human Uses of Power among the Indians of the Americas.* Oxford: Blackwells.

CODEH-PA. 1983. *La Selva y su Ley: Lavadores de Oro.* Sicuani: Comite de Defensa de los Derechos Humanos de las Provincias Altas.

Colchester, M., 1981: Ecological modelling and Indigenous Systems of Resource Use: Some Examples of Southern Venezuela. *Antropologica* 55. pp. 57-72.

Crocker, J.C., 1985. *Vital Souls: Bororo Cosmology, Natural Symbolism and Shamanism.* Tucson; University of Arizona Press.

Davis, J. 1992. History and the People without Europe. in K. Hastrup, ed. *Other Histories* pp.14-28. London: Routledge.

Davis, S. 1977. *Victims of the Miracle: Development and the Indians of Brazil.* Cambridge University Press.

Dean, B. 1995. Forbidden Fruit: Infidelity, Affinity and Brideservice among the Urarina of Peruvian Amazonia. *Journal of the Royal Anthropological Institute*, 1:87-110.

Denevan, W. 1976. The Aboriginal Populations of Amazonia. In *The Native Population of the Americas in 1492*. W. Denevan (ed) pp.205-234. University of Wisconsin Press.

Descola, P. 1989. *La Selva Culta: Simbolismo y praxis en la ecología de los Achuar*. Quito: Coedición Abya-Yala/MLAL.

Descola, P. 1992. Societies of nature and the nature of society. In A. Kuper (ed.) *Conceptualising Society* pp.107-126). London: Routledge.

Dostal, W. (ed.) 1972. *The Situation of the Indian in South America*. Geneva: World Council of Churches with the Ethnological Institute of the University of Berne.

Dumont, L. 1972. *Homo Hierarchicus*. London: Paladin.

Eliade, M. 1951. *Shamanism*. Princeton University Press.

Erikson, P. 1988. Politics in Amazonia *Man* Vol. 23: pp.164-5

Fejos, P. 1941. La región del Río Colorado. *Boletín de la Sociedad Geográfica de Lima* LVIII, 221-42.

Fernandez Moro, W. 1952. *Cincuenta anos en la Selva Amazónica*. Madrid.

Firth, R. 1951. *Elements of Social Organisation*. London: Watts.

Firth, R. 1959. *Social Change in Tikopia*. London: George Allen & Unwin.

Fortes, M & E.E. Evans-Pritchard (eds.). 1940. *African Political Systems*. Oxford University Press.

Friedman, J. 1975. Tribes, States and Transformations. in M. Bloch (ed.) *Marxist Analyses and Social Anthropology*. Association of Social Anthropologists Studies 3, pp. 161-202. London: Malaby Press.

Fuentes, A. 1982. *Parentesco y Relaciones de Producción en Una Comunidad Harakmbut en el Sur-Oriente Peruano*. Centro Amazónico de Antropología y Aplicación Práctica, Peru mss.

Godelier, M. 1977. *Perspectives in Marxist Anthropology*. Cambridge Studies in Social Anthropology.

Gow, P. 1991. *Of Mixed Blood: Kinship and History in Peruvian Amazonia*. Oxford: Clarendon Press.

Gray, A. 1976, *Structural Transformations in Nagaland*. M.A. thesis. Edinburgh University.

Gray, A. 1983. *The Amarakaeri: an Ethnographic Description of an Harakmbut people from Southeastern Peru*. D. Phil. thesis. Oxford University.

Gray, A. 1984. Los Amarakaeri: Una noción de Estructura Social *Amazonía Peruana*, Vol. V, No. 10, pp.47-64, Lima.

Gray, A. 1986. And After the Gold Rush? ... Human Rights and Self-Development among the Amarakaeri of Southeastern Peru. *Document* No. 55. Copenhagen: IWGIA International Work Group for Indigenous Affairs.

Gray, A. 1987. Perspectives on Amarakaeri History In *Natives and Neighbours in South America*. H.Skar & F. Salomon (eds.) pp.299-328. Goteborgs Etnografiska Museum.

Gray, A. 1992. 'It is Time to Act!' say the Peruvian Arakmbut. In *Anti-Slavery Reporter*. 1992-3. pp 111-114. London.

Guillen-Marroquin, J. 1990. 'El Trabajo Infantil en el Perú: La Explotación de Aluviones Auríferos en Madre de Dios'. In J. Boyden (ed.) *La Lucha contra el Trabajo Infantil.* Geneva: International Labour Organisation.

Hastrup, K. (ed.) 1992. *Other Histories.* European Association of Social Anthropologists. London: Routledge.

Harner, M.J. 1972. *The Jivaro. People of the Sacred Waterfalls.* Garden City, N.Y: Doubleday.

Harner, M.J. (ed.) 1973. *Hallucenogens and Shamanism.* New York: Oxford University Press.

Helberg Chavez, H. 1984. *Skizze einer Grammatik des Amarakaeri.* Ph.D. thesis. Eberhard-Karls-University, Tübingen.

Helberg Chavez, H. 1989. Análisis Funciónal del Verbo Amarakaeri. In *Temas de Linguistica Amerindia* R. Cerron-Palomino and G. Solis Fonseca (eds.) , CONCYTEC & GTZ, Lima.

Helberg Chavez, H. 1993. Terminología de Parentesco Harakmbut. *Amazonía Peruana* 23:107-140. Lima: Centro Amazónica de Antropología y Aplicación Práctica.

Helberg Chavez, H. Forthcoming. *Baysik.* Lima: *CAAAP*

Hemming, J. 1978. *Red Gold: The Conquest of the Brazilian Indians.* London: Macmillan.

Hemming, J. 1987. *Amazon Frontier: The Defeat of the Brazilian Indians.* London: MacMillan.

Henley, P. 1982. *The Panare: Tradition and Change on the Amazonian Frontier.* Yale University Press.

Holdsworth, C. 1994. *The Revolution in Anthropology: A Comparative Analysis of the Metaphysics of E.B. Tylor (1832-1917) and Bronislaw Malinowski (1884-1942).* D.Phil. thesis, University of Oxford.

Holzmann, G. 1951/6 La Tribu Mashca *Misiones Dominicanas del Perú* (during 1956 the publication became *Misiones Dominicanas*) XXXII 2-4, 53-6; XXXIII 51-3, no. 193 no page number; XXXIV 17-19; XXXV 64-66; XXXVI 340-3; XXXVII 97-99. Lima.

Hornborg, A. 1986. *Dualism and hierarchy in Lowland South America: Trajectories of Indigenous Social Organisation.* Uppsala University.

Howell, S. & R. Willis (eds.). 1989. *Societies at Peace: Anthropological Perspectives.* London: Routledge.

Hugh-Jones, C. 1978. Food for Thought: Patterns of Production and Consumption in Pira Pirana Society. In J.S. La Fontaine (ed.) *Sex and Age as Principles of Social Differentiation.* Association of Social Anthropologists Monograph 17.pp. 41-66. London: Academic Press.

Hugh-Jones, S. 1993. Clear Descent or Ambiguous Houses? A Re-examination of Tukanoan Social Organisation. *L'Homme 126-128, XXXIII: pp. 95-120.*

Kahn, J., & J. Llobera. 1981. Towards a New Marxism or a New Anthropology? in J. Kahn & J. Llobera (eds.) *The Anthropology of Pre-Capitalist Societies.* pp. 263-329. London: Macmillan.

Kensinger, K. 1973. Banisteriopsis Usage among the Peruvian Cashinahua. in M. Harner (ed.) *Hallucinogens and Shamanism.* New York. Oxford University Press.

Kensinger, K. 1977. Cashinahua Notions of Social Time and Social Space. *Actes du XLIIe Congrès International des Americanistes.* Vol. II, 233-244. Paris.

Kensinger, K., 1984. An Emic Model of Cashinahua Marriage. In *Marriage Practices in Lowland South America.* K.M. Kensinger (ed.) Illinois Studies in Anthropology No. 14. University of Illinois Press.

Kracke, W.H. 1978. *Force and Persuasion: Leadership in an Amazonian Society.* University of Chicago Press.

Kuklick, H. 1993. *The Savage Within: The Social History of British Anthropology 1885-1945.* Cambridge University Press.

Kuper, A. 1988. *The Invention of Primitive Society: Transformations of an Illusion.* London: Routledge.

Lambert, C., 1948. *Music Ho!* London: Pelican Books.

Lea, V. 1992. Mebengokre (Kayapó) Onomastics: A Facet of Houses as Total Social Facts in Central Brazil. *Man* 27:129-153.

Leach, E.R. 1954. *Political Systems of Highland Burma: A Study of Kachin Social Structure.* London School of Economics Monographs on Social Anthropology, 44. London: The Athlone Press.

Leach, E.R. 1961. *Rethinking Anthropology.* London: The Athlone Press.

Lévi-Strauss, C. 1963. 'The Sorcerer and his Magic'. In *Structural Anthropology.* pp. 167-185. Penguin.

Lévi-Strauss, C. 1969. *The Elementary Structures of Kinship.* London: Eyre and Spottiswoode.

Lévi-Strauss, C, 1974. *The Savage Mind.* London: Weidenfeld and Nicolson.

Lyon, P.J. 1967. *Singing as Social Interaction among the Wachipaeri of Eastern Peru.* Unpublished PhD Thesis. University of California.

Lyon, P.J. 1976. Tribal Movement and Linguistic Classification in the Madre de Dios Zone. Typewritten corrected version of the paper published in the XXXIX Congreso Internaciónal de Americanistas, Lima, *Actas y Memorias,* Vol. 5, 185-207. Lima.

Lyon, P.J. 1984. Change in Wachipaeri marriage patterns. In *Marriage Practices in Lowland South America.* K. Kensinger (ed.) Illinois Studies in Anthropology 14. University of Illinois Press.

Marx, K. 1977. 'The German Ideology'. in D. McLellen (ed.) *Karl Marx: Selected Writings.* Oxford University Press.

Maybury-Lewis, D. 1974. *Akwe-Shavante Society.* Oxford University Press.

Maybury-Lewis, D. 1979. *Dialectical Societies. The Gê and Bororo of Central Brazil.* Cambridge MA. and London: Harvard University Press.

McCarthy, T. 1985. *The Critical Theory of Jurgen Habermas.* The MIT Press.

Metraux, A., 1949: 'Religion and Shamanism', *Handbook of South American Indians* 5: 559-599. Washington: Smithsonian Institute

Monnier, A. 1982. Evangelisation Structurale. *Bulletin de Société Suisse des Americanistes* 46, 31-35 Geneva.

Moore, T.R. nd. 'Algunas Notas sobre la Organisación Social y Religion de los Harakmbut'. mss.

Moore, T.R. 1979. Sil and a New-found Tribe. The Amarakaeri Experience. *Dialectical Anthropology* 4, 113-125. Amsterdam.

Moore, T.R. 1985. Movimientos Populares en Madre de Dios y Regionalización. In *Promoción Campesina, Regionalización y Movimientos Sociales*, María Isabel Remy (ed.). Centro de Estudios Rurales Andinos 'Bartolomé de las Casas' y Centro de Estudios y Promoción de Desarrollo (DESCO). Lima.

Morin, F., 1973. *Les Shipibo de L'Ucayali*. These de Doctorat de 3eme Cycle presentée a L'École Practique des Hautes Études (6eme Secion). Paris.

Morgan, L.H. 1877. *Ancient Society*. New York: Holt.

Murphy, R.F. 1978. *Headhunter's Heritage: Social and Economic Change among the Mundurucu Indians*. New York: Octagon Books.

Needham, R. 1973. Prescription *Oceania* 43, 166-181.

Olivera, J.M. 1907. Informe. In *Ultimas Exploraciónes ordenadas por la Junta de Vias Fluviales a los ríos Ucayali, Madre de Dios, Paurcartambo y Urubamba.* pp. 395-429. Lima: Oficina tipográfica de La Opinión Naciónal.

Overing, J. 1989. Styles of manhood: an Amazonian contrast in tranquility and violence. In S. Howell & R. Willis (eds.) *Societies at Peace: Anthropological Perspectives.* pp. 79-99. London. Routledge.

Parry, J. & M. Bloch. 1989. *Money and the Morality of Exchange*. Cambridge University Press.

Radda Barnen. 1991. *Area Chica.* No. 6, Ano II. Lima.

Ramos, A. & B. Albert. 1977. Yanoma descent and affinity: The Sanuma/Yanoman Contrast. In. J. Overing Kaplan, (ed.). *Social Time and Space in Lowland South America.* Actes de Congrès International des Americanistes. Vol. II pp.71-90. Paris.

Reichel-Dolmatoff, G. 1971. *Amazonian Cosmos. The Sexual and Relgious Symbolism of the Tukano Indians.* University of Chicago Press.

Ribeiro, D. 1970. *Os Indios e a Civilizaçao: a integraçao das populaçoes indigenas no Brasil moderno.* Rio de Janeiro: Civilizaçao Brasileira.

Ribeiro, D. & M.R. Wise, 1978. *Los Grupos Etnicos de la Amazonía Peruana Comunidades y Culturas Peruanas* No. 13. Instituto Linguistico de Verano.

Rival, L. 1993. The Growth of Family Trees: Understanding Huaorani Perception of the Forest *Man* (NS) 28:635-652.

Rivers, W.H.R. 1914. *The History of Melanesian Society.* Cambridge University Press.

Rivière, P.G. 1984. *Individual and Society in Guiana. A Comparative Study of Amerindian Social Organization.* Cambridge University Press.

Rivière, P.G. 1995. *Absent-minded Imperialism: Britain and the Expansion of Empire in Nineteenth-century Brazil.* London: Tauris Academic Studies.

Roe, P.G. 1982. *The Cosmic Zygote. Cosmology in the Amazon Basin.* Rutgers: State University of New Jersey.

Rosengren, D. 1983. Proximity and Interaction: The Case of the Matsigenka of the upper Urubamba, Southeastern Peru. *Annals 1981-1982.* pp.48-63. Gothenburg: Gothenburg Ethnographic Museum.

Rosengren, D. 1987. *In the Eyes of the Beholder. Leadership and the Social Construction of Power and Dominance among the Matsigenka of the Peruvian Amazon.* Göteborgs Etnografiska Museum.

Rummenhöller, K. 1987. *Tieflandindios im Goldrausch: Die Auswirkungen des Goldbooms auf die Harakmbut im Madre de Dios, Peru.* Mundus Reihe Ethnologie, Band 12, Bonn.

Rummenhöller, K., M. Lazarte y C. Cardenas. 1991. *Diagnóstico de las Comunidades Natives del Madre de Dios.* Instituto Indigenista Peruana.

Russell, J. 1985. *Francis Bacon.* London: Thames and Hudson.

Sahlins, M.D. 1974. *Stone Age Economics.* London: Tavistock

Santos Granero, F. 1986 Power, Ideology and the Ritual of Production in Lowland South America. *Man* 21. 657-79

Santos Granero, F. 1991. *The Power of Love. The Moral Use of Knowledge amongst the Amuesha of Central Peru.* LSE Monographs on Social Anthropology No. 62. London: The Athlone Press.

Seddon, D. (ed.) 1978. *Relations of Production: Marxist Approaches to Economic Anthropology.* Frank Cass.

Siskind, J. 1973a. Tropical Forest Hunters and the Economy of Sex. In D.Gross (ed.). *People and Cultures of Native South America.* pp. 226-240. New York: Doubleday/ The Natural History Press.

Siskind, J. 1973b. *To Hunt in the Morning.* New York: Oxford University Press.

Siskind, 1973c. 'Visions and Cures among the Sharanahua' in M. Harner (ed.) *Hallucenogens and Shamanism.* New York: Oxford University Press.

Skar, S.L. 1994. *Lives Together – Worlds Apart: Quechua Colonization in Jungle and City.* Oslo Studies in Social Anthropology. Oslo: Scandinavian University Press.

Stocks, A.W. 1981. *Los Nativos Invisibles. Notas sobre la historia y Realidad Actual de los Cocamilla del Río Huallaga, Perú.* Lima: CAAAP.

Steward, J., & L. Faron. 1959. *Native Peoples of South America.* New York: McGraw Hill Books.

Sueyo, H. 1995. The Harakmbut People Reclaim their Traditional Culture. *Indigenous Affairs* No. 1 pp.42-45. International Work Group for Indigenous Affairs. Copenhagen.

Taussig, M. 1986. *Shamanism, Colonialism and the Wild Man. A Study in Terror and Healing.* University of Chicago Press.

Taylor, A-C. 1981. God-Wealth: The Achuar and the Missions. In Norman Whitten (ed.). *Cultural Transformations and Ethnicity in Modern Ecuador.* pp.647-676. University of Illinois Press.

Taylor, A-C. 1993. Remembering to Forget: Identity, Mourning and Memory among the Jivaro. *Man*, ns.28:653-678. London.

Tedlock, B. (ed.). 1987. *Dreaming: Anthropological and Psychological Interpretations.* Santa Fe: School of American Research Advanced Seminar Series.

Torralba, A. 1979. Los Harakmbut. Nueva Situación Misionera. *Antisuyo*, 3. Publicación de los Misiones Dominicanas en la Selva Sur-Oriente del Perú. pp. 83-141. Lima.

Torralba, A. 1981, Sharanahua, *Antisuyo*, 4. Publicación de los Misiones Dominicanas en la Selva-Oriente del Perú. pp. 37-84. Lima.

Townsley, G., 1993. Song Paths: The Ways and Means of Yaminahua Shamanic Knowledge. *L'Homme* 126-128 XXXIII (2-4) pp. 449-468.

Tripp, R., nd. *Amarakaeri Grammar* Mss.

Turner, B.S. 1985. The Practices of Rationality: Michel Foucault, Medical History and Sociological Theory. In R Fardon (ed.) *Power and Knowledge: Anthropological and Sociological Approaches.* Edinburgh: Scottish Academic Press.

Tylor, E.B. 1871. *Primitive Culture.* New York.

Urban, G. & J. Sherzer. 1991. *Nation States and Indians in Latin America.* Austin: University of Texas.

Varese, S. 1972. *The Forest Indians in the Present Political Situation of Peru.* IWGIA Document 8. Copenhagen: International Work Group for Indigenous Affairs.

Vickers, W.T. 1978. Meat is Meat. The Siona-Secoya and the Hunting Prowess – Sexual Reward Hypothesis. *Latin Americanist*, Vol. 11, No.I, 1-5. Florida.

Von Brandenstein, C.G. 1971. The Phoenix Totemism. *Oceania* 41, 39-49.

Von Hassel, J.M. 1905. Las Tribus Salvajes de la Región Amazonica del Perú. *Boletín de la Sociedad Geográfica de Lima* XXVII. pp. 27-75. Lima.

Wahl, L. 1985. La Federación Nativa del Madre de Dios: Informe de un Congreso. *Amazonía Indígena* Año 5 No. 8 Enero.

Wahl, L. 1987. *Pagans into Christians. The Political Economy of Religious Conversion among the Harakmbut of Lowland Southeastern Peru, 1902-1982.* PhD. thesis, The City University of New York.

Wallenstein, I. 1979. *The Capitalist World Economy.* Cambridge University Press.

Weiss, G. 1975. *Campa Cosmology: The World of a Forest Tribe in South America.* Anthropological Papers of the American Museum of Natural History, 52/5. New York.

Whitehead, N. 1993. Ethnic Transformation and Historical Discontinuity in Native Amazonia and Guyana, 1500-1900. *L'Homme* 126-128. XXXIII.285-305. Paris.

Whittaker, A. 1985. Slavery and Gold in Peru. *Anti-Slavery Reporter* Series VII, Vol.13 No.2. pp.63-70.

INDEX